The Concept of Ordered Liberty and the Common-Law Due-Process Tradition

The Concept of Ordered Liberty and the Common-Law Due-Process Tradition

Slaughterhouse Cases through *Obergefell v. Hodges* (1872–2015)

Matthew W. Lunder

LEXINGTON BOOKS
Lanham • Boulder • New York • London

Published by Lexington Books
An imprint of The Rowman & Littlefield Publishing Group, Inc.
4501 Forbes Boulevard, Suite 200, Lanham, Maryland 20706
www.rowman.com

6 Tinworth Street, London SE11 5AL, United Kingdom

British Library Cataloguing in Publication Information Available

Library of Congress Cataloging-in-Publication Data

ISBN 978-1-7936-2634-9 (cloth)
ISBN 978-1-7936-2635-6 (electronic)

With gratitude to my friend and colleague Thomas P. Huff, emeritus professor of philosophy and professor of law, whose support and insight were integral to The Concept's realization. In the alembic of our conversations the metaphors of this story were literalized.

Though the legislative [power] . . . be the supreme power in every common-wealth; yet . . . [i]t is not, nor can possibly be absolutely arbitrary over the lives and fortunes of the people: for it being but the joint power of every member of the society given up to that person, or assembly, which is legislator[.]

—John Locke, *Second Treatise on Government*,
Chapter XI, § 135.

The nature, and ends of legislative power will limit the exercise of it. This fundamental principle flows from the very nature of our free Republican governments[.] . . . There are acts which the Federal, or State, Legislature cannot do, without exceeding their authority. There are certain vital principles in our free Republican governments, which will determine and over-rule an apparent and flagrant abuse of legislative power; as to authorize manifest injustice by positive law; or to take away that security for personal liberty, or private property, for the protection whereof the government was established. An Act of the Legislature (for I cannot call it a law) contrary to the great first principles of the social compact, cannot be considered a rightful exercise of legislative authority. The obligation of a law in governments established on express compact, and on republican principles, must be determined by the nature of the power, on which it is founded.

—*Calder v. Bull*, 3 U.S. 386, 388 (1798).

Contents

Prologue

Readers acquainted with American constitutional law know that twentieth-century personal-liberty cases were some of the most controversial the U.S. Supreme Court decided. Individuals alleged that States violated the due-process guarantee of the Fourteenth Amendment—"No State shall . . . deprive any person of life, liberty, or property, without due process of law"[1]—when attempting to regulate their most intimate relationships. These were claims that States impermissibly interfered with decisions about family, marriage, procreation, and sexuality.[2] The issue of *how* the federal courts should evaluate these claims—according to what theory or method—was just as controversial as the claims themselves and the social policies they challenged.

The Court used the incorporation doctrine to enforce against the States certain requirements of federal due process. This notion that the Fourteenth Amendment applied to the States all and only (or, as it turned out, most) provisions of the original Bill of Rights, promised to constrain judges' discretion when deciding whether the federal constitution prohibited a State's interference with an individual's liberty.[3] But the incorporation doctrine's efficacy became applying it to questions of criminal procedure. It allowed what seemed a straightforward policing of civil rights—the governments of the States had to observe due process in their criminal courts like the federal government did in its.[4]

But incorporation did not as easily address allegations that the very subject matter a law addressed—its *substance*—impermissibly infringed the liberty of an individual. These were claims that the substantive content of a law lay beyond the ambit of legislative authority, because the State's objective was illegitimate, or the means it chose to accomplish it exceeded the legislative authority, or both. If an allegedly offending statute impacted a right already mentioned in the Bill of Rights, like the freedom of speech, incorporation might provide an answer.[5] But some on the Court struggled to develop a broader theory of "fundamental rights," insisting that the Amendment's due-process guarantee meant federal protection against the States for certain substantive rights, whether enumerated or not.

Using a controversial analysis the incorporation doctrine made possible, in 1965, the Court in *Griswold v. Connecticut*[6] found an impermissible deprivation of liberty in the State's criminalizing married couples' using contraceptives. The Court said penumbras emanating from some Bill of Rights provisions formed a "zone of privacy," and held that the liberty to use contraceptives was a "right" within it.[7] This strange spatial metaphor ostensibly connected the protections of the Fourteenth Amendment's due-process guarantee to an extant jurisprudence of substantive rights the federal constitution already recognized. Within the "zone," the Court would in subsequent cases find additional "fundamental rights." The most controversial consequence of this doctrine was *Roe v. Wade*,[8] in which the Court identified, as such a "right" lying within the zone, a woman's decision to abort a fetus.[9]

Not long thereafter, a countervailing modern conservative doctrine of fundamental rights appeared in the jurisprudence. Justice Antonin Scalia would spearhead the effort to implement it during the last two decades of the century.[10] According to this doctrine, there was no need for metaphysical inquiry into the nature of liberty interests to determine if they qualified as fundamental rights. This inquiry focused on "history and tradition"—a right was fundamental if its proponent could show that throughout the Nation's history the American States had traditionally recognized it as such.[11] A right's location vis-a-vis the "zone of privacy" was irrelevant. The zone itself was a myth—a far too capacious understanding of the "liberty" that due process protected. This was evident in the Court's striking down as unconstitutional state laws regulating aspects of social life many believed lay within the authority of the States to regulate. Modern conservatism adopted a method aimed at thwarting federal judicial displacement of state-legislative judgments about personal liberties.

But in the service of their respective aims, both the liberal and conservative doctrines of fundamental rights misappropriated a traditional understanding of due process. Surveying the last half-century of our jurisprudence for a coherent approach to evaluating personal-liberty claims, we find instead the consequences of the Court's quasi-incorporation in *Griswold*. Both so-called "liberal" and "conservative" factions on the Court advocated for a categorical approach to fundamental rights. They just disagreed about *how* to determine which liberties were included. What an incredible misunderstanding was the resulting dialectic that defined the jurisprudence throughout the second half of the twentieth century. And it cost the Court dearly in undermining its reputation as insulated from the corrupting influence of partisan ideologies.

In the twenty-first century, the dialectic resolved into Justice Anthony Kennedy's personal-liberty doctrine. A strange mixture of history and tradition on the one hand, and progressive conceptions of liberty and equality on the other,[12] Justice Kennedy culled his doctrine from both the liberal and conservative twentieth-century doctrines. So it not surprisingly exhibits its antecedents' foibles. Like them, it applies a theory of due process disintegrated from pre-*Griswold* jurisprudence, offering no coherent account of how the doctrine connects to a century-and-a-half of federal precedent that came before it.

Justice Kennedy applied the doctrine most recently in his opinion for the Court in *Obergell v. Hodges*, which vindicated the right of same sex couples to marry.[13] The decision leaves us with a personal-liberty jurisprudence that to some reflects broad principles of justice properly applied. But others level at it a serious criticism: while justified in terms of important principles of justice, it could not have happened without disregarding other important principles that limit the exercise of American judicial power. The decision connects to our concern for liberty and equality here in the twenty-first century, but it also disconnects us from some basic principles of our legal tradition that protect democracy against a federal judiciary impermissibly encroaching upon self-government in the States. We ought to examine this foundation closely, if upon it we are to safely rest such important liberties.

***

The understanding of due process presented here is likely unfamiliar to readers acquainted with modern personal-liberty jurisprudence. In it dissolves the distinction between oxymoronic "substantive due process" and its procedural counterpart. There are no substantive rights which, although unenumerated, are nevertheless fundamental. And "deeply rooted in history and tradition" means something far different than it did to either Justices Scalia or Kennedy. These cryptic features of personal-liberty jurisprudence make sense only in light of what came before them. Seen as part of a longer story we must know to understand them, these familiar trappings of due-process analysis are recent innovations, corresponding to the Court's mid twentieth-century break from the tradition of reasoned judgment.

But seven centuries of due process jurisprudence preceded the modern-liberal and conservative personal-liberty doctrines, over 100 years of which was American federal jurisprudence. Throughout it, the voices of great jurists remind us that there is a coherent and principled practice for resolving controversies about legislative interference with basic liberties. And within this tradition, we discover the origin of the due-process guarantee: The Concept of Ordered Liberty. What follows here is a story of this special judicial concept and its inextricable relationship to the meaning of due process. It tells of how a common-law practice implementing the concept appeared in federal jurisprudence in the nineteenth century, and explores the judicial opinions through which it developed during the late nineteenth century through the end of the twentieth.

To one familiar with today's personal-liberty cases, the concept might seem obscure—like discovering a sacred relic of jurisprudential arcana. But it was not always an esoteric mystery. The reader will meet a lineage of common-law judges that preserved its connection to its origins while developing its application at the cutting edge of the American legal tradition. The story cannot help but pay homage to three of them—a giant, a sage, and a hero—a special order of twentieth-century luminaries who together produced the modern canon of common-law due-process review.[14]

But even as they worked to infuse it with the light of the tradition's grand ideals, this precious gem of reasoned judgment fell into dubious hands. Through misunderstanding, mishap, and deliberate misuse, it was co-opted and defiled. And today, this remarkable theory of individual liberty and its relationship to democratic social order has been forgotten. The tale that follows here nevertheless dares to anticipate its rediscovery in this century.

So the ending is for now uncertain.

But as any properly told story must, this one starts at the beginning.

NOTES

1. U.S. Const. amend. XIV § 1.

2. *See, e.g., Griswold v. Connecticut*, 381 U.S. 479 (1965); *Moore v. City of East Cleveland*, 431 U.S. 494 (1977); *Loving v. Virginia*, 388 U.S. 1 (1967); *Roe v. Wade*, 410 U.S. 113 (1973); *Bowers v. Hardwick*, 478 U.S. 186 (1986).

3. *See, e.g., Adamson v. California*, 332 U.S. 46, 67–71 (1947) (Black, J., dissenting).

4. *See, e.g., Pointer v. Texas*, 380 U.S. 400 (1965); *Klopfer v. North Carolina*, 386 U.S. 213 (1967); *Washington v. Texas*, 388 U.S. 14 (1967); *Duncan v. Louisiana*, 391 U.S. 145 (1968).

5. *See, e.g., De Jonge v. Oregon*, 299 U.S. 353, 364 (1937); *Herndon v. Lowry*, 301 U.S. 242, 259 (1937).

6. 381 U.S. 479 (1965).

7. *Id.* at 483–485.

8. 410 U.S. 113 (1973).

9. *Id.* at 154.

10. *See Bowers v. Hardwick*, 478 U.S. 186 (1986), discussed in chapter 8, *infra*; *Michael H. v. Gerald D.*, 491 U.S. 110 (1989), discussed in chapter 9, *infra.*

11. *See, e.g., Reno v. Flores*, 507 U.S. 292, 303 (1993); *see also Washington v. Glucksberg*, 521 U.S. 702 (1997), discussed in chapter 11, *infra.*

12. *See, e.g., United States v. Windsor*, 570 U.S. 744 (2013), discussed in chapter 14, *infra*; *Obergefell v. Hodges*, 135 S.Ct. 2584 (2015), discussed in chapter 15, *infra*.

13. 135 S.Ct. 2584 (2015).

14. *See Palko v. Connecticut*, 302 U.S. 319 (1937); *Poe v. Ullman*, 367 U.S. 497 (1961) (Harlan, J., dissenting); and *Washington v. Glucksberg*, 521 U.S. 702 (1997) (Souter, J., concurring), discussed *infra*.

Part I

THE COMMON-LAW TRADITION

And it appears in our books, that in many cases, the common law will controul acts of parliament, and sometimes adjudge them to be utterly void: for when an act of parliament is against common right and reason, or repugnant, or impossible to be performed, the common law will controul it, and adjudge such act to be void.

—*Bonham's Case*, 8 Co. Rep. 114a (C.P. 1610).

Chapter 1

A Bulwark against Arbitrary Legislation

There is no more important figure to our understanding the common-law due-process tradition than the sage of this story, Justice John Marshall Harlan II (1899–1971). He served as an associate justice of the Supreme Court from 1955 to 1971, occupying a peculiar position in American legal history. He dissented from the Court's 1961 ruling in *Poe v. Ullman*[1] that rejected for lack of standing the claim that would reappear in the landmark case of *Griswold v. Connecticut*[2]—that a Connecticut law impermissibly interfered with the liberty of married couples to use contraceptives. Harlan's *Poe* dissent provided the first example of properly applying the common-law due-process tradition to a modern personal-liberty question.[3]

As the controversy raged over how to adjudicate claims to liberty under the Fourteenth Amendment, Justice Harlan judged them from a peculiar perspective. The emerging doctrines—both incorporation and fundamental-rights—were unprincipled departures from the American legal tradition. Harlan would reach the same results as the mid-twentieth-century Court in some important cases, including *Griswold.* But he would do so with a very different method. Harlan demonstrated a common-law sensibility, asking in each case whether in light of the importance of the particular liberty interest and under the circumstances of its alleged violation, the State's interference could be adjudged reasonable.

Rejecting the incorporation doctrine, Harlan insisted the due-process guarantee could not "be reduced to any formula."[4] "Its content," he argued, could not "be determined by reference to any code."[5] When considering an individual's claim that a State impermissibly infringed a basic liberty, "[n]o formula could serve as a substitute . . . for judgment and restraint."[6] Despite its promise to contain judicial discretion, the mechanistic ease of incorporation belied its abrogating a critical obligation the American legal tradition imposed on its judges—the delicate balancing of interests in each unique case where individual liberty challenged democratic authority. The common-law due-process tradition, Harlan said mysteriously, "is a living thing."[7]

His approach likewise eschewed what the twentieth-century Court would nevertheless embrace—a category of rights worthy of heightened federal protection. Like incorporation this was an improper substitute for evaluating contending interests in discrete cases and controversies under the liberty provision of the Due Process Clause. Justice Harlan described the provision as "a rational continuum which, broadly speaking, includes a freedom from all substantial arbitrary impositions and purposeless restraints[.]"[8] State laws often interfered with individual liberties, and it was not the work of the Court to determine which were categorically untouchable. The Court's obligation in personal-liberty cases was to decide whether a State had run into the "bulwark against arbitrary legislation" that was the due-process guarantee.[9]

The guarantee "represented the balance which our Nation, built upon postulates of respect for the liberty of the individual, has struck between that liberty and the demands of organized society."[10] This balancing of order and liberty was a dynamic feature of American democracy—one suitable to a rapidly changing nation in which novel claims to liberty inevitably arose. The fledgling American Nation had not merely substituted majority rule for monarchy and its penchant for tyranny. It chose self-government as the means to establish social order. But it did so within a legal paradigm that imposed limitations on majority rule. The people consented to American democracy because it promised to secure each person's liberty. According to its corresponding legal tradition, an arbitrary—or, unreasonable—legislative infringement of an individual's basic liberty was against the law. Like his forbears, Justice Harlan recognized the due-process guarantee as a textual distillation of this basic value underlying American society.[11]

His federal ancestors had applied it to post-Reconstruction controversies under the Fourteenth Amendment. They did so recognizing that judicial review of legislation for arbitrariness originated in the common law that the colonists had brought to the New World.[12] Even before Reconstruction, the common law protected basic civil liberties against unreasonable government intrusion. In the colonies and then the Confederated States, the resolutions of such controversies lay within the jurisdictions of the colonial and state courts.[13] These pre-constitutional political communities applied the due-process or law-of-the-land clauses in their founding documents, which prohibited arbitrary legislative interference with basic liberties.[14]

The lineage of judges to which Harlan belonged honored this history and connected Fourteenth-Amendment jurisprudence to the tradition of reasoned judgment. There they found meaningful constraints on judicial discretion when evaluating the balance struck between democratically wielded governmental power and individuals' basic liberties. And they obeyed the common law's command that the reasons resolving discrete cases and controversies comprise the Nation's ongoing justification for consenting to democratic self-governance in the first instance.

***

As the War Between the States ended, the American Nation made the most significant changes to its constitution since ratifying the Bill of Rights in 1791. The Reconstruction Amendments abolished slavery,[15] prohibited denying the right to vote on account of race,[16] and gave individuals residing within the Union protections against the legislatures of the States in which they resided.[17] The Fourteenth Amendment guaranteed that "no State shall deprive any person of . . . liberty . . . without due process of law."[18] This created a new cause of action. Individuals could challenge, in the federal courts, acts of their own States' legislatures as violative of the due-process guarantee. It did not take long for such claims to make their way to the Nation's highest Court.

In March of 1869, one year after ratification of the Fourteenth Amendment, the Louisiana legislature approved "[a]n act to protect the health of the City of New Orleans[.]"[19] The law required "locat[ing] the stock landings and slaughter-houses, and [it] incorporate[d] the Crescent City Live-Stock Landing and Slaughter-House Company" ("the Company").[20] It prohibited slaughtering any animals within the City of New Orleans and adjacent parishes, except for the Company—seventeen persons exempted from the Act's prohibition.[21] The Act required the Company to build a slaughtering facility large enough to accommodate all New-Orleans butchers and process 500 animals each day.[22]

It gave the Company the exclusive right to build and operate livestock landings, and to have all livestock intended for sale in New Orleans and the adjacent parishes landed at its sites and slaughtered in its slaughterhouse.[23] The Company would open its slaughterhouse to local butchers to use according to a fee schedule.[24] The governor of the State would appoint an inspector to monitor the quality of animals intended for slaughter, and, for a fee, certify whether they were fit for human consumption.[25] The regulations applied to an area covering 1,154 square miles, with a population of between 200,000 and 300,000 persons and approximately 100 of them employed in the daily business of procuring and selling meat.[26]

In litigation known as the *Slaughterhouse Cases*, the Butchers' Benevolent Association of New Orleans sued the State, alleging that the Act violated the Fourteenth Amendment.[27] The Association claimed the Act prevented its members from making a living according to their trade, and thus violated the Fourteenth Amendment's guarantee that "[n]o state shall make or enforce any law which shall abridge the privileges or immunities of citizens of the United States[.]"[28] The Act interfered with its members' basic right to work and to use their own property in doing so, and it granted a monopoly in violation of the common laws in the States and England.[29] It violated the Amendment's guarantee of equal protection of the laws and its due-process guarantee.[30] As citizens of the post-Reconstruction federal Union, the butchers sought shelter in the provisions of the recent Amendment, from an onerous law their own State's legislators passed.

The Association's claims rested on the proposition that the Amendment had recalibrated the relationships among the citizens of the States and of the federal Union and their governments.[31] Prior to the formation of the Union and the War establishing its supremacy over them, the States were the "highest political organization[s]" and, therefore, the protectors of civil liberties.[32] The Union had "no existence save as an incomplete combination among several integers."[33] The Association argued that the Fourteenth Amendment had "forever destroyed . . . all such doctrines."[34] Now, it claimed, "State laws must be so framed as to secure life, liberty, [and] property from arbitrary violation and secure protection of law to all[.]"[35] Because of the Fourteenth Amendment, they claimed,

> The tie between the United States and every citizen in every part of its own jurisdiction has been made intimate and familiar. To the same extent the confederate features of the government have been obliterated. The States in their closest connection with the members of the State, have been placed under the oversight and restraining and enforcing hand of Congress. The purpose is manifest, to establish through the whole jurisdiction of the United States one people, and that every member of the empire shall understand and appreciate the fact that his privileges and immunities cannot be abridged by State authority[.][36]

The Association insisted the Amendment provided federal protection for basic liberties formerly entrusted solely to the States. As the colonies and States had recognized before the War, these liberties were traceable to the English Magna Carta, but now the federal constitution also secured them. A U.S. citizen's rights "must not be impaired, and all the privileges of the English Magna Charta in favor of freemen are collected upon him and overshadow him as derived from this amendment."[37] To the people of the United States, the Amendment was a declaration: "Take and hold this your certificate of status and of capacity, the Magna Charta of your rights and liberties . . . . The States must not weaken nor destroy them."[38]

In 1872, the U.S. Supreme Court rejected this seminal post–Civil War claim that the Fourteenth Amendment authorized federal-judicial displacement of the State's law infringing these citizens' liberties.[39] It dismissed the contention that persons throughout the postwar Union could find federal protection for their basic liberties against the States.[40] And it held that security for basic liberties, as before the War and the post-Reconstruction Amendments, remained the States' concern.[41] The impact of the opinions in the *Slaughterhouse Cases* would ripple throughout Fourteenth-Amendment jurisprudence for the next 150 years. The concept of ordered liberty would appear in the opinions of the dissenting justices, at this point only a hint of what it would become in its full federal manifestation. Soon thereafter, it would appear in a majority opinion of the Court, and begin a century-and-a-half-long journey toward its full realization.

PRIVILEGES AND IMMUNITIES

Writing for the majority in *Slaughterhouse*, Justice Samuel Freeman Miller began with two observations. First, Section 1 of the Fourteenth Amendment recognized dual citizenship—an individual was a citizen of his or her state of residence, and also a citizen of the United States.[42] Second, "the distinction between citizenship of the United States and citizenship of a state [was] clearly recognized and established."[43] The Court saw the Association's argument as resting on the incorrect "assumption that [state and federal] citizenship [were] the same, and the privileges and immunities guaranteed by the [Fourteenth Amendment's Privileges or Immunities] clause [were] the same."[44] The Court recognized that the right to earn a living according to one's trade was a privilege or immunity of citizenship, but it rejected the Association's claim that the federal government, as well as the States, was obligated to protect it.[45] Any redress of the butchers' grievances would have to come from the State of Louisiana.

In construing the privileges or immunities of citizenship, Justice Miller looked to an early-nineteenth-century case, *Corfield v. Coryell*.[46] In *Corfield*, the Court discussed privileges and immunities protected under Article IV of the Constitution. Section 2 of Article IV guaranteed that "[t]he citizens of each state are entitled to all Privileges and Immunities of citizens in the several States."[47] A citizen of Pennsylvania challenged a New Jersey law pursuant to which the latter State impounded his vessel while in the possession of a lessee raking for oysters off the New Jersey coast.[48] The law reserved the right to harvest oysters to "actual inhabitant[s] and resident[s]" in New Jersey, and required they do so on vessels "wholly owned by some person, inhabitant of, and actually residing in this state[.]"[49] The vessel's owner argued that the law violated Article IV Section 2 because New Jersey granted to its own citizens what it denied to the citizens of other States. He argued that access to the oyster beds of the New Jersey coast was a "privilege and immunity of the citizens in the several States," and, therefore, New Jersey could not exclude out-of-staters or impound their vessels if they raked for oysters.

In evaluating the vessel owner's claim, Justice Bushrod Washington, writing for the Court in *Corfield*, described the privileges and immunities that Article IV guaranteed as:

> [T]hose privileges and immunities which are fundamental; which belong of right to the citizens of all free governments, and which have at all times been enjoyed by citizens of the several States which compose this Union, from the time of their becoming free, independent, and sovereign.[50] [T]hese fundamental principles are . . . comprehended under the following general heads: Protection by the government; the enjoyment of life and liberty, with the right to acquire and access property of every kind, and to pursue and obtain happiness and safety; subject nevertheless to such restraints as the government may justly prescribe for the good of the whole.[51]

This description reflected the basic values the several American States shared, now as members of the United States under the Constitution, as they had as members of the Confederated States under the Articles of Confederation.[52] The state governments were established to secure citizens' civil liberties—those basic guarantees that "all free governments" honored, but that were at the same time subject to reasonable restraints in protecting the interests of the political community. The *Corfield* Court interpreted Article IV Section 2 to mean that, like all free governments, the American States were obligated to honor individuals' basic liberties—"the privileges and immunities of citizens in the several States"—and so the citizens in each State were constitutionally entitled to them. But it rejected the vessel owner's contention that the inverse of this proposition were true.

> But we cannot accede to the proposition which was insisted on by the counsel, that, under this provision of the constitution, the citizens of the several states are permitted to participate in all the rights which belong exclusively to the citizens of any other particular state, merely upon the ground that they are enjoyed by those citizens[.][53]

Section 2 did not entitle every citizen of every State to all the political benefits of citizenship in every other. It provided a federal cause of action for a citizen in one of the several States to challenge another State as unreasonably restraining a basic liberty, but "co-tenancy in the common property of the [S]tate of New Jersey" was not one.[54]

After discussing *Corfield*, the *Slaughterhouse* opinion noted that in *Ward v. The State of Maryland*,[55] the Court had "adopted in the main"

Corfield's "definition of the privileges and immunities of the States[.]"[56] But it concluded these were not the privileges or immunities the Fourteenth Amendment protected.

> [This] description, when taken to include others not named, but which are of the same general character, embraces nearly every civil right for the establishment and protection of which organized government is instituted. . . . And they have always been held to be the class of rights which the State governments were created to establish and secure.[57]

Unlike the vessel owner's claim in *Corfield*, the butchers' contention in *Slaughterhouse* was uncontroversial—the freedom to make a living was a purpose for which individuals established civil society under government. But the federal constitution did not protect the butchers' liberty against their own State's interference with it. While Article IV Section 2 provided a federal cause of action to a citizen of one of the several States to challenge another State's alleged violation of his basic liberties, the Fourteenth Amendment did not provide a federal cause of action for a citizen to challenge a similar violation of his own State's government. "[I]n [recent history] is found," Justice Miller explained, "the occasion and the necessity for recurring again to the great source of power in this country, the people of the States, for additional guarantees of human rights."[58]

The Court distinguished the privileges and immunities that Article IV Section 2 guaranteed from the privileges or immunities the Fourteenth Amendment prohibited the States from abridging. Article IV privileges and immunities—those guaranteed to citizens in the several States—were those fundamental to the purposes for which governments were established. The privileges and immunities of federal citizenship were not. Consequently, the butchers' right to make a living according to their trade, while a privilege and immunity of state citizenship, was not a privilege or immunity of federal citizenship, and, therefore, the Fourteenth Amendment did not protect it.[59]

> It is quite clear, then, that there is a citizenship of the United States, and a citizenship of a State, which are distinct from each other, and which depend upon different characteristics or circumstances in the individual.[60]

> The privileges and immunities relied on in the [Association's] argument are those which belong to citizens of the States as such, and that they are left to the State governments for security and protection, and not by [the Fourteenth Amendment] placed under the special care of the federal government.[61]

The Court found untenable the proposition at the heart of the Association's argument, that the Fourteenth Amendment had so radically altered American federalism. The Court asked, rhetorically,

> Was it the purpose of the fourteenth amendment, by the simple declaration that no State should make or enforce any law which shall abridge the privileges and immunities of citizens of the United States, to transfer the security and protection of all the civil rights which we have mentioned, from the States to the Federal government? And where it is declared that Congress shall have the power to enforce that article, was it intended to bring within the power of Congress the entire domain of civil rights heretofore belonging exclusively to the states?[62]

And it answered,

> The argument we admit is not always the most conclusive which is drawn from the consequences urged against the adoption of a particular construction of an instrument. But when, as in the case before us, these consequences are so serious, so far reaching and pervading, so great a departure from the structure and spirit of our institutions; when the effect is to fetter and degrade the State governments by subjecting them to the control of Congress, in the exercise of powers heretofore universally conceded to them of the most ordinary and fundamental character; when it in fact radically changes the whole theory of the relations of the State and Federal governments to each other and of both these governments to the people; the argument has a force that is irresistible, in the absence of language which expresses such a purpose too clearly to admit of doubt.[63]

The Fourteenth Amendment had not altered federalism as the Association argued. It did not transfer the security and protection of civil liberties from the States to the federal government.

> Unquestionably this [Civil War] has given great force to the argument, and added largely to the number of those who believe in the necessity of a strong National government. But, however pervading this sentiment, and however it may have contributed to the adoption of the [Thirteenth, Fourteenth, and Fifteenth] amendments we have been considering, we do not see in those amendments any purpose to destroy the main features of the general system.[64]

Recognizing the implication of its decision, the Court offered some examples of privileges or immunities of federal citizenship. "[L]est it should be said that no such privileges and immunities are to be found if those we have been considering are excluded," Miller wrote, "we venture to suggest some which owe their existence to the Federal government[.]"[65] The Amendment protected a U.S. citizen's right to assert "any claim he may have upon that government, to seek its protection, to share its offices, to engage in administering its functions."[66] It guaranteed the use of seaports and the navigable waters of the United States, and access to courts of justice.[67] It protected a citizen's life, liberty, and property "when on the high seas or within the jurisdiction of a foreign government."[68] It guaranteed the right to peaceably assemble and petition the government for redress of grievances, and to become a citizen of a State.[69]

***

For the dissenting justices, the majority's conception of federal privileges or immunities belied the empty conclusion it reached: the Fourteenth Amendment was a redundancy. It protected rights already federally protected before its ratification. In his dissent, Justice Stephen Field wrote,

> If this inhibition . . . only refers, as held by the majority of the court in their opinion, to such privileges and immunities as were before its adoption specially designated in the Constitution or necessarily implied as belonging to citizens of the United States, it was a vain and idle enactment, which accomplished nothing, and most unnecessarily excited Congress and the people on its passage.[70]

Field recognized what the majority refused to acknowledge. The Fourteenth Amendment fundamentally changed federalism.

> The question presented is, therefore, one of the gravest importance, not merely to the parties here, but to the whole country. It is nothing less than the question whether the recent amendments to the Federal Constitution protect the citizens of the United States against the deprivation of their common rights by State legislation. In my judgement the fourteenth amendment does afford such protection[.][71]

He agreed with the majority that *Corfield* had correctly described the purpose and character of the privileges and immunities of citizenship—the basic liberties "which of right belong to the citizens of all free governments."[72] But he rejected the conclusion that the responsibility for protecting these "common rights" remained solely with the States. "The amendment was adopted," he argued, "to place the common rights of American citizens under the protection of the National government."[73]

Justice Field emphasized the significance of the Amendment's granting federal citizenship.[74] Citizenship and the basic liberties attendant to it no longer depended upon an individual's relationship to any State.

> A citizen of a State is now only a citizen of the United States residing in that State. The fundamental rights, privileges, and immunities which belong to him as a free man and a free citizen, now belong to him as a citizen of the United States, and are not dependent upon his citizenship of any State.[75]

Citizens now enjoyed protection for their basic liberties as citizens of the post-Reconstruction federal Union. Just as Article IV Section 2 protected a state citizen's fundamental liberties against the governments of other States, the Fourteenth Amendment protected them against a U.S. citizen's own, as well as every other, State's government. "[I]f under the fourth article of the Constitution equality of privileges and immunities is secured between citizens of different States," Field argued, then "under the fourteenth amendment the same equality is secured between citizens of the United States."[76]

Field argued further that in this case, the Louisiana legislature had unjustifiably infringed a basic liberty. He recognized that state governments legitimately exercised traditional police powers in the public interest. Describing state power as "exercised on a great number of subjects, and in almost numberless ways[,]" he observed that "[a]ll sorts of restrictions and burdens [were] imposed under it," and it justified "regulations affecting the health, good order, morals, peace, and safety of society[.]"[77] When such exercises of state power did not "conflict with any constitutional prohibitions, or fundamental principles, they [could] not be successfully assailed in a judicial tribunal."[78] This conception of the States' powers echoed *Corfield*'s description of fundamental liberties as "subject nevertheless to such restraints as the government may justly prescribe for the good of the whole."[79] The question *Slaughterhouse* presented was whether the restraints the Act imposed on the butchers' livelihood were so prescribed. For Justice Field, the butchers' position—that the Act did not meet this standard—"ha[d] some support in the fundamental law of the country."[80]

To demonstrate this, he tested the law's application in the case before the Court for fitness with the State's justification for it. Not surprisingly, Louisiana contended the Act represented nothing more than a traditional exercise of state power. "It was adopted," the State argued, "in the interest of the city, to promote its cleanliness and protect its health, and was a legitimate exercise of what is termed the police power of the State."[81] Evaluating each consequence of the Act in light of this proffered justification, Justice Field concluded that the provisions requiring the landing and slaughtering of animals down river of New Orleans and requiring inspection of animals before slaughter were justified in light of their ostensible purpose. "When these requirements are complied with," he concluded, "the sanitary purposes of the act are accomplished."[82]

Considering its remaining provisions, however, Field concluded the Act was "a mere grant to a corporation created by it of special and exclusive privileges by which the health of the city is in no way promoted."[83] He reasoned that if the Crescent City Live-Stock Landing and Slaughter-House Company could do business within the prescribed area without endangering the public, so could others. The health of the City was a legitimate legislative objective, but "no such object could possibly justify legislation removing [slaughtering facilities] from a large part of the State for the benefit of a single corporation. The pretence [*sic*] of sanitary regulations for the grant of the exclusive privileges [was] a shallow one[.]"[84] The State could not use an otherwise legitimate regulation as a pretext to "encroach upon any of the just rights of the citizen, which the Constitution intended to secure against abridgement."[85] This common-law analysis, which examined the fit between the law's as-applied consequences to liberty and the State's justification for it, revealed that in granting a monopoly of the slaughterhouse and related industries, the legislature unjustifiably violated the common rights of these U.S. citizens.[86]

Consistent with his view of post-Reconstruction federalism—the federal constitution now protected basic liberties formerly entrusted solely to the States—Field cited to pre-Reconstruction state cases to support the proposition that a grant of exclusive privileges to select citizens, infringing the liberty of others to make a living, was not a legitimate exercise of the legislative power.[87] In *Norwich Gaslight Company v. The Norwich City Gas Company*,[88] the Supreme Court of Connecticut held that a city-council resolution granting to a private company exclusive use of "the streets for the purpose of distributing gas by means of pipes"[89] violated the first section of Connecticut's Bill of Rights declaring "that no man or set of men, are entitled to exclusive public emoluments, or privileges from the community."[90] But it recognized that even in the absence of any enumerated state or federal constitutional provisions prohibiting such grants of exclusive economic privileges (and resonant with *Corfield*'s conception of fundamental liberties), "the whole theory of a free government is opposed to such grants[.]"[91]

> As stated by the Supreme Court of Connecticut . . . grants of exclusive privileges, such as is made by the act in question, are opposed to the whole theory of free government, and it requires no aid from any bill of rights to render them void. That only is a free government, in the American sense of the term, under which the inalienable right of every citizen to pursue his happiness is unrestrained, except by just, equal, and impartial laws.[92]

Norwich recognized this settled common-law principle[93]—the same principle Justice Field applied in concluding that the federal constitution, as recently amended, protected the butchers from the portion of the Act that unreasonably infringed their freedom to make a living.[94]

Field would emphasize the "common rights" of citizens again a decade later in *Butcher's Union Co. v. Crescent City Co.*[95] In *Butcher's Union Co.*, the Court evaluated whether the new Louisiana Constitution, ratified in 1874, which included (as a response to the *Slaughterhouse* decision) a prohibition against grants of monopolies, violated the Contracts Clause of the federal constitution.[96] The new Louisiana Constitution recognized that local municipalities would regulate the slaughterhouse industry, and the Company claimed that local ordinances impaired its "contract" with Louisiana that *Slaughterhouse* upheld. The Court rejected the argument, and in his *Butcher's Union Co.* concurrence, Justice Field said again that the Act challenged in *Slaughterhouse*, "in creating the monopoly in an ordinary employment and business, was to that extent against common right, and void."[97]

Significantly, Field's analysis in both *Slaughterhouse* and *Butcher's Union Co.* rested on a conception of democracy in which principles restraining legislative power were so deeply rooted in the legal tradition that no overt expression of them in the organic laws of government was required. The common rights of citizens were "the purposes (of securing) which men enter into society."[98] To the extent these principles were made explicit in the foundational declarations and constitutions of free governments, they were expressions of preexisting immunities against government, and not grants of them.[99] They came before governments, the purpose of which was "not [to] grant them, but [to] secure them[.]"[100] As Justice Field explained in *Butcher's Union Co.*, in the American political tradition, "certain principles of morality are assumed to exist without which society would be impossible, so certain inherent rights lie at the foundation of all action and upon a recognition of them alone can free institutions be maintained[.]"[101]

Justice Joseph Bradley joined Field's *Slaughterhouse* opinion, and, in a dissent of his own offered "a few observations for the purpose of more fully illustrating [his] views . . . and the special grounds on which they rest[ed]."[102] He elaborated Field's observations about the Fourteenth Amendment's treatment of citizenship. The Amendment, he wrote, "settled . . . that citizenship of the United States is the primary citizenship in this country[,] and . . . State citizenship is secondary," derived from a U.S. "citizen's place of residence."[103] Bradley disagreed with the Court's distinguishing the rights attendant to federal citizenship from those of state citizenship.

> In this free country, the people of which inherited certain traditiona[l] rights and privileges from their ancestors, citizenship means something. It has

> certain privileges and immunities attached to it which the government, whether restricted by express or implied limitations, cannot take away or impair. It may do so temporarily by force, but it cannot do so by right. And these privileges and immunities attach as well to citizenship of the United States as to citizenship of the States.[104]

The "traditiona[l] rights and privileges" the American people "inherited . . . from their ancestors" were those *Corfield* recognized—the fundamental rights the citizens of all free governments held inviolately. The American people now held them as citizens of governments, state and federal, established for the purpose of securing them.[105] Many of the basic liberties of citizens, therefore, "would be the same in the one capacity as in the other."[106]

Before the ratification of the Fourteenth Amendment, the Constitution protected the basic liberties of citizens against federal-government incursion, while "the protection of the citizen in the enjoyment of his fundamental privileges and immunities . . . was largely left to State laws and State courts."[107] Historically, "the laws of the State" were "the great body of municipal laws intended for the protection of person and property[.]"[108] Only in circumstances where the Constitution expressly authorized it could "the General Government [interfere] between a State and its citizens[.]"[109] But, whereas "formerly the States were not prohibited from infringing any of the fundamental privileges and immunities of citizens of the United States, except in a few specified cases," Justice Bradley observed, "that cannot be said now, since the adoption of the fourteenth amendment."[110] The federal government now had the "requisite authority" to "administer relief to citizens of the United States" when their basic liberties "were actually invaded by the unconstitutional acts or delinquency of the State governments themselves."[111] "In my judgment," he wrote, "it was the intention of the people of this country in adopting that amendment to provide National security against violation by the States of the fundamental rights of the citizen."[112]

THE GUARANTEE OF DUE PROCESS

Justice Bradley criticized the *Slaughterhouse* majority's "very narrow and insufficient estimate of constitutional history" and of the fundamental "rights of . . . the American people."[113] These rights were, at the time the "people of this country [came] to its shores[,] the rights of Englishmen; the rights which had been wrested from English sovereigns at various periods of [that] nation's history."[114] Bradley focused on one of these rights now enshrined in the Fourteenth Amendment—the guarantee of due process—and its origin in the twenty-ninth chapter of the English Magna Carta:

> No freeman shall be taken or imprisoned, or be disseized of his freehold or liberties or free customs, or be outlawed or exiled, or any otherwise destroyed; nor will we pass upon him or condemn him but by lawful judgment of his peers or by the law of the land.[115]

"English constitutional writers," Bradley explained, "expound this article as rendering life, liberty, and property inviolable, except by due process of law."[116] In America, this guarantee was something more than a sovereign's mere concession to the people, sanctioned by the English Parliament and therefore one it "[t]heoretically . . . might repeal[.]"[117] For the colonists brought to the New World an "unwritten constitution"—the English common law—into which the guarantee of due process, among other fundamental principles of government, had been assimilated.[118]

The guarantee had already become in England an "acknowledged . . . and frequently declared . . . privilege of . . . the people, to violate which in any a material respect would produce revolution in an hour."[119] And when they declared their independence from the British sovereign, the American people incorporated this common-law principle into the foundation of their new political experiment.

> [T]he Declaration of Independence, which was the first political act of the American people in their independent sovereign capacity, lays the foundation of our National existence upon this broad proposition: "That all men are created equal; that they are endowed by their creator with certain inalienable rights; that among these are life, liberty, and the pursuit of happiness." Here again we have the great threefold division of the rights of freemen, asserted as the rights of man. Rights to life, liberty, and the pursuit of happiness are equivalent to the rights of life, liberty, and property.[120]

This "broad proposition" was "specified in . . . the amendments to . . . the original Constitution . . . as among the privileges and immunities of citizens of the United States," and then in the Reconstruction Amendments.[121] According to Justice Bradley, "This [was] the very right which the [Association] claim[ed] in this case" under the Fourteenth Amendment's due-process provision.[122]

Like Justice Field, Bradley saw this right as so basic to the reasons for establishing American governments that it required no explicit textual expression. "[E]ven if the Constitution were silent," he wrote, "the fundamental privileges and immunities of citizens, as such, would be no less real and no less inviolable than they are now."[123] He argued that "the right of any citizen to follow whatever lawful employment he chooses to adopt" was one of the most valuable rights.[124] To preserve, exercise, and enjoy the basic rights to life, liberty, and property, "the individual citizen['s] . . . free[dom] to adopt

[a] calling, profession, or trade . . . most conducive to th[ese] ends" was a necessary condition.[125] "Without this right," Bradley argued, a person was not free.[126] This was a basic liberty—one implicating the reasons why American governments were established. "This right to choose one's calling[,]" he said, "is an essential part of that liberty [that] it is the object of government to protect."[127]

An infringement of even a basic liberty, however, was no automatic warrant for the post-Reconstruction federal judiciary to supplant the will of the State's people expressed in its laws. Like Justice Field, who recognized that now-nationally secured basic liberties were not absolute rights against state interference, Bradley acknowledged the "broad and extensive . . . right of a State to regulate the conduct of its citizens[.]"[128] The citizen was obligated to "submit[] . . . to all lawful regulations[.]"[129] At the same time, the fundamental rights to life, liberty, and property meant nothing if a legislature could "arbitrarily assail[]" them.[130] While a State could "prescribe the manner of [the] exercise" of these basic liberties, it could "not subvert the rights themselves."[131] The basic liberties of citizens were not absolute, but they could "only be interfered with, [and] the enjoyment of [them could] only be modified, by lawful regulations necessary or proper for the mutual good of all[.]"[132]

As *Corfield* had explained, laws impacting basic liberties were subject to a special scrutiny. They must honor the process due the citizens of all free governments—they must be "justly prescribe[d] for the good of the whole."[133]

> That portion of the act which requires all slaughter-houses to be located below the city, and to be subject to inspection, etc., is clearly a police regulation. That portion which allows no one but the favored company to build, own, or have slaughter-houses is not a police regulation, and has not the faintest semblance of one. It is one of those arbitrary and unjust laws made in the interest of a few scheming individuals.[134]

The State's reasons here addressed its pursuit of the public's health. But the law's application had an impact on a basic liberty collateral to the State's pursuit of this otherwise legitimate objective. And the State's reasons did not address the collateral impact, on the butchers' freedom to make a living, of granting a monopoly over the slaughtering industry to seventeen persons—an already questionable legislative objective. Such an arbitrary state action violated the due-process guarantee. The common-law test of the Act's as-applied consequences for fitness with the State's justification for them revealed the law's *ultra vires* application here.

Justice Bradley thus proceeded through a two-part analysis.[135] Having invoked *Corfield*'s conception of basic liberties, he asked first if the butchers' freedom to pursue a living was "one of the rights and privileges of a citizen of the United States[.]"[136] Was the liberty for which the Association pleaded recognition a basic liberty that the post-Reconstruction federal government was obligated to protect? Bradley concluded that it was, but even so, it was "subject to such reasonable regulations as may be prescribed by law[.]"[137] The second step in the analysis asked whether the abridgment of the butchers' liberty here was reasonable—within the authority of the legislature to impose.[138] If the legislature arbitrarily impacted a basic liberty, it violated the fundamental guarantee of due process that the Fourteenth Amendment required the federal government to enforce.[139]

With its origin in the common law, the due-process guarantee promised protection for the "common rights" that Justice Field identified, against arbitrary, or, unreasonable, legislative encroachments.[140] Here, the law as applied had consequences collateral to the State's legitimate objectives, impacting a basic liberty with no legitimate power of any free government—including the American States'—to justify it. That portion of the Act responsible for these consequences—"material[] interfer[ence]" with an otherwise lawful trade—was "onerous, unreasonable, arbitrary, and unjust[,]"[141] and violated the due-process guarantee.

***

When the Court decided *Butcher's Union* Co. in 1884, alongside Field in a concurring opinion of his own, Bradley again explained his understanding of the due-process guarantee as effectuating the common-law prohibition against arbitrary legislative interference with basic liberties.[142] During the same term, the Court decided *Hurtado v. People of California*,[143] in which a defendant challenged a California criminal procedure as violative of the Fourteenth Amendment's due-process guarantee. Significantly, *Hurtado*'s analysis, like Bradley's in *Slaughterhouse* and in *Butcher's Union Co.*, recognized due process as substantiating a fundamental value underlying the American democratic experiment—one its legal tradition taught was the reason for establishing governments: protecting individual liberty against arbitrary exercises of democratic power.

Hurtado challenged in federal court his state conviction of first-degree murder and corresponding death sentence. He was charged under California law by information, and not on indictment or presentment to a grand jury as the Fifth Amendment required for individuals charged with federal felonies or capital crimes.[144] After losing his appeal to the California Supreme Court, Hurtado appealed to the U. S. Supreme Court, arguing that the Fifth Amendment's requirement of indictment by grand jury was essential to "that due process of law . . . secured and guaranteed by [the Fourteenth

Amendment], and which accordingly it [was] forbidden to the States respectively to dispense with in the administration of criminal law."[145] Hurtado argued that the "due process" the federal constitution guaranteed had "a fixed, definite, and technical meaning"[146]—it referred to particular forms of procedure and institutions that "immemorial usage" validated.[147] Because California charged him without a grand jury returning an indictment, Hurtado argued that allowing his conviction and sentence to stand would deprive him of life or liberty without due process of law.[148]

The Court recognized, as it had in *Slaughterhouse*, that the question before it was "one of grave and serious import . . . and involve[d] a consideration of what additional restrictions [the Fourteenth Amendment placed] upon the legislative policy of the States."[149] Writing for the majority, Justice Stanley Matthews concluded that California's criminal procedure met the requirements of due process under the Fourteenth Amendment. This conclusion was consistent with the *Slaughterhouse* majority's maintenance of prewar federalism, insofar as it recognized the State's discretion to decide what particular forms of judicial procedure its criminal justice system required. But the opinion resonated with the *Slaughterhouse* dissenters' analyses in two important respects, bringing Justice Bradley's understanding of the guarantee into the Court's jurisprudence. First, reasonable criminal procedures protected the liberties belonging to the citizens of all free governments. And second, the due-process guarantee's origin was the English Magna Carta's prohibition against arbitrary, or, unreasonable, interference with basic liberties.

Justice Matthews did not evaluate California's charging procedure, as Hurtado argued the Court should, against the Fifth Amendment's guarantee of felony or capital indictment by grand jury in federal criminal proceedings. He evaluated Hurtado's challenge to California's criminal procedure like the *Slaughterhouse* dissenters evaluated the Association's claim that the Act in that case violated a fundamental liberty. The question in each case was the same—whether the common-law analysis showed that the State's action violated a fundamental principle of liberty and justice inherent to the American democratic experiment—governments may not arbitrarily deprive individuals of their basic liberties.

Rejecting Hurtado's primary argument, Matthews invoked a well-settled canon of construction. It was "forbidden to assume, without clear reason to the contrary, that any part of this most important amendment [was] superfluous."[150] The Fifth Amendment's Due Process Clause was among other guarantees enumerated in the same Amendment, including the requirement of indictment by grand jury, so "due process" in the Fifth Amendment could not be a redundant reference to the grand jury requirement. The identical clause in the Fourteenth Amendment indicated that the federal prohibition against deprivation of liberty without due process of law now bound the federal and state governments, as it did the federal government before the Reconstruction Amendments. The due-process guarantee referred not to forms of procedure employed in the federal courts, but to fundamental principles of American government and law.

> Due process of law in the [Fifth Amendment] refers to that law of the land which derives its authority from the legislative powers conferred upon congress by the constitution of the United States, exercised within the limits therein prescribed, and interpreted according to the principles of the common law. In the fourteenth amendment, by parity of reason, it refers to that law of the land in each state which derives its authority from the inherent and reserved powers of the state, exerted within the limits of those fundamental principles of liberty and justice which lie at the base of all our civil and political institutions[.][151]

Justice Matthews approved of the California Supreme Court's conclusion that the Fourteenth Amendment did "not confine the States to a particular mode of procedure in judicial proceedings."[152] The due-process guarantee, he wrote, was "designed to protect the citizen against all mere acts of power, whether flowing from the legislative or executive branches of the government."[153] It was "intended to secure the individual from the arbitrary exercise of the powers of government, unrestrained by the established principles of private right and distributive justice."[154] *Hurtado*'s articulation of the limits that due process imposed on the States in prescribing their own judicial proceedings was identical to Bradley and Field's understanding of the limits the Fourteenth Amendment imposed on substantive legislation.[155]

> It necessarily happened, therefore, that as these broad and general maxims of liberty and justice held in our system a different place and performed a different function from their position and office in English constitutional history and law, they would receive and justify a corresponding and more comprehensive interpretation. Applied in England only as guards against executive usurpation and tyranny, here they have become bulwarks also against arbitrary legislation; but, in that application, as it would be incongruous to measure and restrict them by the ancient customary English law, they must be held to guarantee not particular forms of procedure, but the very substance of individual rights to life, liberty, and property.[156]

The twenty-ninth chapter of Magna Carta had been in England a bulwark against arbitrary exercises of executive power.[157] In the United States, where constitutions—state and federal—vested lawmaking power in legislatures, the due-process guarantee protected citizens against arbitrary legislative interference with their basic liberties.[158] *Hurtado* identified a necessary limitation on the exercise of legislative power in a self-governing political community ordered under republican principles. Matthews explained: "Arbitrary power, enforcing its edicts to the injury of the persons and property of its subjects, is not law, whether manifested as the decree of a personal monarch or of an impersonal multitude."[159]

Law was not merely what a majority through its representatives said it was.[160] "It is not every act," Matthews observed, "legislative in form, that is law. Law is something more than mere will exerted as an act of power."[161] It was law only if it honored a foundational principle upon which American governments were erected. Individuals consented to live within a political community that governed itself for the purpose of securing their basic liberties. An arbitrary legislative infringement of a basic liberty, therefore, was not an authentically legislative act. Those who consented to democracy for the purpose of securing their basic liberties did not—indeed, could not—authorize arbitrary infringements of them.

Hurtado's suggestion that due process was limited to particular forms of procedure employed in the past ignored the common-law origins of the concept, and threatened to undermine its ability to address new circumstances and situations.[162]

> [T]o hold that such a characteristic is essential to due process of law, would be to deny every quality of the law but its age, and to render it incapable of progress or improvement. It would be to stamp upon our jurisprudence the unchangeableness attributed to the laws of the Medes and Persians.[163]

> There is nothing in Magna Charta, rightly construed as a broad charter of public right and law, which ought to exclude the best ideas of all systems and of every age; and as it was the characteristic principle of the common law to draw its inspiration from every fountain of justice, we are not to assume that the sources of its supply have been exhausted. On the contrary, we should expect that the new and various experiences of our own situation and system will mould [*sic*] and shape it into new and useful forms.[164]

The age of a particular form of procedure did not determine whether it afforded due process.

> It follows that any legal proceeding enforced by public authority, whether sanctioned by age and custom, or newly devised in the discretion of the legislative power . . . which regards and preserves these principles of liberty and justice, must be held to be due process of law.[165]

And following Justice Field's example, Justice Matthews looked to state cases—where prior to Reconstruction the common-law due-process tradition developed—to elaborate the concept and connect it to the English common law.[166]

> The supreme court of Mississippi, in a well-considered case, speaking of the meaning of the phrase "due process of law," says: "The principle does not demand that the laws existing at any point of time shall be irrepealable, or that any forms of remedies shall necessarily continue. The principle . . . refers to certain fundamental rights which [the English] system of jurisprudence, of which ours is a derivative, has always recognized. If any of these are disregarded in the proceedings by which a person is condemned to the loss of life, liberty, or property, then the deprivation has not been by 'due process of law.'"[167]

Matthews evaluated the means California chose to charge Hurtado with criminal offenses, and found safeguards sufficient to defeat Hurtado's claim that he was denied due process.

> Tried by these principles, we are unable to say that the substitution for a presentment or indictment by a grand jury of the proceedings by information after examination and commitment by a magistrate, certifying to the probable guilt of the defendant, with the right on his part to the aid of counsel, and to the cross-examination of the witnesses produced for the prosecution, is not due process of law.[168]

Implicit in this conclusion was the *Slaughterhouse* dissenters' common-law analysis. The answer to the first question, whether the liberty at stake implicated the due-process guarantee, was obvious. The consequences to Hurtado here—incarceration and death—were the most basic deprivations of liberty and life. Reasonable criminal procedures prevented governments from arbitrarily depriving persons of liberty and life. The question was whether the means through which California charged this defendant with a capital offense were reasonable. Answering it required the very inquiry the common-law test for arbitrariness made, evaluating the means the State chose for fitness with its objective. *Hurtado*'s explanation of the due-process guarantee made clear that the objective of reasonable criminal procedures was to effectuate a principle of justice fundamental to American government—the same principle the *Slaughterhouse* dissenters invoked.

Here, the protections the State afforded Hurtado before charging him with a capital offense included a hearing before a magistrate who evaluated probable cause, the right to confront and cross-examine the witnesses supporting the charges, and the aid of counsel throughout the proceeding. These features arguably left liberty at least as secure as did the federal protection of indictment after presentment to a grand jury. Post-Reconstruction, American federalism was still intact. Matthews quoted Justice Bradley:

> The Fourteenth Amendment does not profess to secure to all persons in the United States the benefit of the same laws and the same remedies. Great diversities in these respects may exist . . . . Each state prescribes its own mode of judicial proceedings.[169]

California was not required to mimic the federal government's criminal procedures, and the means it employed in this case were not an arbitrary exercise of the State's power. They were reasonable, and so afforded due process.

***

Whether evaluating substantive legislation alleged to deprive persons of basic liberties without due process (as in the *Slaughterhouse* dissents), or criminal procedures ostensibly suffering from the same defect (as in *Hurtado*), the answer to the question of whether a State transgressed the limits of its reserved powers lay in the common-law tradition of arbitrariness review. This venerable methodology implemented a core concept of American governments, testing the validity of legislative resolutions of the tension between the States' interests in maintaining social order and individuals' interests in liberty. Despite the *Slaughterhouse* holding, *Hurtado*'s majority opinion freed the concept from the realm of dissent. Another fifty years would pass before a legendary giant of American law would speak its name in the twentieth century.[170] Even as yet unnamed, this elegant concept captured a central insight of the American political experiment in its postwar manifestation. The States were free to govern themselves democratically, but the federal courts could review for arbitrariness the balance they struck between maintaining social order and respecting the basic liberties of individuals.

NOTES

1. 367 U.S. 497 (1961).
2. 381 U.S. 479 (1965).
3. *See Poe*, 367 U.S. at 545–555 (Harlan, J., dissenting), discussed in chapter 4, *infra*.
4. 367 U.S. at 542 (Harlan, J., dissenting).
5. *Id.*
6. *Id.*
7. *Id.*

8. *Id.* at 543.

9. *See Hurtado v. California*, 110 U.S. 516, 532 (1884), discussed *infra*.

10. 367 U.S. at 542 (Harlan, J., dissenting).

11. The protection against majoritarian abuse of the federal government's power appears in the Fifth Amendment to the U.S. Constitution; the protection against such abuse of state power appears in the Fourteenth. *See* U.S. Const. amend. V; U.S. Const. amend. XIV § 1.

12. *See Slaughterhouse Cases*, 83 U.S. 36 (1872); *Hurtado v. California,* 110 U.S. 516 (1884), discussed *infra*.

13. Examples follow throughout part I; s*ee also* Edward S. Corwin, *Liberty Against Government* (Baton Rouge: Louisiana State University Press, 1948), 64–66, 90–94.

14. *See* Corwin, *Liberty Against Government*, 90–91. After the formation of the United States in 1789, as before it, this review remained primarily a matter of state jurisprudence. But the nascent federal judiciary signaled that it too had the power to review legislation for fitness with first principles of American government. *See, e.g.*, *Calder v. Bull*, 3 U.S. 386, 388 (1798); *cf. Marbury v. Madison*, 1 Cranch 177 (1803).

15. U.S. Const. amend. XIII.

16. U.S. Const. amend. XV.

17. U.S. Const. amend. XIV.

18. *Id.* at § 1.

19. *Slaughterhouse Cases*, 83 U.S. at 38.

20. *Id.*

21. *Id.*

22. *Id.*

23. *Id.* at 40–41.

24. *Id.* at 42.

25. *Id.* at 41–42.

26. *Id.* at 43.

27. *Id.* at 58.

28. U.S. Const. amend. XIV, §1.

29. *Slaughterhouse Cases*, 83 U.S. at 48–49.

30. *Id.* at 49–57; *see also id.* at 66.

31. *Id.* at 51–52.

32. *Id.* at 51.

33. *Id.* at 52.

34. *Id.*

35. *Id.* at 53.

36. *Id.*

37. *Id.* at 54.

38. *Id.* at 54–55.

39. *Id.* at 61.

40. *Id.* at 77–78.

41. *Id.* at 67.

42. *Id.* at 73.

43. *Id.*
44. *Id.* at 74.
45. *Id.*
46. 6 F. Cas. 546 (1823).
47. *See* U.S. Const. art. IV, §2.
48. 6 F. Cas. at 546.
49. *Id.* at 547.
50. *Id.* at 551.
51. *Id.* at 551–552.
52. *See id.* at 552 ("[T]he enjoyment of [privileges and immunities] by the citizens of each state, in every other state, was manifestly calculated (to use the expressions of the preamble of the corresponding provision of the old articles of confederation) 'the better to secure and perpetuate the mutual friendship and intercourse among the people of the different states of the Union'.").
53. *Id.* at 552.
54. *Id.*
55. 79 U.S. 418 (1871).
56. *Slaughterhouse Cases*, 83 U.S. at 76.
57. *Id.*
58. *Id.* at 67.
59. The Court's maintaining this distinction between state and federal citizenship—which Section 1 of the Fourteenth Amendment arguably eliminated—allowed it to avoid the obvious conclusion that the language of the Fourteenth Amendment meant securing for citizens throughout one nation what Art. IV, Section 2 guaranteed them within the several States. *See, e.g.*, Jack Balkin, *Living Originalism* (Cambridge: Belknap Press of Harvard University Press, 2011), 189. ("The new language now protected the 'privileges or immunities of Citizens *of the United States*' instead of guaranteeing 'the *citizens of each State* all privileges and immunities of citizens *in the several States*'.") (emphasis in original).
60. 83 U.S. at 74.
61. *Id.* at 78; *see id.* at 75–78.
62. *Id.* at 77.
63. *Id.* at 78.
64. *Id.* at 82.
65. *Id.* at 79.
66. *Id.*
67. *Id.*
68. *Id.*
69. *Id.*
70. *Slaughterhouse Cases,* 83 U.S. at 96 (Field, J., dissenting).
71. *Id.* at 89.
72. *Id.* at 97.
73. *Id.* at 93.
74. *Id.* at 94–95.
75. *Id.* at 95.

76. *Id.* at 101. The central mistake of the *Slaughterhouse* majority was its bifurcating basic liberties that *necessitated* government for their protection—and were thus antecedent *to* governments—into those *derived* from (or at least attendant to) state and federal citizenship, respectively. Justice Washington's reasoning about basic liberties in *Corfield* was a natural place for the Court to look in construing Section 1 of the Fourteenth Amendment. The language of Section 1 had evolved from an original version that deliberately paralleled Article IV Section 2. The *Slaughterhouse* majority looked to the correct precedent, but misapplied the principle it specified. *See* Balkin, *Living Originalism*, 188–190 (noting that "many Republicans, including John Bingham himself, believed that Article IV, section 2, also protected substantive constitutional rights such as habeas corpus and the Bill of Rights").

77. *Id.* at 87.

78. *Id.*; *see* Thomas Cooley, *The General Principles of Constitutional Law in the United States*, ed. Andrew McLaughlin (Boston: Little, Brown, and Company, 1898), 241 ("The Fourteenth Amendment did not give the national government the general authority to regulate the relations between individuals. That power still inheres in the State; but the national government can now protect the individual against State action that would be subversive of fundamental rights.").

79. 6 F. Cas. at 552.

80. *Slaughterhouse Cases*, 83 U.S. at 87 (Field, J., dissenting).

81. *Id.*

82. *Id.*

83. *Id.*

84. *Id.* at 87–88.

85. *Id.* at 87.

86. *Slaughterhouse* would come to stand for the proposition that Justice Field recognized: "The Fourteenth Amendment is held not to have taken from the States the police power reserved to them at the time of the adoption of the Constitution." Cooley, *The General Principles of Constitutional Law in the United States*, 251. But the federal judicial power that Field argued the Fourteenth Amendment activated, to protect basic liberties that all free governments must observe, against American state action subversive of such liberties, became a settled feature of American constitutional law. *Id.* ("In the exercise of this [police] power regard must be paid to the fundamental principles of civil liberty, and to processes that are adapted to preserve and secure civil rights; persons cannot arbitrarily be deprived of equal protection of the laws, or of life, liberty, or property, because the State purports to be exercising the police power."). *See, e.g.*, *Mugler v. Kansas*, 123 U.S. 623, 661 (1887) (Harlan, J.) ("It belongs to [the legislative] department to exert what are known as the police powers of the state, and to determine, primarily, what measures are appropriate or needful for the protection of the public morals, the public safety, and the public health. It does not at all follow that every statute enacted ostensibly for the promotion of these ends is to be accepted as a legitimate exertion of the police power of the state. There are, of necessity, limits beyond which legislation cannot rightfully go. While every possible presumption is to be indulged in favor of the validity of a statute, the courts must obey the constitution rather than the law-making department of government, and

must, upon their own responsibility, determine whether, in any particular case, these limits have been passed.").

87. 83 U.S. at 106–107 (Field, J., dissenting) (citing *City of Chicago v. Rumpff*, 45 Illinois 90 (1867)); *id.* at 108–109 (citing *Norwich Gaslight Company v. The Norwich City Gas Company*, 25 Connecticut 19 (1856)); *id.* at 109 (citing *Mayor of the City of Hudson v. Thorne*, 7 Paige 261 (1838)). This practice of looking to state cases for the common-law understanding of the limits of legislative power would remain a feature of federal due-process jurisprudence. *See, e.g.*, *Lawton v. Steele*, 152 U.S. 133, 136–137 (1894) ("The extent and limits of what is known as the 'police power' have been a fruitful subject of discussion in the appellate courts of nearly every state in the Union. It is universally conceded to include everything essential to the public safety, health, and morals, and to justify the destruction or abatement, by summary proceedings, of whatever may be regarded as a public nuisance. . . . Beyond this, however, the state may interfere wherever the public interests demand it, and in this particular a large discretion is necessarily vested in the legislature to determine, not only what the interests of the public require, but what measures are necessary for the protection of such interests. To justify the state in thus interposing its authority in behalf of the public, it must appear—First, that the interests of the public generally, as distinguished from those of a particular class, require such interference; and, second, that the means are reasonably necessary for the accomplishment of the purpose, and not unduly oppressive upon individuals. The legislature may not, under the guise of protecting the public interests, arbitrarily interfere with private business, or impose unusual and unnecessary restrictions upon lawful occupations; in other words, its determination as to what is a proper exercise of its police powers is not final or conclusive, but is subject to the supervision of the courts.") (citing *Barbier v. Connolly*, 113 U.S. 27 (1884); *Kidd v. Pearson*, 128 U.S. 1 (1888)).

88. 25 Connecticut 19 (1856).

89. 25 Connecticut at 38.

90. *Id.*

91. 83 U.S. at 109 (Field, J., dissenting) (quoting 25 Connecticut at 38).

92. *Id.* at 110–111 (quoting 1 Sharswood's Blackstone, 127, note 8 ("Civil liberty, the great end of all government, is that state in which each individual has the power to pursue his own happiness according to his own views of his interest, and the dictates of his conscience, unrestrained, except by equal, just, and impartial laws.")).

93. 25 Connecticut at 38 ("The statute of 21 James I., C. 3, which declares such monopolies to be contrary to law and void . . . has always been considered as merely declaratory of the common law.").

94. 83 U.S. at 111 (Field, J., dissenting).

95. 111 U.S. 746 (1884) (Field, J., concurring).

96. U.S. Const. art. I, §10.

97. 111 U.S. at 760 (Field, J., concurring).

98. *Calder v. Bull*, 3 U.S. 386, 388 (1798) (as quoted in *Poe v. Ullman*, 367 U.S. 497, 541 (1961) (Harlan, J., dissenting)).

99. 111 U.S. at 757 (Field, J., concurring).

100. *Id.*

101. *Id.* at 756.
102. *Slaughterhouse Cases*, 83 U.S. at 111 (Bradley, J., dissenting).
103. *Id.* at 112.
104. *Id.*
105. Justice Bradley acknowledged the American tradition's notion that basic liberties necessitated governments to protect them, and thus preceded their formation, suggesting that a person's basic liberties did not depend on citizenship in *any* political community. These were basic liberties that belonged of right to all persons, and necessarily *including* the citizens of those free governments instituted to secure them. *See id.* at 118–119 ("[A]nd above all, and including almost all the rest, the right of not being deprived of life, liberty, or property without due process of law. These and still others are specified in the original Constitution, or in the early amendments of it, as among the privileges and immunities of citizens of the United States, or, what is still stronger for the force of the argument, the rights of all persons, whether citizens or not.") *See also* Balkin, *Living Originalism*, 192–193 ("The best reading . . . is that the phrase 'privileges or immunities of citizens of the United States' does not refer to rights exclusive to citizens; rather, it assumes that citizens' rights necessarily include the rights that the Constitution bestows on non-citizens.").
106. 83 U.S. at 121 (Bradley, J., dissenting).
107. *Id.*
108. *Id.*
109. *Id.*
110. *Id.* at 122.
111. *Id.* at 121.
112. *Id.* at 122; *see id.* at 121–123.
113. *Id.* at 116.
114. *Id.* at 114.
115. *Id.* (quoting Magna Carta, 1215).
116. *Id.* at 115.
117. *Id.*
118. *Id.*; *see* Corwin, *Liberty Against Government*, 22–23 ("Certain it is that the contribution of medieval England to the American theory of Liberty versus Government exhibits some striking similarities to the strictly American phase of the subject. There is to begin with a fundamental document, Magna Carta, to symbolize the subordination of political authority to law. Then ensues the slow absorption of this document into judge-made law, a process which is attended by the projection of a portion of the latter into a higher law of liberty.").
119. *Id.*
120. *Id.* at 116.
121. *Id.* at 116–119.
122. *Id.* at 115. The law-of-the-land clause of the English Magna Carta as the origin of the due-process guarantee was a settled understanding of the Nation's legal history. *See, e.g.*, Cooley, *The General Principles of Constitutional Law in the United States*, 241–242 (describing "due process of law" as "implying correct and orderly proceedings, which are due because they observe all the securities for private right

which are applicable in the particular case. In this sense it is synonymous with 'law of the land,' as used in the famous twenty-ninth chapter of Magna Carta[.] . . . The identity of the two in meaning and purpose is now well-settled.") (citing *Murray's Lesee v. Hoboken Land Co.*, 18 How. 272, 276 (1855) ("The words, 'due process of law' were undoubtedly intended to convey the same meaning as the words 'by the law of the land,' in Magna Charta. Lord Coke, in his commentary on those words (2 Inst. 50), says they mean due process of law. The Constitutions which had been adopted by the several States before the formation of the federal Constitution, following the language of the great charter more closely, generally contained the words, 'but by the judgment of his peers, or the law of the land.' The ordinance of Congress of July 13, 1787, for the government of the territory of the United States northwest of the River Ohio, used the same words."); *see also, e.g.*, *Taylor v. Porter & Ford*, 4 Hill (N.Y.) 140, 146 (1843) ("The [New York constitution's law-of-the-land] section was taken with some modifications from a part of the 29th chapter of Magna Charta, which provided, that no freeman should be taken, or imprisoned, or be disseised of his freehold etc., but by lawful judgment of his peers, or *by the law of the land*. Lord Coke in his commentary upon this statute says, that these words, 'by the law of the land,' mean 'by the due course and process of law[.]'").

123. *Id.* at 119.

124. *Id.* at 113–114.

125. *Id.* at 116.

126. *Id.*

127. *Id.*

128. *Id.* at 114.

129. *Id.*

130. *Id.* at 116.

131. *Id.* at 114.

132. *Id.* at 115–116.

133. *Corfield*, 6 F. Cas. at 551–552.

134. *Slaughterhouse Cases*, 83 U.S. at 120 (Bradley, J. dissenting).

135. *Id.* at 112.

136. *Id.*

137. *Id.*

138. *Id.*

139. Justice Bradley's analysis appeared to accomplish under the Due Process Clause what might have more appropriately been done under the Privilege or Immunities Clause, had the majority not foreclosed the opportunity. *See* Balkin, *Living Originalism*, 192 ("Even if courts stick with the due process clause as the source of basic liberties . . . they could learn a great deal about how the Constitution protects fundamental rights by applying the theory and history of the privileges or immunities clause to their construction of the due process clause."). But as Balkin also observes, "[T]here is no reason why the three clauses should not overlap substantially in their coverage[.]" Balkin, *Living Originalism*, 198. The three clauses of section 1 of the Fourteenth Amendment "were designed to serve the structural goals of equal citizenship and equality before the law." *Id.* The drafters of the Fourteenth

Amendment recognized the basic freedoms—the essential civil liberties—of those living under the rule of free governments as equally distributed and impartially protected. The three clauses were descriptively enumerated aspects of political principles already deeply rooted in the American legal tradition.

140. *See* Cooley, *The General Principles of Constitutional Law in the United States*, 244 ("The common law is over and above all tribunals administering any other code, and is watchful and vigilant to keep them within the limits of their jurisdictions, and to punish members if they usurp authority not belonging to them.") (citing Joseph Story, *Commentaries on the Constitution of the United States*, 4th ed., §§ 1943–1946.).

141. 83 U.S. at 119 (Bradley, J. dissenting).

142. 111 U.S. 746, 760–766 (1884) (Bradley, J., concurring) ("The monopoly clause in the act . . . had nothing of the character of a police regulation. . . . The police regulations proper were hitched on to the charter as a pretext.").

143. 110 U.S. 516 (1884).

144. *Id.* at 519. *See* U.S. Const. amend. V ("No person shall be held to answer for a capital, or otherwise infamous crime, unless on a presentment or indictment of a Grand Jury[.]").

145. *Id.* at 519–520 (internal quotation marks omitted).

146. *Id.* at 521.

147. *Id.*

148. *Id.* at 519.

149. *Id.*

150. *Id.* at 534.

151. *Id.*

152. *Id.* at 520.

153. *Id.* at 527 (quoting *Westervelt v. Gregg*, 12 N.Y. 202, 212 (1854)).

154. *Id.* (quoting *Bank of Columbia v. Okely*, 17 U.S. 235 (1819)); *see also Yick Wo v. Hopkins*, 118 U.S. 356, 369–370 (1886) (writing for the Court, Justice Matthews observed, "When we consider the nature and the theory of our institutions of government . . . we are constrained to conclude that they do not mean to leave room for the play and action of purely personal and arbitrary power.").

155. *See, e.g.*, *Hagar v. Reclamation Dist.*, 111 U.S. 701, 708 (1884) (writing for the Court the same term and citing to Justice Matthews' opinion in *Hurtado*, Justice Field wrote: "That clause of the fourteenth amendment is found in almost identical language in the several state constitutions, and is intended as additional security against the arbitrary deprivation of life and liberty and the arbitrary spoliation of property. . . . It is sufficient to observe here that by 'due process' is meant one which, following the forms of law, is appropriate to the case, and just to the parties to be affected. It must be pursued in the ordinary mode prescribed by the law; it must be adapted to the end to be attained; and wherever it is necessary for the protection of the parties, it must give them an opportunity to be heard respecting the justice of the judgment sought. The clause in question means, therefore, that there can be no proceeding against life, liberty, or property which may result in the deprivation of either, without the observance of those general rules established in our system of jurisprudence for the security of private rights.").

156. 110 U.S. at 532.

157. *See* F.W. Maitland, *The Constitutional History of England* (Cambridge: University Press, 1908), 15–16 ("Now Magna Carta came to be reckoned as the beginning of English statute law . . . . The lawyers of the latter middle ages had no occasion to go behind that instrument; the earlier ordinances so far as they had not become obsolete had worked themselves into the common law; but every word of the charter was still of great importance.").

158. *See, e.g., Dent v. State of West Virginia*, 129 U.S. 114, 123–124 (1889) (Field, J.) ("As we have said on more than one occasion, it may be difficult, if not impossible, to give to the terms 'due process of law' a definition which will embrace every permissible exertion of power affecting private rights, and exclude such as are forbidden. They come to us from the law of England, from which country our jurisprudence is to a great extent derived; and their requirement was there designed to secure the subject against the arbitrary action of the crown, and place him under the protection of the law. They were deemed to be equivalent to 'the law of the land.' In this country the requirement is intended to have a similar effect against legislative power; that is, to secure the citizen against any arbitrary deprivation of his rights, whether relating to his life, his liberty, or his property. . . . The great purpose of the requirement is to exclude everything that is arbitrary and capricious in legislation affecting the rights of the citizen.").

159. 110 U.S. at 536.

160. *See* Cooley, *The General Principles of Constitutional Law in the United States*, 242 ("[T]he question presents itself whether anything may be made the law of the land, or may become due process of law, which the legislature under proper forms may see fit to enact? To solve this question we have only to consider for a moment the purpose of the clause under examination. That purpose, as is apparent, was individual protection by limitation upon power; and any construction which would leave with the legislature this unbridled authority . . . 'would render the restriction absolutely nugatory, and turn this part of the Constitution into mere nonsense.[']") (quoting *Taylor v. Porter & Ford*, 4 Hill (N.Y.) 140, 143 (1843) ("The people would be made to say to the [legislature], 'You shall be vested with the legislative power of the state; but no one shall be disfranchised, or deprived of any of the rights or privileges of a citizen, unless you pass a statute of that purpose:' in other words, 'You shall not do the wrong, unless you choose to do it.'"); *see also Westervelt v. Gregg*, 12 N.Y. 202, 209 (1854) (Edwards, J.) ("The constitution of this state declares that 'no person shall be deprived of life, liberty or property without due process of law.' Due process of law undoubtedly means, in the due course of legal proceedings, according to those rules and forms which have been established for the protection of private rights. Such an act as the legislature may, in the uncontrolled exercise of its power, think fit to pass, is, in no sense, the process of law designated by the constitution. This construction has heretofore been adopted; and it is so obviously sound, that the mere statement of it is sufficient. Its correctness cannot be made more apparent by argument or illustration.") (citing *Taylor v. Porter & Ford*, 4 Hill (N.Y.) 140 (1843)) (internal citations omitted).

161. 110 U.S. at 535.

162. *Id.* at 530 ("[W]e shall be ready to acknowledge that it is better not to go too far back into antiquity for the best securities for our 'ancient liberties.' It is more consonant to the true philosophy of our historical legal institutions to say that the spirit of personal liberty and individual right which they embodied was preserved and developed by a progressive growth and wise adaptation to new circumstances and situations of the forms and processes found fit to give, from time to time, new expression and greater effect to modern ideas of self-government.").

163. *Id.* at 528–529.

164. *Id.* at 531.

165. *Id.* at 537.

166. *Id.* at 520–521 (citing *Kalloch v. Super. Ct.*, 56 Cal. 229 (1880) (citing *Rowan v. State*, 30 Wis. 129 (1872))).

167. *Id.* at 536 (quoting *Brown v. Levee Comrs.*, 50 Miss. 468 (1874)).

168. *Id.* at 538.

169. *Id.* at 535 (quoting *Missouri v. Lewis*, 101 U.S. 22 (1879)).

170. *See Palko v. Connecticut*, 302 U.S. 319 (1937), discussed in chapter 3, *infra.*

Chapter 2

Liberty and Economic Ideology

Hurtado brought the concept of ordered liberty and its implementing a bulwark against arbitrary legislation into the new light of post-Reconstruction constitutional law. But like a rough-hewn precious stone, not yet cut and polished, its value was invisible to those oblivious to the rich tradition from which it was mined. And it was soon co-opted into serving an ideology reflecting the extent to which the rapid and momentous changes of the American industrial revolution influenced the Court's judgment. The Court's dubious use of the concept to supplant certain state laws as violative of due process would be the first of two significant turns the jurisprudence would take during the twentieth century.

In 1897, thirteen years after *Hurtado* and *Butcher's Union Co.* and twenty-five years after *Slaughterhouse*, the Court decided *Allgeyer v. Louisiana.*[1] The Court struck down as violative of the due-process guarantee a Louisiana law prohibiting any person, firm, or corporation from entering into an insurance contract with any insurance company that had not complied with the State's insurance regulations.[2] Writing for the majority, Justice Rufus Peckham quoted a short passage from Justice Bradley's concurring opinion in *Butcher's Union Co.*,[3] without discussing the principles the *Slaughterhouse* dissenters and the *Hurtado* opinion so carefully articulated and applied. Adumbrating the Court's fundamental-rights doctrine, which would appear seventy years later, Peckham's opinion contained no common-law analysis testing the Louisiana law's application for fitness with the State's justification for it. It did not determine whether the law was either a legitimate exercise of the State's reserved powers or arbitrary and unreasonable. Instead, the Court announced that the federal constitution protected a categorical "right to contract outside of the state for insurance."[4] Because the Louisiana law interfered with this "liberty to contract," it violated the Fourteenth Amendment's due-process guarantee.[5]

***

A group of cotton exporters, doing business as E. Allgeyer & Co., purchased an open marine insurance policy from a New York insurance company to cover cotton shipments from the port of New Orleans to destinations across the Atlantic.[6] The insurer was domiciled in New York, had no agent in Louisiana, and had not complied with the requirements of Louisiana law for doing business within the State.[7] To obtain coverage for shipments, the exporters would mail letters to New York containing descriptions of the property and other information the insurer required.[8] When they sent two letters requesting coverage for two separate shipments of cotton, the State of Louisiana fined them for violating the provision of its law prohibiting "any act in this state to effect for himself . . . insurance on property then in this state, in any marine insurance company which has not complied in all respects with the laws of this state[.]"[9] The exporters challenged the law in state court, and the trial court ruled in their favor.[10]

The Louisiana Supreme Court reversed the trial court. Like the state-court opinions that Justice Field and the *Hurtado* Court cited, Louisiana's highest court recognized the common-law principle that a State had the authority to establish its own policies "unless there is some inhibition in the federal or state constitution," or if the policy "violates one of those inalienable rights relating to persons and property that are inherent, although not expressed, in the organic law."[11] The court noted the settled proposition that States had the authority to enact public policy setting the conditions under which foreign companies could do business within their borders.[12] Although it recognized that the law "interfered with the liberty of [the] defendants in restricting their rights to place insurance on property of their own whenever and in what company they desired[,]"[13] the court held that the law did so reasonably, because "[i]ndividual liberty of action must give way to the greater right of the collective people in the assertion of well-defined policy, designed and intended for the general welfare."[14] As support for this principle, the Louisiana Supreme Court cited the U.S. Supreme Court opinion in *Hooper v. California*, in which the Court had upheld a California law similar to Louisiana's.[15]

The U.S. Supreme Court reversed the Louisiana Supreme Court's ruling. Writing for the Court, Justice Peckham distinguished the facts of *Allgeyer* from those of *Hooper*. In *Hooper*, the insurance contract was executed in California; in *Allgeyer*, it was executed "beyond the territory of the state of Louisiana."[16] According to Peckham, this distinction rendered *Hooper* inapplicable. The exporters merely mailed letters of notification from Louisiana, and this "did not constitute a contract made or entered into within the [S] tate."[17] "In this case," he wrote, "the company did no business within the state and the contracts were not therein made."[18] Put simply, the ourt seemed to conclude that the exporters had not violated the State's law.

Without explaining why, Peckham went further: "[W]e think the statute is a violation of the fourteenth amendment of the federal constitution, in that it deprives the defendants of their liberty without due process of law."[19] He cited Justice Bradley's *Slaughterhouse* and *Butcher's Union Co.* arguments that the due-process guarantee prevented the Louisiana legislature from granting to selected persons a monopoly over the butchering trade. And he wrote, "It is true that these remarks were made in regard to questions of monopoly, but they well describe the rights which are covered by the word 'liberty' as contained in the Fourteenth Amendment."[20] Peckham concluded that the Fourteenth Amendment recognized a "right to contract . . . of which state legislation c[ould not] deprive" a citizen.[21] The Louisiana law interfered with the exporters' liberty to contract for insurance, and so violated the due-process guarantee.

Allgeyer opened the "*Lochner* Era," named after the 1905 case that would come to exemplify a forty-year period of federal judicial interference, via the due-process guarantee, with the States' policies addressing labor-related and economic issues associated with the American industrial revolution. The cases illustrative of the Era would ignore the common-law tradition of arbitrariness review, while nominally acknowledging the need to test the application of a challenged law for fitness with a State's justification for it. But instead of evaluating for reasonableness the balance struck between an individual's interest in liberty and a State's interest in order, the Court would invoke the concept as authority for supplanting state legislation that interfered with the categorical liberty to contract it identified in *Allgeyer.*

In *Lochner v. New York*,[22] the New York legislature had enacted a law limiting the maximum working hours of bakers to sixty a week, based on its findings regarding "white-lung disease," a vocational hazard peculiar to bakers and associated with their long working hours. The Court held that the statute violated the due-process guarantee and struck down this arguably mild and rational labor regulation. Again writing for the Court, Justice Peckham identified the "right to purchase and sell labor" as "part of the liberty protected by [the Fourteenth] amendment."[23] As in the *Allgeyer* opinion, Peckham nominally invoked Justice Bradley's *Slaughterhouse* example. The question was whether the law was "a fair, reasonable, and appropriate exercise of the police power of the state," or "an unreasonable . . . and arbitrary interference with the right of the individual to his personal liberty[.]"[24] Due process required that the means the State had chosen have a direct relation to its end, and that the end "itself be appropriate and legitimate."[25]

But like *Allgeyer*, *Lochner* did not follow Bradley's example and test the means the State chose in pursuit of its objective for fitness with its justification for them. Instead, the Court decided the New York legislature and courts had incorrectly concluded that the occupation of baking involved a real health risk.[26] The opinion did not ask, as the common-law tradition required, whether limiting the working hours of bakers to sixty per week reasonably infringed an employer-employee contract, in light of the legislature's finding that white-lung disease was a serious risk to the public's health. It simply substituted for these findings its own judgment about the health effects of baking.

> We think that there can be no doubt that the trade of a baker, in and of itself, is not an unhealthy one to that degree which would authorize the legislature to interfere with the right to labor, and with the right of free contract on the part of the individual, either as employer or employee.[27]

Because the Court concluded that baking was in fact *not* unhealthy, the public-health justification for the law was a mere pretext for interfering with the liberty to buy and sell labor; therefore, the legislature had wielded its power arbitrarily in violation of the due-process guarantee.

> This, we think, is unreasonable and entirely arbitrary. When assertions such as these we have averted to become necessary in order to give, if possible, a plausible foundation for the contention that the law is a 'health law', it gives rise to the suspicion that there was some other motive dominating the legislature than the purpose to subserve the public health or welfare.[28]

The Court declared that it was protecting the liberty of employees as much as that of employers, ignoring the factual context that generated the controversy—laws like the working-hour maximum for bakers reflected the labor movement's success at furthering the interests of employees through state legislation in a highly competitive and employer-friendly industrial marketplace.

> We think that such a law as this, although passed in the assumed exercise of the police power, as relating to the public health . . . is not within that power, and is invalid. The act is not, within any fair meaning of the term, a health law, but is an illegal interference with the rights of individuals, both employers and employees, to make contracts regarding labor upon such terms as they may think best, or which they may agree upon with the other parties to such contracts.[29]

In his famous dissent in *Lochner*,[30] Justice Oliver Wendell Holmes, Jr., criticized the Court for promoting a particular economic ideology. He argued that American democracy in the States would produce all kinds of policies, and it was not the task of the federal judiciary to decide whether they were correct.

> [A] constitution is not intended to embody a particular economic theory, whether of paternalism and the organic relation of the citizen to the state or of laissez faire. It is made for people of fundamentally differing views, and the accident of our finding certain opinions natural and familiar, or novel, and even shocking, ought not to conclude our judgment upon the question whether statutes embodying them conflict with the Constitution of the United States.[31]

Justice Holmes expressly rejected supplanting the will of democratic majorities when justices on the Court decided they made an unwise policy choice. The constitutionality of state policy did not turn on the ideological preferences of Supreme Court justices: "This case is decided upon an economic theory which a large part of the country does not entertain. . . . I strongly believe that my agreement or disagreement has nothing to do with the right of a majority to embody their opinions in law."[32] The personal opinions of federal judges were beside the point: "Some of these laws embody convictions or prejudices which judges are likely to share. Some may not."[33]

Holmes dismissed what he called the "shibboleth" of libertarianism—"[t]he liberty of the citizen to do as he likes so long as he does not interfere with the liberty of others to do the same"—observing that a host of state laws, long recognized as within the power of legislatures, interfered with individual liberties.[34] The Court's duty was to review state legislation according to the common-law tradition, like Justices Field and Bradley. Only when a State's interference with a basic liberty was unreasonable did it violate the Fourteenth Amendment. Concluding his dissent, Justice Holmes concisely articulated this theory of due process, juxtaposing it against what he saw as the Court's anti-democratic impulse to preserve the laissez-faire character of early-American capitalism.

> I think that the word 'liberty', in the Fourteenth Amendment, is perverted when it is held to prevent the natural outcome of a dominant opinion, unless it can be said that a rational and fair man necessarily would admit that the statute proposed would infringe fundamental principles as they have been understood by the traditions of our people and our law.[35]

Justice John Harlan—grandfather to Justice John Marshall Harlan II, who would join the Court a half century later—also dissented from the majority opinion. His reasoning followed *Corfield*, Justices Field and Bradley, *Hurtado*, and the state cases on which they relied illustrating the common-law approach to evaluating policies challenged as violating basic liberties.[36] As his namesake would, too, Justice Harlan recognized the tradition as requiring deference to the consequences of democracy within the States, so long as legislation did not exceed the scope of their authority as institutions integral to a government established for the purpose of securing liberties basic to a free society. The federal courts' authority to declare a state-legislative act void extended only so far as the law was arbitrary.

> Regulations respecting the pursuit of a lawful trade or business are of very frequent occurrence . . . and what such regulations shall be . . . are questions for the state to determine, and their determination comes within the proper exercise of the police power by the state, and, unless the regulations are so utterly unreasonable and extravagant in their nature and purpose that the property and personal rights of the citizen are unnecessarily, and in a manner wholly arbitrary, interfered with or destroyed, they do not exceed beyond the power of the state to pass, and they form no subject for Federal interference.[37]

Justice Harlan concluded that the law's public-health objective was squarely within the traditional powers of the State, and found it "impossible . . . to say that there is no real or substantial relation between the means employed by the state and the end sought to be accomplished by its legislation."[38] Concluding his opinion, and offering the wisdom his grandson would inherit and magnify sixty years hence, he reminded his colleagues of the respect for federalism, separation of powers, and institutional proficiency that the tradition demanded they observe.

> Therefore I submit that this court will transcend its functions if it assumes to annul the statute of New York.[39]

> [T]he New York statute . . . cannot be held to be in conflict with the 14th Amendment, . . . without bringing under the supervision of this court matters which have been supposed to belong exclusively to the legislative departments of the several states[.][40]

> No evils arising from such legislation could be more far reaching than those that might come to our system of government if the judiciary, abandoning the sphere assigned to it by the fundamental law, should enter the domain of legislation[.][41]

The *Lochner* Era stands now as one example of the Court's disregarding basic institutional restraints in favor of promoting a particular ideology in Fourteenth Amendment jurisprudence. Even at the time, it was an ironic legal development in light of the *Slaughterhouse* opinion. According to

Slaughterhouse, the Fourteenth Amendment had not fundamentally altered federalism—it left the security of basic civil liberties to the States. But it had, according to the *Lochner*-Era Court, transferred the oversight of local economic policy from the States to the federal judiciary.

***

Not all due-process cases decided during the Era exemplify federal interference with the States' economic policies. Perhaps portending its end, in two significant cases decided late in the Era, *Meyer v. Nebraska*[42] (1923) and *Pierce v. Society of Sisters* (1925),[43] the Court properly applied the common-law analysis that the *Lochner* dissenters defended as the proper approach to federal judicial review of the States' legislative judgments. Neither *Meyer* nor *Pierce* involved economic legislation, and so neither triggered the Court's penchant during the Era for supplanting such laws. In these two cases, the tradition of arbitrariness review was implicitly present, and quietly surviving, awaiting emancipation from its ideological servitude.

In *Meyer*, a teacher at a parochial school challenged his criminal conviction under a Nebraska statute that made it a misdemeanor to "teach any subject to any [child who had not passed the eighth grade] in any language [other] than the English language."[44] Robert Meyer was convicted of using German versions of bible stories to teach the German language.[45] The Nebraska legislature passed the law in the wake of World War I, to address the "emergency" of the "baneful effects of permitting foreigners" residing in the United States to "rear and educate their children in the language of their native land[,]" which the legislature determined was "inimical to our own safety."[46] Aimed at Nebraska's large German-speaking population, the legislation's objective was to promote cultural assimilation—to prevent the inculcation of "ideas and sentiments foreign to the best interests of this country."[47] The Nebraska Supreme Court affirmed the conviction, and Meyer appealed to the U.S. Supreme Court, arguing that his conviction violated the Fourteenth Amendment's due-process guarantee.

The Court stated the question before it as "whether the statute as construed and applied unreasonably infringes the liberty guaranteed . . . by the Fourteenth Amendment: No state . . . shall deprive any person of life, liberty, or property without due process of law."[48] Writing for the Court, Justice James McReynolds cited *Slaughterhouse*, *Butcher's Union Co.*, and *Allgeyer*, recognizing that the liberty of the Due Process Clause, while not "define[ed] with exactness," had "received much consideration and some of the included things ha[d] been definitely stated."[49] Synthesizing prior decisions and alluding to *Corfield*'s conception of fundamental liberties, he wrote:

> Without a doubt, it denotes not merely freedom from bodily restraint but also the right of the individual to contract, to engage in any of the common occupations of life, to acquire useful knowledge, to marry, establish a home and bring up children, to worship God according to the dictates of his own conscience, and generally to enjoy those privileges long recognized at common law as essential to the orderly pursuit of happiness by free men.[50]

The "established doctrine" held that the liberty the Due Process Clause protected "may not be interfered with, under the guise of protecting the public interest, by legislative action which is arbitrary or without reasonable relation to some purpose within the competency of the state to effect."[51]

Consistent with the common-law analysis, McReynolds first evaluated the weight of the liberty interest asserted as worthy of protection. Citing the Ordinance of 1787, he noted the "supreme importance" of "education and acquisition of knowledge" to "[t]he American people."[52] He recognized that with respect to the upbringing of children, the right and duty to control religious training, moral instruction, and the acquisition of knowledge belonged to parents.[53] And he noted that "nearly all the states, including Nebraska, enforce this obligation by compulsory laws."[54] Because the education of children required schools where "especially qualified persons" devoted themselves to the task, Meyer's right to teach was also implicated. McReynolds concluded that the teacher's "right to teach and the right of parents to engage him so to instruct their children . . . are within the liberty of the amendment."[55]

Turning to the statute, the opinion examined its scope, noting that it did not apply to "the so-called ancient or dead languages" like Latin, Greek, or Hebrew, but "German, French, Spanish, Italian, and every other alien speech [were] within the ban."[56] McReynolds described the statute's effect as "materially interfering with the calling of modern language teachers, with the opportunities of pupils to acquire knowledge, and with the power of parents to control the education of their own."[57] And following the *Slaughterhouse* dissenters' examples, he examined the State's justification for the statute.

> It is said the purpose of the legislation was to promote civic development by inhibiting training and education of the immature in foreign tongues and ideals before they could learn English and acquire American ideals, and that the English language should be and become the mother tongue of all children reared in this state. It also affirmed that the foreign born population is very large, that certain communities commonly use foreign words, follow foreign leaders, move in a foreign atmosphere, and that the children are hereby hindered from becoming citizens of the most useful type and the public safety is imperiled.[58]

Like Field and Bradley, McReynolds expressly acknowledged the broad ambit of legitimate legislative action to promote the general welfare. The State could "go very far . . . to improve the quality of its citizens, physically, mentally, and morally," but, at the same time, "the individual ha[d] certain fundamental rights which must be respected."[59] The legislature was, therefore, subject to the limitation that "a desirable end cannot be promoted by prohibited means."[60] Specifically, while it might be "highly advantageous if all had ready understanding of our ordinary speech . . . this cannot be coerced by methods which conflict with the Constitution."[61]

The opinion tested the means the State had chosen for fitness with its objective. In post-World-War-I America, it was "easy to appreciate" the "desire to foster a homogeneous people with American ideals prepared readily to understand current discussions of civic matters[.]"[62] There was no question of "[t]he power of the state to compel attendance at . . . school and to make reasonable regulations for all schools, including a requirement that they shall give instructions in English," or to "prescribe a curriculum for institutions which it supports."[63] The interference via the criminal law, however, with Meyer's right to teach and the parents' right to employ him to do so, was not reasonably related to the State's legitimate objectives. The State presented no evidence of an emergency "render[ing] knowledge by a child of some language other than English so clearly harmful as to justify its inhibition with the consequent infringement of rights long freely enjoyed."[64] The statute as applied was, therefore, "arbitrary and without reasonable relation to any end within the competency of the state."[65]

Two years later in *Pierce*, a private Catholic school and a military school challenged an Oregon law that required any parent or person having control or custody of a child between the ages of eight and sixteen to send the child to public school.[66] The law made failure to do so a misdemeanor offense.[67] The schools argued that the law impermissibly interfered with the right of parents to control their children's education, and with the schools' and teachers' right to engage in a useful business.[68] The state court ruled in their favor, holding that the guarantees of the Fourteenth Amendment protected the schools, and parents choosing to send their children to them, from being held criminally accountable. The Supreme Court agreed, and Justice McReynolds wrote this opinion, too. Following *Meyer*'s analysis, *Pierce* held that the law "unreasonably interfere[d] with the liberty of parents and guardians to direct the upbringing and education of children under their control."[69] Criminalizing the parents' decision to send their children to private schools unreasonably interfered with a basic liberty.

The reasoning of *Meyer* and *Pierce* would become a critical connection between the traditional common-law method and its post-*Lochner* redemption. In 1937, the Court repudiated its *Lochner*-Era practice of supplanting state laws regulating business and employment relations. As the Court revived the due-process guarantee as a bulwark against arbitrary legislation, *Meyer* and *Pierce* would become central precedents in the twentieth-century debate over how to decide due-process cases. Proponents of the common-law tradition, and of the incorporation and fundamental-rights doctrines, would each invoke them when interpreting the due-process guarantee.

***

The case of *West Coast Hotel v. Parrish*[70] marked the Era's end. The Court rejected a challenge to the State of Washington's minimum-wage law alleged to violate the liberty to contract. It held that "liberty implies the absence of arbitrary restraint, not immunity from reasonable regulations and prohibitions imposed in the interests of the community."[71] And it overruled its decision in *Adkins v. Children's Hospital,*[72] a *Lochner*-Era invalidation of a District of Columbia minimum-wage law.[73] The Court concluded that *Adkins* represented a "departure from the true application of the principles governing the regulation by the state of the relation of employer and employed," and was, therefore, wrongly decided.[74]

Overruling *Adkins* freed the concept of ordered liberty from the stilted contrivance it had become in the hands of ideologically spellbound justices. The Court explained that while the liberty that due process protected was an essential feature of the American political tradition, so was the requirement of social order. State legislatures could establish and maintain order, without the federal courts interfering, so long as the means they chose bore a reasonable relation to an objective within their power to pursue—so long as implementing public policy did not arbitrarily impact basic liberties.[75] The Court recognized the common-law principle that liberty was subject to restraints that did not violate the demands of due process.

> The Constitution does not speak of freedom of contract. It speaks of liberty and prohibits the deprivation of liberty without due process of law. In prohibiting that deprivation, the Constitution does not recognize an absolute and uncontrollable liberty. Liberty in each of its phases has its history and connotation. But the liberty safeguarded is liberty in a social organization which requires the protection of law against the evils which menace the health, safety, morals, and welfare of the people. Liberty under the Constitution is thus necessarily subject to the restraints of due process, and regulation which is reasonable in relation to its subject and adopted in the interests of the community is due process.[76]

Holmes's and Harlan's arguments were vindicated. The wisdom of state policies was not the business of the federal courts. Within the design of

American federalism, only an arbitrary state law was subject to a federal-judicial veto.

> [W]ith the wisdom of the policy adopted, with the adequacy or practicability of the law enacted to forward it, the courts are both incompetent and unauthorized to deal.[77]

> The adoption of similar requirements by many states evidences a deepseated conviction both as to the presence of the evil and as to the means adapted to check it. Legislative response to that conviction cannot be regarded as arbitrary or capricious and that is all we have to decide.[78]

So powerful was the ordered-liberty concept's vindication that it reverberated even beyond the Court's due-process cases. In *United States v. Carolene Products Co.*,[79] decided during the same term as *West Coast Hotel*, the Court rejected a challenge under the Commerce Clause[80] to federal legislation regulating the contents of milk substitutes. Congress had outlawed the sale of "filled milk"—milk skimmed of its fat and supplemented with another fat or oil[81]—responding to evidence, presented during congressional hearings, regarding the inferior quality of filled milk and corresponding deleterious health effects.[82] Like many of the States' laws at issue in the *Lochner*-Era cases, the federal filled-milk statute was ostensibly enacted to protect public health. Although decided primarily under the Commerce Clause, the *Carolene Products* analysis paralleled the Court's approach in *West Coast Hotel*. The Court rejected the challenge to the statute and concluded the law was a reasonable response to a legitimate legislative objective.[83]

In so holding, the Court articulated the "presumption-of-constitutionality" principle. When a litigant challenged a legislative act as violative of the Constitution, so long as a plausible explanation reasonably connected a proper legislative goal to the means chosen to accomplish it, the Court would not supplant the judgment of the legislature. Here, there was "affirmative evidence [that] sustain[ed] the [filled-milk] statute."[84] But, the Court explained:

> [E]ven in the absence of [legislative committee reports], the existence of facts supporting the legislative judgment is to be presumed, for regulatory legislation affecting ordinary commercial transactions is not to be pronounced unconstitutional unless in the light of the facts made known or generally assumed it is of such a character as to preclude the assumption that it rests upon some rational basis within the knowledge and experience of the legislators.[85]

> [S]uch inquiries, where the legislative judgment is drawn in question, must be restricted to the issue whether any state of facts either known or which could reasonably be assumed affords support for it.[86]

With this presumption in place, as Justice Harlan had argued in his *Lochner* dissent, the burden was on the party challenging the statute to demonstrate the absence of a rational relationship between the means chosen and the purported end.[87]

But in footnote 4 of the *Carolene Products* opinion, the Court identified an important distinction. While it would presume fact-findings demonstrating a rational relation of means to ends, where laws impacted essential civil liberties the Court might make a "more searching judicial inquiry."[88] In cases where, for example, legislation "appear[ed] on its face to be within a specific prohibition of the Constitution," there might be "narrower scope for operation of the presumption of constitutionality."[89] The filled-milk statute was not one that "should be subjected to more exacting judicial scrutiny under the general prohibitions of the Fourteenth Amendment"—laws "restrict[ing] those political processes which can ordinarily be expected to bring about repeal of undesirable legislation."[90] But the opinion cited a string of examples in which the Court had recognized, as constitutionally protected against state infringement, liberties implicating the purposes for which American governments were established.[91] "Nor need we enquire," the Court said, citing *Meyer* and *Pierce*, "whether similar considerations enter into the review of statutes directed at particular religious, . . . national, or racial minorities[.]"[92] Echoing *Corfield*'s teaching that laws impacting basic liberties must be "justly prescribed for the good of the whole,"[93] the Court noted that "special condition[s]" could require a "correspondingly more searching judicial inquiry"; for example, "prejudice against discrete and insular minorities . . . tend[ing] seriously to curtail the operation of those political processes ordinarily to be relied upon to protect [them]."[94]

Even as it adopted a deferential post-*Lochner*-Era position with respect to legislatures, the Court in footnote 4 unmistakably repudiated the *Slaughterhouse* majority's conclusion that in post-Reconstruction America the federal courts had no role in protecting essential civil liberties. Footnote 4 made clear that the Court had not, in renouncing its *Lochner*-Era invasion of democratic processes and recognizing the broad ambit of state-legislative power, simply abdicated to political majorities on issues of constitutional import. The Privileges or Immunities Clause would remain nearly as empty as the *Slaughterhouse* majority left it. But the Fourteenth Amendment's due-process guarantee was established as the source of federal protection against arbitrary interference with basic liberties, despite the Court's absolutist application of it during the *Lochner*-Era. The Court's rekindling deference to federalism would subsequently show in its scrutinizing both the States' substantive laws and their self-prescribed judicial proceedings. This same year, in the case of *Palko v. Connecticut*,[95] the Court would reaffirm *Hurtado*'s respect for the tradition of arbitrariness review in evaluating a State's criminal procedure allegedly violative of due process.

NOTES

1. 165 U.S. 578 (1897).
2. *Id.* at 579.
3. *Id.* at 590.
4. *Id.* at 590–591.
5. *Id.* at 591.
6. *Id.* at 580–581.
7. *Id.*
8. *Id.*
9. *Id.* at 579, 583.
10. *Id.* at 583.
11. *Id.* at 584–585.
12. *Id.* at 585.
13. *Id.*
14. *Id.*
15. *Id.* at 586 (citing 155 U.S. 648 (1895)).
16. *Id.* at 586–587.
17. *Id.* at 588.
18. *Id.* at 589.
19. *Id.*
20. *Id.* at 590.
21. *Id.* at 590–591.
22. 198 U.S. 45 (1905).
23. *Id.* at 53.
24. *Id.* at 56.
25. *Id.* at 57.
26. *Id.* at 59.
27. *Id.*
28. *Id.* at 62–63.
29. *Id.* at 61.
30. *Lochner*, 198 U.S. at 65 (Holmes, J., dissenting).
31. *Id.* at 75–76.
32. *Id.* at 75.
33. *Id.*
34. *Id.*
35. *Id.* at 76.
36. *Lochner*, 198 U.S. at 65 (Harlan, J., dissenting).
37. *Id.* at 66–67 (quoting *Gundling v. Chicago*, 177 U.S. 183 (1900)) (internal quotation marks omitted).
38. *Id.* at 69.
39. *Id.* at 69–70 (internal citations omitted).
40. *Id.* at 73.
41. *Id.* at 74 (quoting *Atkin v. Kansas*, 191 U.S. 207, 223 (1903)).
42. 262 U.S. 390 (1923).

43. 268 U.S. 510 (1925).
44. 262 U.S. at 397.
45. *Id.*
46. *Id.* at 397–398.
47. *Id.* at 398.
48. *Id.* at 399.
49. *Id.*
50. *Id.*
51. *Id.* at 399–400.
52. *Id.* at 400.
53. *Id.*
54. *Id.*
55. *Id.*
56. *Id.* at 400–401.
57. *Id.* at 401.
58. *Id.*
59. *Id.*
60. *Id.*
61. *Id.*
62. *Id.* at 402.
63. *Id.*
64. *Id.* at 403.
65. *Id.*
66. 268 U.S. at 530.
67. *Id.*
68. *Id.* at 532–533.
69. *Id.* at 534–535.
70. 300 U.S. 379 (1937).
71. *Id.* at 392.
72. 261 U.S. 525 (1923).
73. 300 U.S. at 400.
74. *Id.* at 397.
75. *See e.g.*, *Dent v. State of West Virginia*, 129 U.S. 114, 125–128 (1889) (Field, J.) (citing *Cummings v. State of Missouri*, 4 Wall. 277 (1866); *Pierce v. Carskadon*, 16 Wall. 234 (1872); and *Ex Parte Garland*, 4 Wall. 333 (1866) as examples of finding legislation arbitrary as applied, that is, lacking a reasonable relation to the legislative power to regulate participation in a public profession. Upholding West Virginia's law regulating who was eligible to practice medicine, Justice Field discussed these cases illustrating the common-law understanding of the limits of legislative power. The cases involved postwar requirements in some States that persons wanting to hold public office take an oath denying having committed past acts associated with the rebellion against the Union. Field wrote, "[T]hese decisions . . . determine that one who is in the enjoyment of a right to preach and teach the Christian religion as a priest of a regular church, and one who has been admitted to practice the profession of the law, cannot be deprived of the right to continue in the exercise of their respective professions by the exaction from

them of an oath as to their past conduct *respecting matters which have no connection with such professions.*"; and "The Constitution of Missouri and the act of Congress in question in those cases were designed to deprive parties of their right to continue in their professions for past acts, or past expressions of desires and sympathies, *many of which had no bearing upon their fitness to continue in their professions.*") (italics added).

76. 300 U.S. at 391.

77. *Id.* at 389 (internal quotation marks and citations omitted).

78. *Id.* at 399.

79. 304 U.S. 144 (1938).

80. U.S. Const. art. I, § 8, cl. 5. ("The Congress shall have power to . . . regulate commerce . . . among the several states[.]").

81. 304 U.S. at 145–146.

82. *Id.* at 148–149.

83. *Id.* at 154. The filled-milk company argued that the statute violated the Fifth Amendment's due-process guarantee because it deprived the company of property, "purport[ing] to make binding and conclusive . . . the legislative declaration that appellee's product 'is an adulterated article of food, injurious to the public health, and its sale constitutes a fraud on the public.'" *Id.* at 147. Citing to *Hebe Co. v. Shaw*, 248 U.S. 297 (1919), the Court explained that "[t]wenty years ago [it had] held that a state law which forbids the manufacture and sale of a product assumed to be wholesome and nutritive, made of condensed skimmed milk, compounded with coconut oil, is not forbidden by the Fourteenth Amendment"; and "the Court thought that there was ample scope for the legislative judgment that prohibition of the offending article was an appropriate means of preventing injury to the public." *Id.* at 150. The Court saw "no persuasive reason for departing from that ruling here," and concluded the legislature's characterization of filled-milk products was nothing "more than a declaration of the legislative findings deemed to support and justify the action taken as a constitutional exertion of the legislative power, aiding informed judicial review, as do the reports of legislative committees, by revealing the rationale of the legislation." *Id.* at 150, 152.

84. *Id.* at 150.

85. *Id.* at 152.

86. *Id.* at 154 ("Here, the demurrer challenges the validity of the statute on its face, and it is evident from all the considerations presented to Congress, and those of which we may take judicial notice, that the question is at least debatable whether commerce in filled milk should be left unregulated, or in some measure restricted, or wholly prohibited. As that decision was for Congress, neither the finding of a court arrived at by weighing the evidence nor the verdict of a jury can be substituted for it.") (citing *Price v. Illinois*, 238 U.S. 446, 452 (1915); *Hebe Co. v. Shaw*, 248 U.S. 303 (1919); *Standard Oil Co. v. Marysville*, 279 U.S. 582, 584 (1929); *South Carolina v. Barnwell Bros., Inc.*, 303 U.S. 177, 191 (1938) (citing *Worcester County Trust Co. v. Riley*, 302 U.S. 292, 299 (1937))).

87. *See* 198 U.S. 45, 68 (1905) (Harlan, J., dissenting) ("[W]hen the validity of a statute is questioned, the burden of proof, so to speak, is upon those who assert it to be unconstitutional.").

88. 304 U.S. at 152 footnote 4.

89. *Id.*

90. *Id.*

91. *Id.* (Identifying as potentially deserving of "a more exacting judicial scrutiny under the general prohibitions of the Fourteenth Amendment . . . legislation which restricts those political processes which can ordinarily be expected to bring about repeal of undesirable legislation[,] . . . restrict[ing] . . . the right to vote, . . . restrain[ing] . . . the dissemination of information, . . . interfer[ing] with political organizations, . . . [and] prohibit[ing] . . . peaceable assembly[.]") (citing *Nixon v. Herndon*, 273 U.S. 536 (1927); *Nixon v. Condon*, 286 U.S. 73 (1932); *Near v. Minnesota ex rel. Olson*, 283 U.S. 697, 713–714, 718–720, 722 (1931); *Grosjean v. American Press Co.*, 297 U.S. 233 (1936); *Lovell v. Griffin*, 303 U.S. 444, 452 (1938); *Stromberg v. California*, 283 U.S. 369 (1931); *Fiske v. Kansas*, 274 U.S. 380 (1927); *Whitney v. California*, 274 U.S. 357, 373–378 (1927); *Herndon v. Lowry*, 301 U.S. 242 (1937); *Gitlow v. New York*, 268 U.S. 652, 673 (1925) (Holmes, J., dissenting); *De Jonge v. Oregon*, 299 U.S. 353, 365 (1937)).

92. *Id.* (citing *Pierce v. Society of Sisters*, 268 U.S. 510 (1925); *Meyer v. Nebraska*, 262 U.S. 390 (1923); *Bartels v. Iowa*, 262 U.S. 404 (1923); *Farrington v. Tokushige*, 273 U.S. 284 (1927); *Nixon v. Herndon*, 273 U.S. 536 (1927); *Nixon v. Condon*, 286 U.S. 73 (1932)).

93. 6 F. Cas. at 551–552.

94. 304 U.S. at 152 footnote 4.

95. 302 U.S. 319 (1937).

Chapter 3

Philosophy, Incorporation, and Natural Law

The States were free to govern themselves, but the federal courts were obligated to protect individuals' basic liberties against arbitrary majoritarian action. The *Slaughterhouse* dissents and *Hurtado* introduced the concept of ordered liberty into Fourteenth Amendment jurisprudence. Justices Holmes and Harlan distilled it in their *Lochner* dissents. *Meyer* and *Pierce* demonstrated it. *West Coast Hotel* vindicated it, and *Carolene Products* reinforced it. The *Lochner*-Era Court had strayed from the common-law tradition, capitulating to an absolutist implementation of the substantive "liberty to contract" that Justice Peckham found in *Allgeyer*. It neglected the initial consideration of whether the liberty a litigant asserted implicated the due-process guarantee, and the common law's corresponding test of the means a State chose for fitness with its objective. Rather than examining whether in each case a State transgressed the limits of its reserved powers, impacting a basic liberty arbitrarily, the Court simply supplanted legislative judgments in the States with its own conception of economic liberty.

The Court had succumbed to this deviation from the tradition for forty years. It now faced the challenge of developing judicial review under the Due Process Clause to protect basic liberties, in light of the federalism principle and the dangers of *Lochner*-Era activism, while demonstrating meaningful judicial restraint. With all the gravitas needed at this point in the story, here enters a legendary giant of the American legal tradition—Justice Benjamin Cardozo, the archetype of the common-law judge. In *Palko v. Connecticut*, the first of three judicial opinions that would constitute the twentieth-century canon of common-law arbitrariness review, he summoned the moral-philosophical pneuma animating the concept and announced its since-renowned appellation. But there would be no respite in the struggle to honor the tradition and protect the concept's integrity. For even as the *Lochner*-Era ended, the persistent harbinger of a most dangerous threat to it appeared again. Like Hurtado's argument presaging the incorporation doctrine, Palko argued the Fourteenth Amendment applied the Fifth Amendment's double jeopardy provision, as it operated in federal criminal proceedings, to the State.[1]

***

The State of Connecticut prosecuted Palko for first-degree murder and sought a death sentence. But Palko was convicted after trial of second-degree murder and sentenced to life in prison.[2] The State appealed Palko's conviction under its law allowing the prosecution to appeal from trial-court rulings it believed were made in error, just as a criminal defendant could.[3] On appeal, the Connecticut Supreme Court of Errors concluded the trial court had erred when it instructed the jury and excluded certain testimony, and the errors had prejudiced the State.[4] Palko was retried, convicted of first-degree murder, and sentenced to death.[5] When the Connecticut Supreme Court affirmed the second conviction, Palko appealed to the U.S. Supreme Court, arguing that the Connecticut law allowing the State to appeal his first conviction violated due process.[6]

An eloquent companion to *Hurtado*, Cardozo's *Palko* opinion recognized the due-process guarantee as a bulwark against arbitrary legislation. Consistent with the Court's post-*Slaughterhouse* precedent, Cardozo quickly dispatched Palko's argument that "[w]hatever would be a violation of the original bill of rights . . . if done by the federal government is now equally unlawful by force of the Fourteenth Amendment if done by a state."[7] He concluded simply, "There is no such general rule."[8] Fifty years of Fourteenth Amendment cases included the Court's rejecting challenges to state criminal procedures that differed from federal procedures with respect to charging documents,[9] the prohibition against self-incrimination,[10] and the jury requirement for criminal and civil trials.[11] Limits that the Fourth Amendment imposed on the federal government, and some provisions of the Sixth, did not bind the States in precisely the same ways.[12] It was well settled that the Fourteenth Amendment did not require the States to adopt the criminal procedures that the Bill of Rights required of the federal government.

But just as clearly, the precedent showed that some basic liberties the Fourteenth Amendment protected against unreasonable state infringements were also expressly mentioned in the Bill of Rights and immunized against unreasonable federal incursion. Justice Cardozo pointed to examples:

> The freedom of speech which the First Amendment safeguards against encroachment by the Congress,[13] . . . the like freedom of the press,[14] or the free exercise of religion,[15] or the right of peaceable assembly, without which speech

> would be unduly trammeled,[16] or the right of one accused of crime to the benefit of counsel.[17]

The Due Process Clause protected basic liberties against the States, and some of these were enshrined in the Bill of Rights as enumerated protections against the federal government. The jurisprudence made clear that the States were not obligated to mimic the federal government's procedures for honoring basic liberties, but the Fourteenth Amendment prohibited the States from violating them.

The overlap of basic liberties protected from unreasonable state and federal intrusion was no accident. Peering into the precedents, Cardozo observed that "[t]here emerge[d] the perception of a rationalizing principle which gives to discrete instances a proper order and coherence."[18]

> In these and other situations immunities that are valid as against the federal government by force of the specific pledges of particular amendments have been found to be implicit in the concept of ordered liberty, and thus, through the Fourteenth Amendment, become valid as against the states.[19]

The common-law practice of arbitrariness review implemented this "concept of ordered liberty." *Corfield*, the *Slaughterhouse* dissenters, *Hurtado*, Justices Holmes, Harlan, and McReynolds, and *West Coast Hotel* had recognized, honored, and applied it. In the American political tradition, individuals consented to democratic social order for the purpose of securing their basic liberties. Immunity against arbitrary legislation was implicit in this concept, for individuals living under the rule of American governments could not consent to unreasonable infringements of their basic liberties—even those accomplished through nominally "democratic" processes.

Mere mechanistic "incorporation" could not possibly explain the coincidence of the Fourteenth Amendment including protections enumerated in the Bill of Rights. The inclusion was a consequence of the values underlying American society and the form of government that organized it.

> We reach a different plane of social and moral values when we pass to the privileges and immunities that have been taken over from the earlier articles of the Federal Bill of Rights and brought within the Fourteenth Amendment by a process of absorption. These in their origin were effective against the federal government alone. If the Fourteenth Amendment has absorbed them, the process of absorption has had its source in the belief that neither liberty nor justice would exist if they were sacrificed.[20]

The Fourteenth Amendment protected, for example, "freedom of speech and thought" against unreasonable state infringement, as the First Amendment protected it against federal interference, because it was "the matrix, the indispensable condition, of nearly every other form of freedom."[21] This freedom was essential, but not *because* it appeared in the Bill of Rights. It appeared in the Bill of Rights, and implicated the due-process guarantee, because the course of the Nation's political history had proved it necessary to effectuating the purposes for which governments—including American ones—were established. And judicial review of legislation for arbitrariness was inherent to the American legal tradition, because according to its corresponding political theory, protection for basic liberties was the reason for ordering society democratically.

> With rare aberrations a pervasive recognition of that truth can be traced in our history, political and legal. So it has come about that the domain of liberty, withdrawn by the Fourteenth Amendment from encroachment by the states, has been enlarged by latter-day judgments to include liberty of the mind as well as liberty of action. The extension became, indeed, a logical imperative when once it was recognized, as long ago it was, that liberty is something more than exemption from physical restraint, and that even in the field of substantive rights and duties the legislative judgment, if oppressive and arbitrary, may be overridden by the courts.[22]

As in *Hurtado*, the challenge in *Palko* was to the State's criminal procedure. And like *Hurtado*, *Palko* recognized that due process protected "the very substance of individual rights."[23] The Court had rejected, and would continue to reject, the idea that the due-process guarantee meant that before violating basic liberties, the government must merely provide a standard legislated process. Arguments for thus limiting the discretion of judges would run up against the affirmation that "liberty" meant "more than exemption from physical restraint."[24] As Justice Harlan II would explain a generation later, for the common-law judge, "Were due process merely a procedural safeguard it would fail to reach those situations where the deprivation of life, liberty or property was accomplished by legislation which by operating in the future could, given even the fairest possible procedure in application to individuals, nevertheless destroy the enjoyment of all three."[25]

The incorporation for which Palko argued—and for which some justices on the Court would advocate—could not explain the precedent as the Court found it at the end of the *Lochner*-Era. Understanding the relationship between the provisions of the Bill of Rights and the due-process guarantee this way would render incoherent fifty years of post-Reconstruction jurisprudence. The Court's "survey of the cases," Cardozo concluded, "justif[ied] the statement that the dividing line between them, if not unfaltering throughout its course, has been true, for the most part to a unifying principle."[26] States were free to govern themselves legislatively unless in doing so they violated "some principle of justice so rooted in the traditions and conscience of our people as to be ranked as fundamental."[27] As the *Slaughterhouse* dissents and *Hurtado* taught, a lesson that *West Coast Hotel* finally affirmed, judicial review of legislation for arbitrariness effectuated just such a "so-rooted" principle. A State's legislative act that arbitrarily deprived a person of a basic liberty was not a legitimate law, and the Fourteenth Amendment obligated the federal courts to say so.

Like Justice Matthews in *Hurtado*, Cardozo evaluated the means Connecticut chose to accomplish its objective of a fair criminal trial. Did allowing the State to appeal from a conviction it believed resulted from legal errors at trial violate the "fundamental principle[] of liberty and justice" that a State may not arbitrarily deprive a person of liberty and life?[28] The case before the Court was not one in which the State attempted "after a trial free from error to try the accused over again or to bring another case against him[.]"[29] Cardozo observed that "the precise limits of the prohibition of double jeopardy in federal prosecutions" was a subject of well-considered debate on the Court.[30] A closely divided Court in 1904 had produced dueling opinions on the question of whether it prevented the federal government from retrying a defendant under the same, or only a second, indictment.[31] "Right-minded men," Cardozo wrote, "could reasonably, even if mistakenly, believe that a second trial was lawful in prosecutions subject to the Fifth Amendment, if it was all in the same case."[32]

Confining his analysis to the discrete issue and the record of the case before the Court, Cardozo concluded that the operation of the challenged statute, as applied in this particular controversy, did not deprive Palko of liberty and life arbitrarily. The State's objective was an error-free trial, and the means it chose to accomplish this—providing appeal rights to the State as well as to the defendant—were reasonably related to it.

> We deal with the statute before us and no other. The state is not attempting to wear the accused out by a multitude of cases with accumulated trials. It asks no more than this, that the case against him shall go on until there shall be a trial free from the corrosion of substantial legal error. This is not cruelty at all, nor even vexation in any immoderate degree. If the trial had been infected with error adverse to the accused, there might have been review at his instance, and as often as necessary to purge the vicious taint. A reciprocal privilege, subject at all times to the discretion of the presiding judge has now been granted to the state. There is here no seismic innovation.[33]

Allowing the State to appeal trial rulings it believed to be erroneous, in a single case against Palko, as a means to its end—a trial free of substantial legal error—was not an arbitrary exercise of the State's power. It did not deprive Palko of liberty and life without due process of law. It did not offend the principle of justice, implicit in the American concept of ordered liberty, that persons are immune from arbitrary government infringement of their basic liberties.[34] Only arbitrary interference with basic liberties justified a federal court supplanting the results of a State's legislative or judicial processes.

Palko crystallized three critical features of due-process jurisprudence. First, the "unifying principle" that Cardozo identified reinforced the *Slaughterhouse/Hurtado* insight that judicial review for arbitrariness applied to state criminal procedures and substantive legislation alike. This reaffirmed the thrust of *Hurtado* (like *Palko*, a case evaluating a state criminal *procedure*) that the "liberty" due process protected was substantive. The process—legislative or judicial—due those who consented to American democracy substantiated their basic liberties. A criminal procedure was evaluated for whether its operation, on the facts of the case in which it was challenged, arbitrarily deprived a person of liberty, the security against which was the purpose of establishing American governments, state and federal. Another thirty years would pass before any formal distinction between analyses for procedural questions and substantive ones would appear in due-process jurisprudence.[35]

Second, the ordered-liberty concept expressed the political theory within which the federal courts reviewed state laws challenged as violative of the due-process guarantee. The enumerated provisions of the Bill of Rights were not the touchstone of judicial review under the Due Process Clause. *Palko* thus reaffirmed, yet again, that the Fourteenth Amendment did not apply to the States the discrete requirements that the Bill of Rights applied to the federal government. It did not "incorporate" them. The due-process guarantee effectuated a principle of justice deeply rooted in the traditions and conscience of the American people, and the common-law test for arbitrariness applied it in discrete controversies brought before the federal courts. An arbitrary legislative act was not a valid law.

Third, this "so-rooted principle of justice" the Due Process Clause prohibited the States from violating was one inherent to the American political experiment and integral to its legal tradition. As Justice Bradley had explained in his *Slaughterhouse* dissent, it was a feature of the Nation's heritage—the common law had assimilated it.[36] It was not an objective—natural-law or otherwise—principle. The language of *Corfield*, the *Slaughterhouse* dissents, and their progeny were perhaps susceptible to interpretation as natural-law arguments—a profound misunderstanding that would influence the due-process debate in the twentieth century.[37] But the *Slaughterhouse* dissenters' objecting to the majority's narrow reading of the Privileges or Immunities

Clause was not based on their subjective opinions about "first principles" of natural law. Instead, the liberties that "belong[ed] of right to the citizens of all free governments"[38] derived from a distinctly American political theory that Cardozo captured succinctly with "the concept of ordered liberty."[39]

As these words themselves made clear, this was not an appeal to natural-law principles, but an expression of the justification, from within American political history and its corresponding legal tradition, for free individuals consenting to self-governance, under the rule of law, in the first instance.[40] It captured the tension within the uniquely American political design between majoritarian and counter-majoritarian concerns. As Justice John Marshall Harlan II would elaborate, the "ordered" aspect of the ordered-liberty concept addressed the majoritarian principle—the State's power to order society ". . . derived from the governed's consent." States must be free to make their own laws through democratic processes. At the same time, as *Hurtado* explained, law was not whatever a political majority decided. The rule of law in America was a non-positivist ideal.[41] It presumed that free individuals could not consent to live under a government where mere majoritarian will justified infringing their basic liberties. The purpose of American governments was that of all free governments—to secure the basic liberties of individuals. So the supreme law necessarily limited the power majorities wielded to make their own temporal laws. It interposed a counter-majoritarian principle—the "liberty" aspect of the ordered-liberty concept—into the democratic processes through which the States established social order.

Some liberties, therefore, called for special scrutiny of the States' justifications for impacting them. These individual interests deserved special recognition *not* because they resonated with any objective natural-law principles. Instead, claims that a majority unreasonably infringed them triggered a judicial obligation to scrutinize whether legislation as applied violated a principle "so rooted in the traditions and conscience of [the American] people as to be ranked as fundamental"[42]—arbitrary legislative infringement of a basic liberty was an *ultra vires* act. A judge's obligation in these cases was to determine whether a particular application of majoritarian will impermissibly impinged the liberty of an individual, who, along with every member of the majority, consented to a system of self-government that promised to secure basic liberties against arbitrary majoritarian invasion.

***

The "concept of ordered liberty" would come to seem a meaningless moniker, rather than a beautifully terse description of the political theory supporting a precise legal methodology—a judicial decision-making practice. Perhaps mistaking it for an amorphous slogan, some feared the concept was unable to impose real constraints on judges' discretion. Some misunderstood it as an appeal to natural law. And despite *Palko*'s rejection of the incorporation doctrine, its proponents, most notably Justice Hugo Black, would argue in post-*Palko* opinions for finding restraint in due-process cases in the discrete provisions of the Bill of Rights, regardless of over sixty years of precedent to the contrary.

During the mid-twentieth century, Justice Black's campaign for total incorporation proved unsuccessful—the Court never held that the Due Process Clause incorporated all of the original Bill-of-Rights provisions. But the Court's embracing a "selective" version of the doctrine seriously disrupted the development of the common-law tradition,[43] and subjected the concept to further peril redolent of the *Lochner*-Era. The incorporation doctrine's influence on the jurisprudence cannot be overstated, for it allowed developments with dire consequences that will show as the story continues. As this saga unfolds steadily into the mid-twentieth century, tension emerges among the ordered-liberty concept, natural-law theory, and the incorporation doctrine.

***

Ten years after *Palko*, in *Adamson v. California*,[44] the Court rejected a challenge to a law allowing the prosecutor in a criminal case to comment on the defendant's decision not to testify in his own defense. Adamson was charged with first-degree murder.[45] California's criminal procedures presented him with the choice of either (1) taking the stand in his own defense, in which case the government could introduce three prior felony convictions as impeachment evidence; or (2) remaining silent, in which case the court and the government could comment on his failure to testify.[46] Adamson did not testify, the prosecutor commented on his silence during closing argument, and he was convicted and sentenced to death. The California Supreme Court affirmed the conviction.[47]

Appealing his conviction to the U.S. Supreme Court, Adamson first argued that the Fourteenth Amendment incorporated the Fifth Amendment's protection against self-incrimination as it applied in federal court.[48] He argued that because the prohibition was enumerated in the Bill of Rights, it was a "personal right" that the Privileges or Immunities Clause protected.[49] The Court rejected this argument, briefly revisiting *Slaughterhouse*, citing to *Palko*, and reaffirming the holding of *Twining v. New Jersey*,[50] a 1908 case in which the Court determined that the Fourteenth Amendment did not categorically apply to the States the protection against self-incrimination as it applied in federal court.[51]

Adamson next argued that this specific form of protection "inhere[d] in the right to a fair trial. . . . a right admittedly protected by the Due Process Clause of the Fourteenth Amendment."[52] The Court saw this argument as similar to the first, although this time situated in the Due Process Clause, and rejected it because the "clause . . . d[id] not draw all the rights of the federal Bill of Rights under its protection."[53] "This contention," the Court said, "was made and rejected in *Palko v. Connecticut*."[54] *Twining* had said the same about the Due Process Clause incorporating the Bill of Rights. It was "possible that some of the personal rights safeguarded by the first eight Amendments against national action may also be safeguarded against state action, because a denial of them would be a denial of due process of law." It was "not because those rights [were] enumerated in the first eight Amendments, but because they are included in the conception of due process of law."[55]

Having rejected Adamson's incorporation arguments, the Court turned to his claim that the choice the California law forced him to make—to testify and reveal his prior convictions or remain silent and let the prosecutor comment on his failure to answer the evidence against him—was unreasonable and violated due process. The Court recognized this claim as appealing to the common-law guarantee originating in Magna Carta's "law of the land" clause: "State action must be consistent with the fundamental principles of liberty and justice which lie at the base of all our civil and political institutions and not infrequently are designated as 'law of the land'."[56] Following the common-law example of Justice Cardozo's *Palko* opinion, the Court narrowed its analysis to California's applying the law as recounted in the record of the case before it. "[W]e must examine[,]" it said, "the effect of the California law applied in this trial to see whether the comment on failure to testify violates the protection against state action that the due process clause does grant to an accused."[57]

> California . . . is one of a few states that permit limited comment upon a defendant's failure to testify. That permission is narrow. The California law . . . authorizes comment by court and counsel upon the failure of the defendant to explain or to deny by his testimony any evidence of facts in the case against him. This does not involve any presumption, rebuttable or irrebuttable, either of guilt or of the truth of any fact, that is offered in evidence.[58]

Like Cardozo's acknowledgment in *Palko* of the State court's role in meeting the requirements of due process, the Court observed, "There is no lack of power in the trial court to adjudge and no denial of a hearing."[59] It noted that under California law, "[f]ailure of the accused to testify [was] not an admission of the truth of the adverse evidence."[60] And it emphasized the trial court's instruction to the "jury that the burden of proof remained upon the state and the presumption of innocence with the accused."[61] Finally, the court noted that the California Supreme Court, in evaluating the trial record, had "called attention to the fact that the prosecutor's argument approached the borderline in a statement that might have been construed as asserting that the jury should infer guilt solely from defendant's silence[,]" but concluded "that it was improbable the jury was misled into such an understanding of their power."[62]

The State had resolved a close question in favor of the government and against Adamson. Against the background of post-Reconstruction federalism, this was not a "ground for intervention in California's administration of criminal justice."[63] As in *Palko*, reasonable persons might disagree about the resolution of the issue Adamson raised, but here the Court could not conclude that Adamson was arbitrarily deprived of his liberty. The Court was obligated to leave the administration of criminal justice to the State, because the means it chose in pursuing its objective of a fair trial were reasonable. The Court concluded, "[A] state may control such a situation in accordance with its own ideas of the most efficient administration of criminal justice. The purpose of due process is not to protect an accused against a proper conviction, but against an unfair conviction."[64]

Both the natural-law and incorporationist reactions to the ordered-liberty concept appeared in concurring and dissenting opinions in *Adamson*. Justice Felix Frankfurter concurred. He agreed with the disposition but insisted the Court should not rely on *Palko*, and instead decide the case on the authority of *Twining* alone. In his view, *Twining* "show[ed] the judicial process at its best."[65] For Justice Frankfurter, meaningful limitations on judges' discretion in due-process cases would be found in "natural law,"[66] and he read *Twining* as illustrative of this approach. This was a stretch, for *Twining* had reaffirmed the *Slaughterhouse/Hurtado* respect for state autonomy while at the same time acknowledging the force of Field'sand Bradley's dissents.[67] Significantly, Frankfurter's position, that the Court should rely on natural-law theory and not on *Palko*, suggested that he understood *Palko*'s "concept of ordered liberty" as something other than an appeal to natural law.

Justice Black dissented, joined by Justice William Douglas. They argued for total incorporation—the Fourteenth Amendment enforced against the States the Bill of Rights along with the federal courts' interpretations of what they demanded.[68] Misconstruing the principles to which *Palko* referred, Black aimed his criticism at his own misunderstanding of the ordered-liberty concept as one under which the "Court [was] endowed by the Constitution with boundless power under 'natural law' periodically to expand and contract constitutional standards to conform to the Court's conception of what at a particular time constitutes civilized decency and fundamental principles of liberty and justice."[69]

Frankfurter's and Black's approaches were both problematic. Black's tethering to the Bill of Rights the protections due process afforded was untenable in terms of precedential integrity. This would require repudiating post-*Slaughterhouse* federalism, *Hurtado*, *West Coast Hotel, Palko*, and every other case affirming the due-process guarantee as a bulwark against arbitrary legislation. And Frankfurter's natural-law argument, while correct in its refusing to equate the guarantee with the provisions of the Bill of Rights, nevertheless risked reviving *Lochner*-Era abuse, leaving federal judges to fill the concept of due process with their own opinions about what natural law's tenets required.[70] In contrast to both of these positions, the ordered-liberty concept provided constraints on a judge's discretion with reference to principles of justice inherent to the American political design and realized throughout its legal tradition—in the written justifications its common-law judges gave for their decisions resolving discrete cases and controversies.

***

Eight years after *Adamson*, the next luminary in the lineage joined the Court. Standing on the shoulders of America's common-law giant, the sage of this tale would author the second of the three major opinions comprising the due-process canon of the twentieth century. He would provide the first modern example of arbitrariness review and connect the mid-twentieth-century jurisprudence through *Palko,* to *Meyer* and *Pierce*, *Hurtado*, and the *Slaughterhouse* dissents. He consciously situated his analysis within the common-law tradition of reasoned judgment, even as his colleagues on the Court capitulated to the pragmatism of the incorporation doctrine. This placed him in the peculiar position of dissenting from many decisions during the national civil rights movement and the Warren Court's using "selective incorporation" to police judicial procedures in the States. He became the "Great Dissenter of the Warren Court."[71]

But he also concurred in many decisions, writing separately to present the common-law justification for concluding that a State deprived an individual of liberty in violation of the due-process guarantee. Countering the incorporationists and attending to precedential integrity, Justice John Marshall Harlan II grounded his arguments against the doctrine in *Palko*'s ordered-liberty concept, the examples of the *Slaughterhouse* dissenters, and the *Slaughterhouse*-through-*Palko* conception of federalism. He argued often that it was not only unprincipled, but also dangerous to use selective incorporation to categorically apply to all of the States some of the precise limits the Bill of Rights required the federal government to observe.

It would not take long for his warnings to prove prophetic.

NOTES

1. 302 U.S. at 322.
2. *Id.* at 320–321.

3. *Id.* at 321.
4. *Id.*
5. *Id.* at 321–322.
6. *Id.*
7. *Id.* at 323.
8. *Id.*
9. *Id.* (citing *Hurtado v. California*, 110 U.S. 516 (1884)).
10. *Id.* at 324 (citing *Twining v. New Jersey*, 211 U.S. 78 (1908)).
11. *Id.* (citing *Walker v. Sauvinet*, 92 U.S. 90 (1875); *Maxwell v. Dow*, 176 U.S. 581 (1900); *New York Central R. Co. v. White*, 243 U.S. 188 (1917); *Wagner Electric Mfg. Co. v. Lyndon*, 262 U.S. 226 (1923)).
12. *Id.* (citing *Weeks v. United States*, 232 U.S. 383 (1913); *West v. Louisiana*, 194 U.S. 258 (1904)).
13. *Id.* (citing *De Jonge v. Oregon*, 299 U.S. 353, 364 (1937); *Herndon v. Lowry*, 301 U.S. 242, 259 (1937)).
14. *Id.* (citing *Grosjean v. American Press Co.*, 297 U.S. 233 (1936); *Near v. Minnesota ex rel. Olson*, 283 U.S. 697, 707 (1931)).
15. *Id.* (citing *Hamilton v. Regents*, 293 U.S. 245, 262 (1934); *Pierce v. Society of Sisters*, 268 U.S. 510 (1925)).
16. *Id.* (citing *DeJonge v. Oregon*, 299 U.S. 353, 364 (1937); *Herndon v. Lowry*, 301 U.S. 242, 259 (1937)).
17. *Id.* (citing *Powell v. Alabama*, 287 U.S. 45 (1932)).
18. *Id.* at 325.
19. *Id.* at 324–335.
20. *Id.* at 326.
21. *Id.* at 327.
22. *Id.*
23. *Hurtado*, 110 U.S. at 532.
24. 302 U.S. at 327.
25. *Poe v. Ullman*, 367 U.S. 497, 541 (1961) (Harlan, J. dissenting).
26. 302 U.S. at 328.
27. *Id.* (citing *Snyder v. Massachusetts*, 291 U.S. 97, 105 (1934) (holding that a state court proceeding denying a criminal defendant the opportunity to attend the jury's viewing of the scene where the crime allegedly occurred did not violate the Due Process Clause); *Brown v. Mississippi*, 297 U.S. 278, 285 (1936) (holding that due process required overturning criminal convictions where confessions were procured by physical torture)).
28. *Id.* (quoting *Herbert v. Louisiana*, 272 U.S. 312, 316 (1926)).
29. *Id.*
30. *Id.*
31. *Id.* at 322–323 (citing *Kepner v. United States*, 195 U.S. 100 (1904)).
32. *Id.* at 323.
33. *Id.* (internal citations omitted).
34. Cardozo's reference to the "discretion of the presiding judge[,]" as a safeguard against a violation of due process in Palko's case, reinforced post-*Lochner*-Era

federalism. Mere disagreement with how a State managed its affairs did not justify federal judicial intervention into them. *See* 302 U.S. at 328. This resonated with *Hurtado*'s quoting of Justice Bradley, that "[e]ach state prescribes its own mode of judicial proceedings." 110 U.S. at 535 (quoting *Missouri v. Lewis*, 101 U.S. 22 (1879)).

35. *See* discussion of *Duncan v. Louisiana*, chapter 6, *infra*.

36. *See* discussion of *Slaughterhouse Cases*, chapter 1, *supra*; *see also* chapter 1 notes 118, 140, and 157.

37. *See, e.g.*, *Adamson v. California*, 332 U.S. 46 (1947) (Black, J., dissenting); *see also* Lawrence H. Tribe, *American Constitutional Law* (St. Paul: Foundation Press, 1988), §81.

38. *Corfield*, 6 Fed. Cas. at 551.

39. This point does not deny the influence of natural-rights theory on Anglo-American political and legal thought, but emphasizes that before *Slaughterhouse* the common law had assimilated the principle that arbitrary legislation was against the rule of law, obviating the need to refer to any criteria external to the tradition, including principles of natural law, when deciding due-process cases. *See* chapter 1 note 157.

40. *See, e.g.*, *Slaughterhouse Cases*, 83 U.S. at 86–87 (Field, J., dissenting) ("No one will deny the abstract justice which lies in the position of the plaintiffs in error; and I shall endeavor to show that the position has some support in the fundamental law of the country.").

41. *See* discussion of *Hurtado v. California*, Chapter 1, *supra*. *See also* Randy E. Barnett, "Who's Afraid of Unenumerated Rights?" *University of Pennsylvania Journal of Constitutional Law* 1, no. 9 (October 2006): 5–11. Barnett defines positivism as meaning "that statutes enacted by popularly-elected legislatures are laws binding on judges, unless they violate an express prohibition in a popularly-enacted constitution." Barnett notes the early shift in American law toward a positivist perspective as American lawyers embraced the influence of Blackstone and his conception of sovereignty, and as some argued for the legality of slavery. But he notes as well that as late as the 1940s, "opinions about the proper role of judges were still fluid enough" that a non-positivist approach "was still possible." (citing Robert M. Cover, *Justice Accused: Antislavery and the Judicial Process* (New Haven and London: Yale University Press, 1975), 8–30 (noting Cover's "describing how the tradition of positivism created the foundation for the notion that judges should be will-less" and adopt a position of extreme deference to legislatures)). The notion that judges should be will-less and extremely deferential to legislatures when adjudicating claims of fundamental rights is one that modern conservatism, promoting a majoritarian positivist conception of American law, would espouse in the late-twentieth century, and is explained in part II, *infra*.

42. *Snyder*, 291 U.S. at 105.

43. *See* discussion of *Duncan v. Louisiana*, chapter 7, *infra*.

44. 332 U.S. 46 (1947).

45. *Id.* at 47.

46. *Id.* at 49.

47. *Id.* at 47–48.

48. *Id.* at 50.
49. *Id.*
50. 211 U.S. 78 (1908).
51. 332 U.S. at 51–53.
52. *Id.* at 53 (citing *Moore v. Dempsey*, 261 U.S. 86, 91 (1923); *Chambers v. Florida*, 309 U.S. 227, 238 (1940); *Buchalter v. New York*, 319 U.S. 427 (1943)).
53. *Id.*
54. *Id.* at 53–54.
55. 211 U.S. at 99.
56. 332 U.S. at 54 n. 13 (citing *Hebert v. Louisiana*, 272 U.S. 312, 316 (1926)).
57. *Id.* at 54.
58. *Id.* at 55–56.
59. *Id.* at 56.
60. *Id.* at 58.
61. *Id.*
62. *Id.* (citing *People v. Adamson*, 27 Cal.2d 494, 495) (internal quotation marks omitted).
63. *Id.* at 59.
64. *Id.* at 57.
65. *Id.* at 59–60.
66. *Id.* at 65.
67. *See Twining*, 211 U.S. at 93–103.
68. 332 U.S. at 71–72 (Black, J., dissenting) ("My study of the historical events that culminated in the Fourteenth Amendment, and the expressions of those who sponsored and favored, as well as those who opposed its submission and passage, persuades me that one of the chief objects that the provisions of the Amendment's first section, separately, and as a whole, were intended to accomplish was to make the Bill of Rights, applicable to the states.").
69. *Id.* at 69 (internal quotation marks omitted).
70. *See* Tribe, *American Constitutional Law*, §114 (noting that Justice Frankfurter believed that he could identify "those liberties of the individual which history has attested as the indispensable conditions of an open as against a closed society," *Kovacs v. Cooper*, 336 U.S. 77, 95 (1949) (Frankfurter, J., concurring), by a "disinterested inquiry pursued in the spirit of science, on a balanced order of facts exactly and fairly stated, on the detached consideration of conflicting claims . . . on a judgment not ad hoc and episodic but duly mindful of reconciling the needs both of continuity and of change in a progressive society," *Rochin v. California*, 342 U.S. 165, 172 (1952)).
71. *See*, *e.g.* Tinsley E. Yarbrough. John Marshall Harlan. *Great Dissenter of the Warren Court* (New York: Oxford University Press, 1992).

Chapter 4

A Reasonable and Sensitive Judgment

When *West Coast Hotel* repudiated the *Lochner*-Era case law, it reinvigorated the concept of ordered liberty. "[T]he liberty" that due process "safeguarded [was] liberty in a social organization which require[d] the protection of law[.]"[1] The guarantee, the court had said, "does not recognize an absolute and uncontrollable liberty[,]" for "[l]iberty in each of its phases has its history and connotation."[2] The common-law analysis thus required evaluating claims to liberty, against those of State interests in social order, with attention to the contexts in which claims arose. It tested a State's chosen means for fitness with its proffered objectives, in light of the importance of the liberty asserted, with the facts of each case providing the details and honing the analysis.

The examples now ranged from the *Slaughterhouse* dissents and *Hurtado*, through the *Lochner*-Era dissents, *Meyer* and *Pierce*, and to *West Coast Hotel*, *Palko*, and *Adamson*. Whether evaluating claims to substantive liberty or procedural fairness, the strength of the common law was its enduring applicability to exigencies arising in an evolving society—one organized around the concept of ordered liberty. The concept had survived the *Lochner*-Era, despite the pressures that early American industrial capitalism brought to bear on the Court's judgment. And even as the proponents of incorporation created the conditions for its next and most trying ordeal, the concept's resilience would show in the reasoning of Justice Harlan II, as he evaluated a controversial claim to liberty during America's mid-twentieth-century social revolution.

***

Pauline Poe had three consecutive pregnancies, each ending with the birth of an infant who died shortly thereafter due to multiple congenital abnormalities.[3]

Pauline and her husband consulted a doctor, a renowned obstetrician and gynecologist, who determined that a genetic factor was to blame, and advised as the best and safest medical treatment the use of contraceptive drugs and devices.[4] The same doctor treated another patient, Jane Doe, whom a recent pregnancy had rendered critically ill for nine weeks, including a two-week period of unconsciousness.[5] The pregnancy had left Jane, twenty-five-years old and living with her husband, partially paralyzed with a speech impairment and emotional instability.[6] Her doctor advised that another pregnancy would be life-threatening, and the best and safest treatment for her was the use of contraceptives.[7]

The Poes and Does lived in the State of Connecticut in the late 1950s. The State's Attorney, Abraham Ullman, publicly expressed his intention to enforce the State's laws, and claimed that the use of contraceptives violated them.[8] Anyone providing advice regarding their use was susceptible to prosecution under Connecticut's general criminal accessory law.[9] Violations carried penalties of up to a year in prison and a fine of at least fifty dollars.[10] The Poes and Doe sought a declaratory judgment from the Superior Court of New Haven County that the statutes were unconstitutional because they deprived them of life and liberty without due process of law.[11] Their doctor sought a declaratory judgment that the laws prohibiting his giving advice to Doe deprived him of liberty and property without due process.[12]

The Superior Court of New Haven County dismissed the claims.[13] The State appellate court upheld the decision. So did the Supreme Court of Connecticut, which agreed with the lower courts that the record showed no justiciable constitutional question—it was unclear whether the statutes had or would in fact be enforced against the plaintiffs.[14] When they appealed to the U.S. Supreme Court, it held that the cases below were properly dismissed for lack of justiciability.[15] Writing for the majority in *Poe v. Ullman*, Justice Frankfurter reasoned that Ullman's stated intention to enforce the laws of the State was insufficient to support the Poes's, Doe's, and their doctor's claims that a threat of prosecution coerced them into foregoing the use of contraceptives and giving advice regarding their use.[16]

The concurring and dissenting Justices emphasized the social climate within which the appellants challenged the Connecticut law and its implication for their claims. In his concurring opinion, Justice William Brennan identified the "true controversy in [the] case" as "the opening of birth-control clinics on a large scale[.]"[17] Justice Douglas, dissenting, noted that a "public clinic dispensing birth-control ha[d] indeed been closed by the State[,]" and "[d]octors and a nurse working in that clinic were arrested by the police and charged with advising married women on the use of contraceptives."[18] And Justice Harlan, in his dissent, criticized the majority's decision "that the appellants are more or less free to act without fear of prosecution because the prosecuting authorities of the State, in their discretion and at their whim, are, as a matter of prediction, unlikely to decide to prosecute."[19]

Regarding the married persons claims, Harlan explained his "disagreement with the present disposition."[20]

> [T]he most substantial claim which these married persons press is their right to enjoy the privacy of their marital relations free of the enquiry of the criminal law . . . . And I cannot agree that their enjoyment of this privacy is not substantially impinged upon, when they are told that if they use contraceptives, indeed whether they do so or not, the only thing which stands between them and being forced to render criminal account of their marital privacy is the whim of the prosecutor.[21]

These circumstances invoked the very purpose of anticipatory relief, and Harlan found it necessary "to consider the merits of appellants' Constitutional claims."[22]

But these particular claims "dr[e]w their basis from no explicit language of the Constitution, and ha[d] yet to find expression in any decision of th[e] Court[.]"[23] "I feel it desirable at the outset[,]" Harlan wrote, "to state the framework of Constitutional principles in which I think the issue must be adjudged."[24]

> [T]he basis of judgment as to the Constitutionality of state action must be a rational one, approaching the text which is the only commission of our power not in a literalistic way, as if we had a tax statute before us, but as the basic charter of our society, setting out in spare but meaningful terms the principles of government.[25]

This "rational process in Constitutional adjudication" was critical. Because the due process guarantee was "not self-explanatory," applying it demanded authentic judicial restraint.[26] Like Justices Field and Bradley, Harlan recognized the weight of the federalism principle—it counseled deference to the "plenary power of [State] government[,]" unless the Constitution permitted "judicial interference in sovereign operations of the State."[27]

The Court had struggled with identifying constraints on its discretion. In its attempt "to delineate [the Due Process Clause's] scope," Harlan explained, the Court had considered and rejected two possible responses to the danger of the federal judiciary inappropriately interfering in the States' affairs. The first, a reaction to perceived "abuses by th[e] Court of its reviewing power, sought to limit the provision to a guarantee of procedural fairness."[28] The second "would have it that the Fourteenth Amendment, whether by way of the Privileges [or] Immunities Clause or the Due Process Clause, applied against the states only and precisely those restraints which had prior to the Amendment been applicable merely to federal action."[29] "[D]ue process in the consistent view of this Court[,]" Harlan observed, "has even been a broader concept than the first view and more flexible than the second."[30] *Slaughterhouse*, *Hurtado*, *Twining*, and *Palko* made clear that the due-process guarantee protected "the very substance of . . . liberty,"[31] and the incorporation doctrine did not explain the relationship between the guarantee and the Bill of Rights.[32]

Invoking the ordered-liberty concept, Harlan stated the political theory within which the tradition required him to analyze the appellants' claims.

> Due process cannot be reduced to any formula; its content cannot be determined by reference to any code. The best that can be said is that through the course of this Court's decisions it has represented the balance which our Nation, built upon postulates of respect for the liberty of the individual, has struck between that liberty and the demands of organized society.[33]

He described a judge's relationship to the common law in terms of the peculiar history that generated it, which in turn informed it in the present—a relationship including limitations on judicial power inherent to the tradition. The notion of insurmountable obstacles to restraint when deciding cases was a chimera.

> If the supplying of content to this Constitutional concept has of necessity been a rational process, it certainly has not been one where judges have felt free to roam where unguided speculation might take them. The balance of which I speak is the balance struck by this country, having regard to what history teaches are the traditions from which it developed as well as the traditions from which it broke. That tradition is a living thing.[34]

This was not about a "living constitution" capable of assimilating shifting social values in order to remain relevant to the current society. The *vitality* of the common law was its power to decide "apparently novel claim[s]"[35]—claims only "apparently" novel because, while emerging from a developing society inevitably producing novel controversies, judges could resolve them within a tradition that provided the applicable principles and examples of properly applying them.

> Each new claim to Constitutional protection must be considered against a background of Constitutional purposes, as they have been rationally perceived and historically developed. . . . The decision of an apparently novel claim must depend on grounds which follow closely on well-accepted principles and

> criteria. The new decision must take its place in relation to what went before and further (cut) a channel for what is to come.[36]

Evaluating due-process claims within the common-law tradition ensured that decisions of the Court that "radically depart[ed]" from it "could not long survive, while . . . decision[s] which build[] on what has survived [are] likely to be sound."[37]

From this perspective, the incorporation doctrine was a *non sequitur.* "Though we exercise limited and sharply restrained judgment," Harlan explained, "there is . . . no mechanical answer[38]. . . . No formula could serve as a substitute . . . for judgment and restraint."[39] The tradition itself provided both.

> The vague contours of the Due Process Clause do not leave judges at large. We may not draw on our merely personal and private notions and disregard the limits that bind judges in their judicial function. Even though the concept of due process of law is not final and fixed, these limits are derived from considerations that are fused in the whole nature of our judicial process. These are considerations deeply rooted in reason and in the compelling traditions of the legal profession.[40]

The tradition required judges "to perceive distinctions in the imperative character" of a constitutional provision like the due-process guarantee.[41] And that character, Harlan said, "must be discerned from [the] provision's larger context"[42] a context "of history and purposes."[43]

> [T]he full scope of liberty guaranteed by the Due Process Clause cannot be found in or limited by the precise terms of the specific guarantees elsewhere provided in the Constitution. This liberty is not a series of isolated points pricked out in terms of the taking of property; the freedom of speech, press, and religion; the right to keep and bear arms; the freedom from unreasonable searches and seizures; and so on.[44]

Harlan described the liberty that due process protected as "a rational continuum which, broadly speaking, include[d] a freedom from all substantial arbitrary impositions and purposeless restraints."[45] He quoted *Hurtado*: "[T] he guarantees of due process, though having their roots in the Magna Carta's 'per legem terrae' and considered as procedural safeguards against executive usurpation and tyranny, have in this country become bulwarks also against arbitrary legislation."[46] And consistent with the post-*Lochner*-Era distinction that *Carolene Products* made, he recognized "what a reasonable and sensitive judgment must, that certain interests require particularly careful scrutiny of the state needs asserted to justify their abridgement."[47]

From this perspective, previous decisions in which the Court evaluated States' laws allegedly interfering with unenumerated liberties—those without explicit mention in the Constitution—fit within the tradition of reasoned judgment. Citing *Meyer* and *Pierce* as examples,[48] Harlan acknowledged the incorporationists' inclination to cast such decisions as based on "concepts derived from the explicit guarantees of the First Amendment against federal encroachment upon freedom of speech and belief."[49] But as Cardozo had explained in *Palko*, a connection to discrete Bill-of-Rights provisions was not a condition precedent to applying the due-process guarantee. These First-Amendment liberties were not essential because they were enumerated as protected against unwarranted federal encroachment. They were enumerated as such, and were also included in the liberty that due process protected, because they were expressions of the "fundamental theory of liberty upon which all governments in this Union repose."[50] So were the liberties at issue in *Meyer* and *Pierce*. Harlan explained, "[I]t is the purpose of those guarantees and not their text, the reasons for their statement by the Framers and not the statement itself, which have led to their present status in the compendious notion of liberty embraced in the Fourteenth Amendment."[51]

Harlan identified the contending interests in the controversy before the Court with reference to the arguments the parties presented—another important restraint the common-law tradition provided. On the liberty side of the concept, the "appellants contend[ed] that the Connecticut statute deprive[d] them . . . of a substantial measure of liberty in carrying on the most intimate of all personal relationships, and that it [did] so arbitrarily and without any rational, justifying purpose."[52] And "[t]he State assert[ed,]" on the ordered side of the concept, "that it [was] acting to protect the moral welfare of its citizenry, both directly, in that it consider[ed] the practice of contraception immoral in itself, and instrumentally, in that the availability of contraceptive materials tend[ed] to minimize 'the disastrous consequence of dissolute action[.]'"[53] The question before the Court was whether the State had reasonably resolved the tension between these contending interests in order and liberty as specified in this particular controversy.

Harlan initially addressed the moral objective the statute ostensibly served. The appellants' argued "that the judgment, implicit in this statute—that the use of contraceptives by married couples is immoral—is an irrational one, that in effect it subjects them in a very important matter to the arbitrary whim of the legislature, and that it does so for no good purpose."[54] But Harlan explained that "the moral soundness of its people" was a traditional and legitimate state concern.[55] To suggest otherwise "would be to withdraw from community concern a range of subjects with which every society in civilized times has found it necessary to deal[]"—including the institution of marriage, sexual behavior, and "the legal and social context in which children are born and brought up[.]"[56]

Considering the broad range of opinions on the morality of contraception, Harlan said, "Connecticut's judgment is no more demonstrably correct or incorrect than are the varieties of judgment, expressed in law, on marriage and divorce, on adult consensual homosexuality, abortion, and sterilization, or euthanasia and suicide."[57] This was no mere list of hypothetical issues the Court might confront; rather, as the story will reveal, it was evidence of this sage's clairvoyance. "The very controversial nature" of such moral questions, he explained, counseled against the Court "concluding that the Constitution precluded Connecticut from choosing as it has among these various views."[58]

So it was not the Court's place to evaluate whatever moral conclusion the State had reached. Harlan explained, however, that the Court was "not presented simply with this moral judgment to be passed on as an abstract proposition."[59] Because the allegation here was that the means the State chose to express its morality had impermissibly impacted a significant personal-liberty interest.

> The secular state is not an examiner of consciences: it must operate in the realm of behavior, of overt actions, and where it does so operate, not only the underlying, moral purpose of its operations, but also the choice of means becomes relevant to any Constitutional judgment on what is done.[60]

He offered examples of means the State might choose to express its judgment about the morality of contraception. It could mandate, for example, "that a marriage in which only contraceptive relations had taken place had never been consummated and could be annulled."[61] It could make the use of contraceptives grounds for divorce, or use tax benefits and subsidies to encourage large families.[62] He focused his analysis on the means the State had chosen here.

> Precisely what is involved here is this: the State is asserting the right to enforce its moral judgment by intruding upon the most intimate details of the marital relation with the full power of the criminal law. . . . Nor could any imaginable elaboration of presumptions, testimonial privileges, or other safeguards, alleviate the necessity for testimony as to the mode and manner of the married couples' sexual relations, or at least the opportunity for the accused to make denial of the charges.[63]

"In sum," Harlan wrote, "the statute allows the State to enquire into, prove and punish married people for the private use of their marital intimacy."[64]

The litigants claimed the State interfered with "a most fundamental aspect of [their] liberty."[65] If so, then consistent with the *Carolene-Products* distinction, "[t]he statute must pass a more rigorous Constitutional test than that going merely to the plausibility of its underlying rationale."[66] The State's justification for its chosen means would "be subjected to strict scrutiny."[67] Harlan found the authority for this proposition—that "certain interests require particularly careful scrutiny of the state needs asserted to justify their abridgement[,]"[68]—in *Skinner v. Oklahoma*,[69] a Fourteenth-Amendment case in which, almost twenty years earlier, the Court had applied the *Carolene-Products* distinction. In *Skinner*, the Court struck down an act of the Oklahoma legislature requiring forced sterilization of persons thrice convicted of "felonies involving moral turpitude."[70] Decided under the Equal Protection Clause, the Court emphasized the "large deference" afforded the States' policy choices, but also that "strict scrutiny" of such a classification was "essential" in light of the danger it could pose to "the constitutional guaranty [*sic*] of just and equal laws."[71]

As Justice Bradley had demonstrated in *Slaughterhouse*, this was a dyadic inquiry, and each part corresponded to one aspect of the concept. The appellants would have to show that the liberty for which they sought protection was a "basic liberty"—one fundamental to the theory upon which all governments in the Union reposed and thus implicating the due-process guarantee. And if they met this burden, the State would have to show that in pursuing its interest in social order, it interfered with this liberty reasonably—its imposition was not arbitrary. Where a basic liberty was at stake, it obviated the presumption of reasonableness that the State's choice would otherwise enjoy, and the Court would strictly scrutinize the State's justification for the means it chose to accomplish its objective. Reasoned judgment required the Court to test the means the State had chosen, as applied in this case, for fitness with its justification for them. The Court had no authority to supplant a reasonable interference, even with a basic liberty, because the due-process guarantee prohibited only an arbitrary one.

***

Beginning with the liberty aspect of the inquiry, Harlan saw the liberty for which the married couples sought protection as "embrac[ing] the concept of the privacy of the home[.]"[72] The Constitution protected it in the Third and Fourth Amendments.[73] "While these Amendments reach only the Federal Government," he argued, "this Court has held in the strongest terms . . . that the concept of 'privacy' . . . is part of the 'ordered liberty' assured against state action by the Fourteenth Amendment."[74] He acknowledged that the Constitution's text expressly addressed "only . . . *methods* of ferreting out substantive wrongs, and the procedure it require[d] presuppose[d] that substantive offenses may be committed and sought out in the privacy of the home."[75] But if the Constitution placed a mere procedural hurdle for the government to clear before invading the privacy of person's homes, the due-process guarantee was "limited to what is explicitly provided in the Constitution, divorced from the rational purposes, historical roots, and subsequent developments of the relevant provisions."[76] To reach this untenable conclusion, one would have to deny the common-law tradition altogether.

Harlan found the "most comprehensive statement of the principle of liberty underlying" the appellants' claim in Justice Louis Brandeis's dissenting opinion in *Olmstead v. United States* (1928).[77] In *Olmstead*, the Court declined to interpret the Fourth Amendment's warrant requirement as applying to government taps of private telephone calls. Echoing Justice Bradley's *Slaughterhouse* dissent, Justice Brandeis had argued:

> [T]he makers of our Constitution undertook to secure conditions favorable to the pursuit of happiness. . . . They sought to protect Americans in their beliefs, their thoughts, their emotions and their sensations. They conferred, as against the government, the right to be let alone—the most comprehensive of rights . . . To protect that right, every unjustifiable intrusion by the government upon the privacy of the individual whatever the means employed, must be deemed a violation[.][78]

"The sweep of the court's decisions" vindicated this view, "amply show[ing] that the Constitution protects the privacy of the home against all unreasonable intrusion of whatever character."[79]

The intrusion the married couples challenged here—"the enactment of a substantive offense"—was decidedly different than those challenged in prior cases.[80] "[H]ere we have not an intrusion into the home[,]" Harlan said, "so much as on the life which characteristically has its place in the home."[81] This distinction did not, however, "preclude the making of a claim based on the right of privacy embraced in the 'liberty' of the Due Process Clause[.]"[82] While specific provisions of the Constitution reflected discrete instances of the principle's applications, they were not an exhaustive list of them. In *Meyer*, *Pierce*, and Brandeis's *Olmstead* opinion, for example, the same principle had been applied in other contexts, for liberty understood as residential and familial privacy served a purpose within the uniquely American design of ordered liberty.

> If the physical curtilage of the home is protected, it is surely as a result of solicitude to protect the privacies of the life within. Certainly the safeguarding of the home does not follow merely from the sanctity of property rights. The home derives its pre-eminence as the seat of family life. And the integrity of that life

> is something so fundamental that it has been found to draw to its protection the principles of more than one explicitly granted Constitutional right.[83]

Harlan emphasized the power of the common law to address issues arising within a developing society, observing that when the Constitution was written, the general warrant and the quartering of soldiers were "two particular threats" to the "Constitutional principle of privacy[.]"[84] But these were not, of course, the *only* intrusions against which the Constitution protected the home. "Legislation, both statutory and constitutional, is enacted from an experience of evils[.] [I]ts general language should not, therefore, be necessarily confined to the form that evil had theretofore taken. A principle, to be vital, must be capable of wider application than the mischief which gave it birth."[85]

Long before *Olmstead*, in *Boyd v. United States* (1886),[86] Justice Bradley explained that the Fourth Amendment should be construed "to effect the purpose of the framers of the Constitution in the interest in liberty."[87] Harlan argued that this principle underlying the Fourth Amendment was also an aspect of the due-process guarantee. "(These) principles affect the very essence of constitutional liberty and security. They reach farther than (a) concrete form of the case before the court, with its adventitious circumstances; they apply to all invasions on the part of the government . . . of the sanctity of [the] home and the privacies of life."[88] "The security of one's privacy against arbitrary invasion by the police," he concluded, "is basic to a free society."[89]

Harlan acknowledged that the "right of privacy . . . [was] not an absolute."[90] Following the examples of Justices Bradley, Field, and Cardozo, he used the details of this particular controversy to hone the breadth of the liberty interest asserted as worthy of triggering strict scrutiny of the State's action. This was not a *Lochner*-esque opportunity to identify an unenumerated "right" to use contraception, to marital or familial privacy, or to sexual intimacy. The jurisprudence would, soon after *Poe*, become a battleground for opposing views on how to identify and categorize such abstract substantive rights. But here, Harlan carefully juxtaposed the appellants' liberty interest against the State's countervailing interest in regulating it.

> It is one thing when the State exerts its power either to forbid extra-marital sexuality altogether, or to say who may marry, but it is quite another when, having acknowledged a marriage and the intimacies inherent in it, it undertakes to regulate by means of the criminal law the details of that intimacy.[91]

Harlan concluded the first step in the analysis, and turned to the second:

> In my view the appellants have presented a very pressing claim for Constitutional protection. Such difficulty as the claim presents lies only in evaluating it against

> the State's countervailing contention that it be allowed to enforce, by whatever means it deems appropriate, its judgment of the immorality of the practice the law condemns.[92]

Scrutinizing the State's justification required little effort. Connecticut asserted that the statute expressed its people's moral judgment on the subject of contraception, and so argued the "[c]onstitutional permissibility of the moral judgment underlying" the law.[93] Harlan had already explained that the State's moral conclusion was not an appropriate object of the Court's scrutiny.[94] And the State offered *only* its morality to justify interfering with the appellants' liberty—an objective supporting every criminal statute in every State. The common-law tradition of reasoned judgment required a judge to scrutinize the State's reasons for choosing in this case, as the means to express its morality, the threat of intruding into the marital bedroom via the criminal law. It was time to test the means the State had chosen for fitness with its objective, in light of the importance of the liberty it impacted. But, "[n]either [the State's] brief, nor its argument, nor anything in any of the opinions of its highest court in these or other cases[,]" Justice Harlan observed, "even remotely suggests a justification for the obnoxiously intrusive means it has chosen to effectuate that policy."[95] For its choice of means the State proffered no reasons. The law was unreasonable. It was a "substantial arbitrary imposition" the due-process guarantee prohibited.[96]

Harlan acknowledged the tradition's respect for federalism as a source of judicial restraint, and its command that the Court supplant a State legislature's judgment only where the common-law analysis exposed an unreasonable interference with a basic liberty.

> Though undoubtedly the States are and should be left free to reflect a wide variety of policies, and should be allowed broad scope in experimenting with various means of promoting those policies . . . There are limits to the extent to which a legislatively represented majority may conduct experiments at the expense of the dignity and personality of the individual. In this instance these limits are, in my view, reached and surpassed.[97]

Concluding his analysis, Harlan narrowed to the facts of the case the holding he would have the Court reach.

> I would adjudicate these appeals and hold this statute unconstitutional, insofar as it purports to make criminal the conduct contemplated by these married women. It follows that if their conduct cannot be a crime, appellant[s' doctor]

cannot be an accomplice thereto. I would reverse the judgment in each of these cases.[98]

***

The Connecticut law criminalized these married couples' using contraceptives, without a justification for the onerous means it chose to effectuate its moral judgment. In light of the purposes of American government, this was a purposeless restraint and thus violated the Fourteenth Amendment's due-process guarantee. Here was a model of restraint that found meaningful limits on judicial discretion in the common-law practice of arbitrariness review. Harlan eschewed the ease of the incorporation doctrine in favor of fidelity to reasoned judgment. There was no appeal to natural law here, and his opinion announced no unenumerated fundamental right. It did the work of common-law judging, and concluded the law as applied in this case was unreasonable.

Like Harlan's contemporaries, successive generations of justices would fail to fully appreciate this elegant demonstration of the common-law method. Its eloquence, humility, and attention to detail were squandered as emerging factions on the Court continued arguing about incorporation and unenumerated substantive rights. And this in turn catalyzed the most significant development yet in personal-liberty jurisprudence. A mere four years hence, when it revisited the criminal prohibition challenged in *Poe*, the Court would merge the two doctrines that Justice Harlan had so gracefully deflected.

NOTES

1. 300 U.S. at 391.
2. *Id.*
3. *Poe v. Ullman*, 367 U.S. 497, 498 (1961).
4. *Id.* at 498–499.
5. *Id.*
6. *Id.*
7. *Id.*
8. *Id.* at 499 (citing Conn. Gen. Stat. Rev. 1958 § 53-32) ("Any person who uses any drug, medicinal article or instrument for the purpose of preventing conception shall be fined not less than fifty dollars or imprisoned not less than sixty days nor more than one year or be both fined and imprisoned.").
9. *Id.* at 500 (citing Conn. Gen. Stat. Rev. 1958 § 54-196) ("Any person who assists, abets, counsels, causes, hires or commands another to commit any offense may be prosecuted and punished as if he were the principal offender.").

10. *Id.* at 499.
11. *Id.* at 497, 500.
12. *Id.* at 500.
13. *Id.* at 497.
14. *Id.*
15. *Id.* at 508–509.
16. *Id.*
17. *Id.* at 509 (Brennan, J., concurring).
18. *Id.* at 511 (Douglas, J., dissenting).
19. *Id.* at 536 (Harlan, J., dissenting).
20. *Id.*
21. *Id.*
22. *Id.*
23. *Id.*
24. *Id.*
25. *Id.* at 539–540 (citing *McCulloch v. Maryland*, 4 Wheat. 316 (1819)).
26. *Id.* at 540.
27. *Id.*
28. *Id.*
29. *Id.* at 540–541.
30. *Id.* at 541.
31. *See Hurtado*, 110 U.S. at 532; *see Poe*, 367 U.S. at 541–542 (Harlan, J., dissenting) (citing *Corfield*, 6 F. Cas. 546, 551 (1823); *Calder v. Bull*, 3 Dall. 386, 388 (1798)).
32. 367 U.S. at 541–542 (citing *Slaughterhouse Cases*, 16 Wall. 36 (1872); *Walker v. Sauvinet*, 92 U.S. 90 (1875); *Hurtado v. California*, 110 U.S. 516 (1884); *Presser v. Illinois*, 116 U.S. 252 (1886); *In re Kemmler*, 136 U.S. 436 (1890); *Twining v. New Jersey*, 211 U.S. 78 (1908); *Palko v. Connecticut*, 302 U.S. 319 (1937)).
33. *Id.* at 542.
34. *Id.*
35. *Id.* at 544.
36. *Id.* (quoting *Irvine v. California*, 347 U.S. 128, 147 (1954) (Frankfurter, J., dissenting) ("'There is all the difference in the world between disposing of a case as though it were a discrete instance and recognizing it as part of the process of judgment, taking its place in relation to what went before and further cutting a channel for what is to come.'")) (internal quotation marks omitted; parentheses are Harlan's).
37. *Id.* at 542.
38. *Id.* at 544 (quoting *Irvine v. California*, 347 U.S. 128, 147 (1954) (Frankfurter, J., dissenting)) (internal quotation marks omitted).
39. *Id.* at 542.
40. *Id.* at 544–545 (quoting *Irvine v. California*, 347 U.S. 128, 147 (1954) (Frankfurter, J., dissenting) (citing Cardozo, *The Nature of the Judicial Process* (1921); *The Growth of the Law* (1927); *The Paradoxes of Legal Science* (1928))) (internal quotation marks omitted).
41. *Id.* at 542.

42. *Id.*
43. *Id.* at 542–543.
44. *Id.* at 543.
45. *Id.*
46. *Id.* at 541 (quoting *Hurtado*, 110 U. S. at 532) (internal quotation marks omitted).
47. *Id.* (citing *Skinner v. Oklahoma*, 316 U.S. 535, 544 (1942)); *see also id.* at 546 ("Where, as here, we are dealing with what must be considered a basic liberty, [t]here are limits to the extent to which the presumption of constitutionality can be pressed, and the mere assertion that the action of the State finds justification in the controversial realm of morals cannot justify alone any and every restriction it imposes.") (citing *Skinner,* 316 U.S. at 541; quoting *Skinner*, 316 U.S. at 544 (concurring opinion) (citing *United States v. Carolene Products Co.*, 304 U.S. 144, 152, footnote 4); citing *Alberts v. California*, 354 U. S. 476 (1957)) (internal quotation marks omitted).
48. *Id.* at 543–544.
49. *Id.* at 544.
50. *Id.* at 543–544 (citing *Pierce*, 268 U.S. at 535).
51. *Id.*
52. *Id.* at 545.
53. *Id.*
54. *Id.*
55. *Id.* at 545–546.
56. *Id.* at 546.
57. *Id.* at 547.
58. *Id.*
59. *Id.*
60. *Id.*
61. *Id.* at 547–548.
62. *Id.* at 548.
63. *Id.*
64. *Id.*
65. *Id.* at 548 (internal quotation marks omitted).
66. *Id.*
67. *Id.* (quoting *Skinner*, 316 U.S. at 541) (internal quotation marks omitted).
68. *Id.* at 543 (citing *Skinner,* 316 U.S. at 541).
69. 316 U.S. 535 (1942).
70. *Id.* at 536.
71. *Id.* at 541.
72. 367 U.S. at 548.
73. *Id.* at 549.
74. *Id.*
75. *Id.* (emphasis added).
76. *Id.*
77. 277 U.S. 438 (1928).
78. *Id.* at 478.

79. 367 U.S. at 550.
80. *Id.*
81. *Id.*
82. *Id.*
83. *Id.* at 551–552.
84. *Id.* at 551.
85. *Id.* (quoting *Weems v. United States*, 217 U.S. 349, 373 (1910)) (internal quotation marks omitted).
86. 116 U.S. 616 (1886).
87. *See Olmstead*, 277 U.S. at 465 (discussing Justice Bradley's view in *Boyd*).
88. 367 U.S. at 550 (quoting *Boyd*, 116 U.S. at 630) (internal quotation marks omitted; parentheses in original).
89. *Id.* (quoting *Wolf v. Colorado*, 338 U.S. 25, 27 (1949)) (internal quotation marks omitted).
90. *Id.* at 552.
91. *Id.* at 553.
92. *Id.*
93. *Id.* at 554.
94. *Id.* at 546–547.
95. *Id.* at 554.
96. *Id.* at 543.
97. *Id.* at 555 (quoting *Skinner*, 316 U.S. at 546 (Jackson, J., concurring)) (internal quotation marks omitted).
98. *Id.*

Chapter 5

A Zone of Substantive Rights

Four years after *Poe*, the State's anti-contraception statute was again before the Court in *Griswold v. Connecticut*.[1] Estelle Griswold, executive director of the Planned Parenthood League of Connecticut, and Dr. Buxton, a licensed physician, had been arrested, and convicted in state court of violating the statute at issue in *Poe*.[2] The State's appellate and supreme courts affirmed the convictions.[3] This time the U.S. Supreme Court resolved the justiciability question in favor of the appellants.[4]

The incorporation debate had reached a fever pitch as the Court faced the ongoing challenge of demonstrating judicial restraint in due process cases. Culling together a plurality, Justice Douglas authored the Court's opinion. While the reasoning of *Griswold* retreated from his total-incorporationist position in *Adamson*, Douglas nevertheless connected to the Bill of Rights the Court's power to invalidate the statute. But this was not a selective-incorporationist solution, with one particular Bill-of-Rights provision as its primary ingredient. Douglas identified in the Court's prior decisions several unenumerated rights emanating from explicit Bill-of-Rights provisions, that formed a "zone of privacy."[5] Because the relationship of married persons was in the zone,[6] the State of Connecticut's intruding into it violated "established Constitutional principles."[7]

Douglas acknowledged the "wide range of questions that implicate[d] the Due Process Clause,"[8] and the danger inherent to federal judicial oversight of the State's policies. Admitting the Court's troubled history, and unaware of the influence the *Griswold* opinion would have on the jurisprudence, he wrote,

> Overtones of some arguments suggest that *Lochner v. State of New York* should be our guide. But we decline that invitation as we did in *West Coast Hotel v.*

> *Parrish.* We do not sit as a super-legislature to determine the wisdom, need, and propriety of laws that touch economic problems, business affairs, or social conditions.[9]

Douglas found the Court's obligation to review the statute in the observation that the "law . . . operate[d] directly on an intimate relation of husband and wife and their physician's role in one aspect of that relation."[10] But he did not discuss why these relationships were important and required scrutiny of the State's interference with them. He turned immediately instead to a discussion of unenumerated rights, identifying the "association of people," the "right to educate a child in a school of the parents' choice," and the "right to study any particular subject or any foreign language," as rights "not mentioned in the Constitution nor in the Bill of Rights."[11] Citing *Meyer* and *Pierce* as examples, Douglas said that the "First Amendment ha[d] been construed to include" them, as well as "freedom of inquiry, freedom of thought, . . . freedom to teach, [and] . . . the freedom of the entire university community."[12] Neither *Meyer* nor *Pierce*, of course, mentioned the First Amendment. Both were examples of the common-law tradition of arbitrariness review under the due-process guarantee of the Fourteenth.[13] This mischaracterization belied the need to reach the challenged statute on a theory connected to the Bill of Rights, ostensibly ensuring judicial restraint and palatable to the incorporationists on the Court.

From an array of precedent affirming "the principle of the *Pierce* and the *Meyer* cases" and addressing various protected "associations," Douglas concluded, "[T]he First Amendment has a penumbra where privacy is protected from government intrusion."[14] And from this conclusion he induced a broader proposition: "[S]pecific guarantees in the Bill of Rights have penumbras, formed by emanations from those guarantees that help give them life and substance."[15] "Various guarantees[,]" he wrote, "create zones of privacy."[16] In addition to the First Amendment, the Third's "prohibition against quartering of soldiers . . . [was] another facet of that privacy."[17] Provisions of the Fourth and Fifth Amendments contributed to this "zone of privacy," as did the Ninth Amendment's assurance that rights existed other than those explicitly mentioned in the Bill of Rights.[18]

Douglas invoked some of the same Bill-of-Rights provisions that Justice Harlan had in *Poe*.[19] But he did not use them to evaluate the importance of the asserted liberty interest in light of the principles they expressed, as "rationally perceived and historically developed" within the common-law tradition. Douglas used them to construct a spatial metaphor within which he located the interest. Having identified the "zone of privacy created by several fundamental constitutional guarantees," Douglas declared, "[T]he present case . . . concerns a relationship lying within" it.[20] And because the State had chosen means having a "maximum destructive impact upon that relationship," the statute violated the principle that "a governmental purpose to control or prevent activities constitutionally subject to state regulation may not be achieved by means which sweep unnecessarily broadly and thereby invade the area of protected freedoms."[21]

From the common-law perspective, this description was accurate. Where a basic liberty was at stake, a State could not adopt means that while achieving its objective had an arbitrary collateral impact on it. But Douglas's analysis did not follow the tradition and test—let alone identify—the State's justification for the means it chose here. Douglas seemed to presume the question was simply whether the freedom to use contraceptives—at least for married couples—was included in the due-process guarantee's protections, and then to declare that it was. He concluded his opinion asking, "Would we allow the police to search the sacred precincts of the marital bedroom for telltale signs of the use of contraceptives?"[22] And he answered, "The very idea is repulsive to the notions of privacy surrounding the marriage relationship."[23] The final sentence of the *Griswold* opinion reaffirmed that the marital relationship enjoyed the protections of other associations and interests suggested in the Ninth Amendment to the Constitution and found within the penumbras of the First, Third, Fourth, and Fifth. "Marriage[,]" Douglas concluded, "is an association for as noble a purpose as any involved in our prior decisions."[24] The State court decision was therefore reversed.[25]

***

Douglas rebuffed the suggestion that *Lochner* should guide the Court's decision. But the "zone of privacy" comprising his penumbral emanations would take the Court in just such a direction. Although apparently intended to extend the incorporation doctrine far enough to capture unenumerated rights, this spatial metaphor suggested a category of substantive liberties—those within the "zone of privacy"—much like *Lochner*-Era decisions relied on a categorical economic liberty. Douglas identified the marital relationship as "lying within" this zone, leaving unclear precisely what "right" the Court had recognized as protected against the State's interference. He referred to the marital relationship as "a right of privacy[.]"[26] But his analysis identified other rights of privacy—familial, informational, and spatial—penumbral to emanations of various Bill-of-Rights provisions. The *Griswold* opinion described a broad right of privacy and narrower rights within it.

But it did not specify precisely what they were. Perhaps marital privacy, or a right to use contraception, or of married persons to use contraception. *Griswold* thus epitomized a controversial issue that would thereafter pervade the Court's fundamental-rights jurisprudence. Whether a right was considered "in" the zone of protected substantive liberties could depend on the level of generality at which it was stated. How a "right" was described could determine whether it was constitutionally protected. Over the next fifty years, the jurisprudence would gradually absorb the full impact of this feature of *Griswold*, as various justices grappled with, or exploited, the problem it created.

Griswold displayed the absence of a coherent theory upon which the justices agreed for reviewing state laws under the liberty provision of the Due Process Clause. And it generated several opinions about the appropriate means of judicial restraint in personal-liberty cases. Justice Black and Justice Potter Stewart dissented, arguing for a stricter version of incorporation and against, as had Black in his *Adamson* dissent, what they saw as "natural law due process philosophy."[27] Justice Arthur Goldberg concurred, joined by Chief Justice Earl Warren and Justice William Brennan, arguing that the Court's reasoning should emphasize the Ninth Amendment.[28] Justices Harlan and Byron White each concurred, arguing for the traditional common-law analysis that Harlan demonstrated in *Poe*.[29]

In his concurrence, Harlan wrote, "[T]he proper constitutional inquiry . . . is whether this . . . statute infringes the Due Process Clause of the Fourteenth Amendment because the enactment violates basic values implicit in the concept of ordered liberty[.]"[30] He explained that the details of the proper analysis under the ordered-liberty concept were found in his dissenting opinion in *Poe*.[31] And he focused his criticism on Douglas's diluted incorporation solution. While it allowed the Court in this case to recognize an unenumerated right and reach the Connecticut statute, it could just as easily do the opposite and restrict the scope of the due-process guarantee.[32] Describing succinctly the result of Douglas's analysis, Harlan wrote, "[T]he Due Process Clause of the Fourteenth Amendment does not touch this Connecticut statute unless the enactment is found to violate some right assured by the letter or penumbra of the Bill of Rights."[33]

> In other words, what I find implicit in the Court's opinion is that the incorporation doctrine may be used to restrict the reach of Fourteenth Amendment Due Process. For me this is just as unacceptable constitutional doctrine as is the use of the incorporation approach to impose upon the States all the requirements of the Bill of Rights as found in the provisions of the first eight amendments and in the decisions of this Court interpreting them.[34]

Acknowledging the problem the incorporation doctrine tried to address, Harlan argued, "While I could not more heartily agree that judicial self restraint is an indispensable ingredient of sound constitutional adjudication, I do submit that the formula suggested for achieving it is more hollow than real."[35] He criticized the "illusory restriction on the content of the Due Process Clause" that the doctrine offered, as if judges would somehow "be confined to 'interpretation' of specific constitutional provisions, and . . . thereby restrained from introducing their own notions of constitutional right and wrong into the 'vague contours' of the Due Process Clause."[36] Other so-called "[s]pecific provisions of the Constitution," he argued, "lend themselves as readily to personal interpretations by judges whose constitutional outlook is simply to keep the Constitution in supposed tune with the times."[37]

> Judicial self-restraint . . . will be achieved in this area, as in other constitutional areas, only by continual insistence upon respect for the teachings of history, solid recognition of the basic values that underlie our society, and wise appreciation of the great roles that the doctrines of federalism and separation of powers have played in establishing and preserving American freedoms.[38]

Throughout the remainder of the twentieth century, various factions on the Court would invoke this passage as authority for points of view that at best misunderstood, and, at worst, deliberately misrepresented the tradition of reasoned judgment that Harlan and his forbears honored. The modern-conservative approach to personal-liberty claims would soon co-opt not only the words "history" and "values" in this passage, but also the very notion of "tradition." But it would do so reacting against the modern-liberal post-*Griswold* fundamental-rights doctrine, itself a significant deviation from the tradition. Modern-conservatism would tailor the fundamental-rights doctrine to serve its own ideological ends in legal controversies arising out of the mid-twentieth-century social revolution, and attempt to use Harlan's presentation of the principles informing the tradition of arbitrariness review to eliminate federal protections against the States for unenumerated substantive liberties.

While Harlan's concurrence reminded the Court of the principles informing proper due-process analysis, Justice White's offered the analysis Douglas neglected. White recognized that the Fourteenth Amendment provided protection for the "basic civil rights of man."[39] Citing *Meyer* and *Pierce* as examples, he argued that establishing a home and decisions pertaining to the rearing of children were among these basic liberties.[40] And the Court's prior decisions "affirm[ed] that there is a realm of family life which the state cannot enter without substantial justification."[41] The proper analysis required evaluating both the liberty interest asserted as worthy of constitutional protection *and* the State's justification for infringing it.

The first step in the common-law analysis identified and evaluated the importance of the liberty interest—being "free of regulation of the intimacies of the marriage relationship[.]"[42] Consistent with the distinction *Carolene Products* made, this interest came to the "Court with a momentum for respect lacking when appeal is made to liberties which derive merely from shifting economic arrangements."[43] Justice Douglas had likewise concluded the liberty interest here was important, but without considering how its weight derived from the purposes of democracy as recognized within the American legal tradition. Douglas had merely proceeded from the conclusory assertion that the interest was important to the conclusion that the Court should, therefore, question the State's interference with it.[44]

Turning to the second step in the analysis, and calling out Douglas's omission, White wrote, "An examination of the justification offered . . . cannot be avoided by saying that the . . . statute invades a protected area of privacy and association or that it demands the marriage relationship."[45] The "nature of the right" mattered, of course, but its importance did not of itself invalidate any state interference with it.[46] Rather, its importance triggered the requirement to scrutinize strictly the means the State chose to accomplish its objective.[47] Because the State had chosen means that substantially interfered with this interest, it bore "a substantial burden of justification when attacked under the Fourteenth Amendment."[48]

White observed, "[T]he State claims but one justification for its anti-use statute."[49] Unlike its position in *Poe*, the State did not argue that contraception was "immoral or unwise in itself."[50] This time, Connecticut claimed the "statute . . . serve[d] the State's policy against all forms of promiscuous or illicit sexual relationships, be they premarital or extramarital, concededly a permissible and legitimate legislative goal."[51] White did not "take[] issue with the premise that the fear of conception operate[d] as a deterrent to such relationships in addition to the criminal proscriptions Connecticut had against such conduct[.]"[52] But as the common law required, White tested the means the State had chosen for fitness with its proffered objective, confining his analysis, as Harlan demonstrated in *Poe*, to the details of this particular controversy.

> I wholly fail to see how the ban on the use of contraceptives by married couples in any way reinforces the State's ban on illicit sexual relationships. Connecticut does not bar the importation or possession of contraceptive devices . . . and their availability in that State is not seriously disputed. The only way Connecticut seeks to limit or control the availability of such devices is through its general aiding and abetting statute whose operation in this context has been quite obviously ineffective and whose most serious use has been against birth-control clinics rendering advice to married, rather than unmarried, persons.[53]

White nevertheless guessed at a plausible reason for the ban. If it prevented married persons from using contraception within their marital relationships, there might be "no or less temptation to use [it] in extramarital ones."[54]

But the Court could not presume a rational connection between means and ends—the liberty interest was too important. White concluded, "At most the broad ban is of marginal utility to the declared objective," and "[a] statute limiting its prohibition on use to persons engaging in the prohibited relationship would serve the [same] end."[55] Concluding his analysis, White could "find nothing in this record justifying the sweeping scope of this statute, with its telling effect on the freedoms of married persons," and he "therefore conclude[d] that it deprive[d] [them] of liberty without due process of law."[56]

White's concurrence situated the analysis within the arbitrary-reasonable framework of the common law and followed its two-part inquiry. It evaluated the weight of the liberty interest asserted and the State's justification for interfering with it, and included the common law's testing the State's choice of means for fitness with its reasons for choosing them. Failing the test in light of the importance of the interest it impacted, the law deprived the appellants of liberty in violation of the due-process guarantee. As Justice Harlan might have put it, as applied in this particular controversy, the law arbitrarily interfered with a liberty the American legal tradition recognized as "basic to a free society."[57]

***

Despite serial deviations from the tradition, a lineage of common-law judges had sustained the concept of ordered liberty from the moment it appeared in post-Reconstruction federal jurisprudence. From Bradley's and Field's *Slaughterhouse* dissents, through Matthews' opinion in *Hurtado* and Cardozo's in *Palko*, to Harlan's *Poe* dissent and Harlan's and White's *Griswold* concurrences, these judges understood the concept's value and their responsibility to realize its potential. In each opinion, they engaged in a thoughtful examination of contending interests. Where an individual's claim to liberty resonated with the reasons, according to the American legal tradition, for which governments were established, they tested the justification the State proffered for the balance it had struck between liberty and the demands of organized society. They scrutinized with particular care, in each controversy, the means the State had chosen in pursuing social order, against the reasons it proffered for choosing them. Each decision then became an ingredient in the admixture informing the next. But this was no mere haphazard incrementalism. The concept of ordered liberty was the talisman counseling this endeavor, grounding it in basic values underlying the American political experiment, and in the caution and moderation inherent to the special discretion the common-law tradition obligated its judges to exercise.

The common-law judges rescued the concept from its *Lochner*-Era co-option, where it had been pounded with a heavy-handed absolutism into an all-or-nothing answer to any democratic regulation of economic liberty. And they successfully protected it against the further impulse of some to reduce it to baser elements and then arrange them into a simple formula. For almost a century, the lineage of judges had guarded, honed, and polished it, bringing it increasingly into consciousness, describing the theory it expressed and providing examples of its proper application.

Under their protection the concept might have served to catch, reflect, and amplify the light of a distinctly American theory of liberal democracy, and thereby illuminate how the Court should consider a host of difficult issues destined to come before it. But although the bargain struck in *Griswold* produced a discrete victory for individual liberty against unreasonable state interference, it was also the moment the modern Court broke from the tradition of reasoned judgment. For *Griswold* let loose the categorical formalism of the late-twentieth-century fundamental-rights doctrine, and created the conditions for modern-conservative political ideology to infiltrate due-process jurisprudence.

NOTES

1. 381 U.S. 479 (1965).
2. *Id.* at 480.
3. *Id.*
4. *Id.* at 481.
5. *Id.* at 482–486.
6. *Id.* at 485.
7. *Id.*
8. *Id.* at 481.
9. *Id.* at 481–482.
10. *Id.* at 482.
11. *Id.*
12. *Id.* (citing *Meyer v. Nebraska*, 262 U.S. 390 (1923); *Pierce v. Society of Sisters*, 268 U.S. 510 (1925)).
13. *See* discussion of *Meyer* and *Pierce*, chapter 2, *supra*.
14. 381 U.S. at 482–483 (citing *Martin v. Struthers*, 319 U.S. 141, 143 (1943); *Wiemann v. Updegraff*, 344 U.S. 183, 195 (1952); *Sweezy v. New Hampshire*, 354 U.S. 234, 249–250, 261–263 (1957); *Barenblatt v. United States*, 360 U.S. 109, 112 (1959); *Baggett v. Bullitt*, 377 U.S. 360, 369 (1964); *NAACP v. Alabama*, 357 U.S. 449, 462 (1958); *NAACP v. Button*, 371 U.S. 415, 430–431 (1963); *Schware v. Board of Bar Examiners*, 353 U.S. 232, 244–246 (1957); *De Jonge v. Oregon*, 299 U.S. 353 (1937); *Board of Education v. Barnette*, 319 U.S. 624 (1943)).
15. *Id.* at 484.
16. *Id.*
17. *Id.*

18. *Id.*
19. *See id.* (citing *Poe*, 367 U. S. 497, 516–522 (Harlan, J., dissenting) for the proposition that "specific guarantees in the Bill of Rights have penumbras, formed by emanations from those guarantees that help give them life and substance."). Justice Douglas's citing Harlan's *Poe* dissent was ironic, considering Harlan's warning in his *Griswold* concurrence regarding the danger of this "incorporation"—the requirement that a protected liberty have a connection to discrete constitutional provisions other than the Due Process Clause of the Fourteenth Amendment. *See Griswold*, 381 U.S. at 499–500 (Harlan, J. concurring).
20. *Id.* at 485.
21. *Id.*
22. *Id.*
23. *Id.* at 486.
24. *Id.*
25. *Id.*
26. *Id.*
27. *Id.* at 507–527 (Black, J., dissenting); *see id.* at 516; *id.* at 527–531 (Stewart, J., dissenting).
28. *Id.* at 486–499 (Goldberg, J., concurring).
29. *Id.* at 499–502 (Harlan, J., concurring); *Id.* at 502–507 (White, J. concurring).
30. *Id.* at 500 (Harlan, J., concurring) (quoting *Palko*, 302 U.S. at 325) (internal quotation marks omitted).
31. *Id.*
32. *Id.*
33. *Id.* at 499.
34. *Id.* at 500.
35. *Id.* at 501.
36. *Id.*
37. *Id.*
38. *Id.*
39. *Id.* at 502 (White, J., concurring) (citing *Skinner v. Oklahoma*, 316 U.S. 535, 541 (1942)).
40. *Id.*
41. *Id.* (citing *Prince v. Massachusetts*, 321 U.S. 158, 166 (1944)).
42. *Id.* 502–503.
43. *Id.* (citing *Kovacs v. Cooper*, 336 U.S. 77, 95 (1949)).
44. *Id.* at 482.
45. *Id.* at 503 (White, J., concurring).
46. *Id.* at 503–504.
47. *Id.*
48. *Id.* at 503.
49. *Id.* at 505.
50. *Id.*
51. *Id.*
52. *Id.*

53. *Id.* at 505–506.
54. *Id.* at 506.
55. *Id.* at 507.
56. *Id.*
57. *Poe*, 367 U.S. at 550.

Part II

FUNDAMENTAL RIGHTS AND MODERN CONSERVATISM

A principle, to be vital, must be capable of wider application than the mischief which gave it birth.

—*Weems v. United States*, 217 U.S. 349, 373 (1910).

Chapter 6

Procedural and Substantive Due Process

Griswold portended the trajectory of mid-to-late twentieth-century due-process jurisprudence. It ignored the State's justification for the statute, and understood the substantive protections the due-process guarantee afforded as coextensive with a zone of liberty emanating from the Bill of Rights. One might generously interpret this union of unenumerated rights and incorporation as an honest attempt to accommodate rival theories and arrive at consensus. A more discerning account, however, is of the *Griswold* opinion as an alembic in which a clever alchemist's experiment went awry, releasing into the jurisprudence a mischievous spirit of unintended consequences. Douglas's penumbras would fade quickly as the explicit justification for recognizing unenumerated rights, but they cast a strange and enduring shadow across the jurisprudential landscape. One that would stretch all the way into the next century.

As part I has told, the due-process guarantee prohibited unreasonable government interference with basic liberties. A law violated the guarantee only if the interference was arbitrary. Whether a law was arbitrary turned on how the means the State chose to pursue its objective, in light of their impact on an individual in a particular controversy, fit with the State's justification for choosing them. Even where the State pursued a legitimate legislative objective, and even where the means chosen were reasonably related to it, the State had to account for the collateral impact on an individual's basic liberty with a justification compelling enough to render the *interference* reasonable. This was precisely the problem in *Poe* with Connecticut's anti-contraception statute. In pursuit of a contraception-free society, the State chose to intrude into the privacy of the marital relationship—to *criminalize* a decision made within it—without proffering a reason for choosing such liberty-impacting means to further its end.

Once a litigant challenging state action showed that it impacted a liberty basic to a free society—one that free governments were established to protect—due process demanded of the State a reasonable justification for the impact.[1] Examples of appropriate judicial displacements of legislative judgments included *Meyer*, where although the means might achieve the objective, they also infringed a basic liberty when other effective means would not,[2] and Justice White's analysis in *Griswold*, where the means chosen impacted a basic liberty without even achieving the State's purported objective.[3] The post-*Griswold* fundamental-rights doctrine captured these examples with the requirement that a State must choose narrowly tailored means in pursuit of a compelling objective if impacting a fundamental right.[4]

The Court borrowed the "narrowly-tailored test" from its equal-protection jurisprudence.[5] This was a natural place to look, as the due-process guarantee was understood to include a guarantee of equal treatment—the processes afforded to those with whose liberty a free government interfered had to be impartial.[6] But as applied in the due-process context, the narrowly tailored test was a meager apparition of the traditional analysis developed over the preceding centuries. Using this stilted shorthand had dire consequences for the jurisprudence and for the Court, as it became hyper-focused on the status of the liberty interests for which litigants claimed protection. Passing the narrowly tailored test was required *if* the challenged state action *impacted a fundamental right*. The question was no longer an initial one—whether a basic liberty had been impacted—with an affirmative answer triggering a particularized scrutiny of the justification for the impact. The first step in the common-law analysis soon morphed into the fundamental-rights doctrine's dispositive question: Was the liberty interest asserted a "fundamental right" the Due Process Clause shielded from state action?

Deciding personal-liberty cases became once again an absolutist enterprise. *Griswold*'s spatial metaphor—the "zone of substantive liberties"—reified into a "category of rights" with the practical effect that the States' governments could not interfere with them. Either an asserted liberty was "in" the category and the state action impinging it was prohibited, or the interest was not in the category and the State could regulate it. During the mid-twentieth century, this burgeoning fundamental-rights category overshadowed the ordered-liberty concept, even as aspiring ideologues once again nominally invoked it to advance their causes. Two methods for deciding which "rights" were worthy of inclusion developed during the twenty-five years after *Griswold*. Both imitated *Griswold*'s emphasizing the asserted liberty and its failing to identify and scrutinize the State's countervailing interests in order.

One of the two approaches concluded that some liberties were fundamental rights and deserved special protection against the States. Eight years after *Griswold*, when the Court in *Roe v. Wade*[7] reviewed a Texas law criminalizing procuring or providing a medically induced abortion, it concluded that "the right of personal privacy includes the abortion decision."[8] Justice Harry Blackmun, writing for the majority, identified the "right of privacy" as "founded in the Fourteenth Amendment's concept of personal liberty and restrictions upon state action."[9] He mentioned *Griswold*'s penumbra metaphor as one of the various theories through which the Court had found a constitutional "guarantee of certain areas or zones of privacy."[10] Equating the ordered-liberty concept with the fundamental-rights category, he concluded, "These decisions make it clear that only personal rights that can be deemed 'fundamental' or 'implicit in the concept of ordered liberty,' are included in this guarantee of personal privacy."[11]

Like the *Griswold* opinion, missing from *Roe* was the common-law analysis of the State's justification that Harlan and White had demonstrated. The Court acknowledged that the "abortion decision . . . must be considered against important state interests in regulation[.]"[12] But instead of scrutinizing whether *this* State's interest must give way to *this* petitioner's liberty in *this* controversy, it announced the point at which *every* individual's privacy trumped *every* State's interest in protecting fetal life.[13] In stark contrast to Harlan's *Poe* example, which would have simply reversed the decisions of the lower courts, the Court in *Roe* presented a statute-like holding, summarizing its response to criminal abortion statutes "of the current Texas type[.]"[14] The Court explained how it would prospectively resolve the tension between individuals' and the States' interests when evaluating abortion legislation in cases yet to come before it.[15]

Now merged with incorporation, the doctrine of unenumerated rights could demand of all the States, in one decision, categorical respect for a "fundamental" substantive liberty, just as incorporation could with respect to federal criminal procedures enshrined in the Bill of Rights. The Court's inquiry was skewed toward the status (fundamental or not) of the personal right asserted, and neglected the careful testing of the concrete application of the law for fitness with the State's justification for it. Such a lopsided analysis arguably resurrected *Lochner*esque interference with state-policy choices, making the Court susceptible to accusations of "legislating from the bench." In *Roe*, after all, the Court plainly supplanted, with its own resolution, the balance the State of Texas had struck between contending interests in order and liberty.

The other approach to evaluating fundamental-rights claims appeared as a reaction to the consequences of this one, objecting to the nature of the rights the Court was recognizing as fundamental. During the twenty-five years after *Griswold*, individuals continued to challenge state laws targeting reproductive choices, and challenged laws regulating familial arrangements.[16] As Justice Harlan had foreseen in *Poe*, the issues of homosexuality and physician-assisted suicide would make their way to the Court.[17] The abortion issue symbolized the political debate over federal-judicial oversight of the States' interfering with personal liberties, and the questionable reasoning of the *Roe* decision became a focal point for conservative criticism. Echoing political conservatism's deriding the federal courts for their complicity in the erosion of "traditional values," the modern-conservative method for deciding personal-liberty cases would eliminate federal protection against the States for individuals who would otherwise live beyond the bounds of conservative social mores.

But even as it reacted against the post-*Griswold* emphasis on personal liberty, modern conservatism used it. As the jurisprudence transformed into a battleground for fights over whether an asserted right was in the fundamental-rights category, the modern-conservative method *always* answered "no." The States should be free from federal interference with legislation implementing conservative social policies in the States—their resolutions of contending interests in order and liberty should be left undisturbed. This echoed conservative criticism of the Court's using selective incorporation to impose upon the States the specific demands of procedural fairness the Bill of Rights required of the federal government. The federal courts were violating the States' right to govern themselves, supplanting the moral judgments of their majorities and dictating their criminal procedures.

The concept of ordered liberty substantiated a non-positivist legal ideal, effectuating a fundamental principle of justice deeply rooted in the traditions and conscience of the American people. Properly applying this limitation on what political majorities could legislatively do required a reasonable and sensitive judgment proceeding with cautious moderation. With *Griswold*'s union of the two modern doctrines, the Court abandoned this restrained approach, even as increasingly controversial cases came before it. Reacting in turn, modern conservatism espoused a revised version of the Nation's history and a corresponding majoritarian-positivist legal tradition. According to it, the legitimacy of not only legislation, but also of any limitation on the power to make it, derived only from a positive democratic sanction. A peculiar series of due-process cases, decided at the Supreme Court between 1968 and 1986, culminated with this ideology infiltrating federal due-process jurisprudence.

***

Despite Justice Black's efforts during the mid-twentieth century, during the almost thirty years between the *Lochner* Era's end and the *Griswold* decision, the Court never embraced the incorporation doctrine's explanation of the relationship between the Bill of Rights and the Fourteenth Amendment. As *Palko* taught, while the protections of some Bill of Rights provisions and those the guarantee afforded might overlap, the latter did not derive from the former. The ordered-liberty concept, as explained and applied in *Palko*, and subsequently in *Poe*, captured a critical insight the *Slaughterhouse* dissents and *Hurtado* had illuminated. The due-process guarantee obligated the federal judiciary to perform common-law arbitrariness review of legislation, when an individual challenged a discrete instance of its application as an unreasonable deprivation of liberty. Reasonable legislation, whether substantive or procedural, was due "the citizens of all free governments."[18]

The incorporation doctrine inverted this insight. The Fourteenth Amendment's due-process guarantee was a portal through which passed the federal courts' interpretations of (at least some) Bill of Rights provisions, now enforceable against the States. As Justice Harlan taught, *Griswold* had applied a version of the incorporation doctrine to an issue of substantive liberty, implicitly embracing the incorporation doctrine's inversion of the *Slaughterhouse/Hurtado* insight. A connection to the Bill of Rights ostensibly contained a judge's discretion, keeping it within the bounds of the Constitution. But as a consequence, the guarantee's protection did not derive from an independent principle with its own history and tradition. Contrary to Harlan's view, the Due Process Clause did not "stand[] on its own bottom."[19] With this restraint removed, the Court could reconfigure post-Reconstruction federalism, with respect to substantive claims, just as the incorporation doctrine allowed with respect to procedural ones. The incorporation doctrine, after all, irrefutably repudiated Justice Bradley's 1879 edict, echoed in *Hurtado* and reaffirmed in *Palko*, that "[e]ach state prescribes its own mode of judicial proceedings."[20] Likewise, the fundamental-rights doctrine would impose categorical restrictions on the States' substantive-legislative options. This was indeed a *Lochner*-Era redux. But it was not about labor relations and the freedom to contract. In the mid-to-late twentieth century, it was about personal and social morality.

Even as *Griswold*'s zone of substantive liberties became the category of fundamental rights, case-by-case the Court continued furthering the cause of national civil rights and requiring of every State some of the identical criminal procedures the Bill of Rights required of the federal government.[21] And because *Griswold* had associated the incorporation doctrine with an *unenumerated* right—a substantive liberty with no express textual recognition in the Constitution—it blurred the conceptual distinction between the Court's mechanistic incorporation of criminal procedures enshrined in the Bill of Rights and its emerging fundamental-rights doctrine. In *Poe*, Justice Harlan had gracefully eschewed both doctrines in favor of the common-law tradition. But *Griswold* then melded them together—fusing two implicitly distinct doctrines through which the jurisprudence had developed during the preceding twenty-five years. Three years after *Griswold*, in his opinion for the Court in *Duncan v. Louisiana*,[22] Justice White tried to separate these conjoined analyses and distill out of the jurisprudence two distinct inquiries—one for analyzing claims that criminal procedures violated due process and another for challenges to substantive legislation.

***

Duncan, a nineteen-year-old black man, was charged with simple battery, a misdemeanor under Louisiana law that carried a sentence of up to two years in prison.[23] Attempting to diffuse a tense confrontation between two of his cousins, who had recently transferred to a formerly all-white high school, and four white boys, Duncan either "touched" or "slapped" one of the white boys on his elbow.[24] Because the Louisiana Constitution provided for jury trials only where the crime charged carried a sentence of death or hard labor, the trial judge denied Duncan's request for a jury trial.[25] After a bench trial, the judge convicted and sentenced him.[26] The Supreme Court of Louisiana refused to hear Duncan's appeal, finding "no error of law in the [trial court's] ruling."[27] On appeal to the U.S. Supreme Court, Duncan argued that the Sixth Amendment's guarantee of trial by jury in criminal cases applied to his case through the Fourteenth Amendment, where the potential sentence corresponding to the crime charged was as much as two years.[28] The Court agreed, and further held that the Fourteenth Amendment guaranteed a right of trial by jury to all criminal defendants in every State for whom, were they tried in federal Court, the Sixth Amendment would afford a jury trial.[29]

Writing for the Court, Justice White confronted *Griswold*'s conjoining the unenumerated-rights and incorporation doctrines. He observed that the "test for determining whether a right" that federal criminal procedures safeguarded was "also protected against state action by the Fourteenth Amendment[,]" had been "phrased in a variety of ways in the opinions of [the] Court."[30] Referring to the Court's practice of selectively incorporating federal criminal procedures enshrined in Bill-of-Rights provisions, he observed that "recent cases applying provisions of the first eight Amendments to the States represent a new approach to the incorporation debate."[31] And he introduced a new analysis for evaluating due-process challenges to state criminal procedures. *Duncan* thus set the stage for the conceptual distinction between analyses for "procedural" and "substantive" due-process claims.

Palko and its progeny were obstacles here. *Palko* had expressly rejected incorporation and elaborated the *Slaughterhouse/Hurtado* ordered-liberty concept in evaluating a State's criminal *procedure* for fitness with the demands of due process. Duncan's plight here, just like Palko's, was a "procedural" one. But Justice White brushed *Palko* aside, observing that trial by jury was not the specific issue there, like here in *Duncan*.[32] He described Cardozo's *Palko* analysis as a counterfactual inquiry, requiring the Court to ask whether, hypothetically, a fair system of justice could exist without the right claimed.[33] Several "recent cases[,]" he observed, "proceeded on the valid assumption[,]" and contrary to *Palko*, "that state criminal processes [were] not imaginary and theoretical . . . but actual systems bearing virtually every characteristic of the common-law system that ha[d] been developing contemporaneously in England and in [America]."[34]

This dismissal of *Palko* notwithstanding, the question White suggested the Court should ask when evaluating procedural fairness included a nominal reference to the ordered-liberty concept. According to White, the "sort of inquiry that c[ould] justify" the Court's recent cases was whether given "this kind of system"—an "Anglo-American regime of ordered liberty"—the procedure was necessary.[35] And to determine whether, in a case like Duncan's, a jury trial was necessary to an Anglo-American regime of ordered liberty, the Court should ask whether most Anglo-American Courts, despite Louisiana's, already required one.

> [I]t might well be said that the limitation in question is not necessarily fundamental to fairness in every criminal system that might be imagined but is fundamental in the context of the criminal processes maintained by the American States. When the inquiry is approached in this way the question [of] whether the States can impose criminal punishment without granting a jury trial appears quite different from the way it appeared in the older cases opining that States might abolish jury trial. A criminal process which was fair and equitable but used no juries is easy to imagine. It would make use of alternative guarantees and protections which would serve the purposes that the jury serves in the English and American systems. Yet no American State has undertaken to construct such a system.[36]

Not *every* requirement of procedural fairness the Bill of Rights enforced against the federal government applied to the States. But those necessary to an Anglo-American criminal justice system did. To discover whether a jury trial for Duncan was necessary, White examined the procedural practices of Anglo-American criminal justice systems. A detailed ten-page exegesis of "past and contemporary standards"[37] justified the Court's holding, revealing the importance and general acceptance of trial by jury in the English and American legal traditions.[38] Consistent with the Court's new approach, White broadened the holding beyond the particular controversy before the Court, concluding that the Fourteenth Amendment incorporated against every State the requirement of trial by jury in every case where the Sixth Amendment would require it of the federal government.[39]

Justice Harlan dissented. He again argued that incorporation was contrary to the Court's precedent, insisting that while "[t]he Bill of Rights [was] not necessarily irrelevant to the [Court's] search for guidance in interpreting the Fourteenth Amendment, . . . the reason for and the nature of its relevance must be articulated."[40] He explained again the common-law due-process guarantee,[41] and reminded the Court of federalism—the Fourteenth Amendment did not preclude "state experimentation and disparity."[42] The Court should not evaluate state procedures in terms of what the Bill of Rights required of the federal government.[43] The incorporation doctrine was an unprincipled pragmatism that allowed "[t]he Court [to] justif[y] neither its starting place nor its conclusion."[44]

> Today's Court still remains unwilling to accept the total incorporationists' view of the history of the Fourteenth Amendment. This, if accepted, would afford a cogent reason for applying the Sixth Amendment to the States. The Court is also, apparently, unwilling to face the task of determining whether denial of trial by jury in the situation before us, or in other situations, is fundamentally unfair. Consequently, the Court has compromised on the ease of the incorporation position, without its internal logic. It has simply assumed that the question before us is whether the Jury Trial Clause of the Sixth Amendment should be incorporated into the Fourteenth, jot-for-jot and case-for-case, or ignored. Then the Court merely declares that the clause is "in" rather than "out."[45]

Harlan saw danger here, in this method for discovering which procedural requirements were necessary. This could be what *Hurtado* had warned against—restricting the meaning of due process to "rules fixed in the past . . . deny[ing] every quality of the law but its age . . . render[ing] it incapable of progress or improvement."[46] Offered just three years before the great sage's passing, this was not just another warning.

It was Justice Harlan's parting prophesy.

NOTES

1. *See Lochner*, 198 U.S. at 68 (Harlan I, J., dissenting); *Carolene Products*, 304 U.S. at 152 footnote 4; *Poe*, 367 U.S. at 543 (Harlan II, J., dissenting).

2. *See* discussion of *Meyer v. Nebraska*, chapter 2, *supra.*

3. *See* discussion of *Griswold v. Connecticut*, chapter 5, *supra.*

4. *See, e.g., Roe v. Wade*, 410 U.S. 113, 115 (1973) ("Where certain 'fundamental rights' are involved, the Court has held that regulation limiting these rights may be justified only by a 'compelling state interest,' *Kramer v. Union Free School District,* 395 U.S. 621, 627 (1969); *Shapiro v. Thompson,* 394 U.S. 618, 634 (1969), *Sherbert v. Verner,* 374 U.S. 398, 406 (1963), and that legislative enactments must be narrowly drawn to express only the legitimate state interests at stake. *Griswold v. Connecticut,* 381 U.S. at 485; *Aptheker v. Secretary of State,* 378 U.S. 500, 508 (1964); *Cantwell*

v. Connecticut, 310 U.S. 296, 307–308 (1940); *see Eisenstadt v. Baird,* 405 U.S. at 463–464 (White, J., concurring).").

5. *See Bearden v. Georgia*, 461 U.S. 660, 665–667 (1983) (noting the relationship between due-process and equal-protection analyses) (citing *Griffin v. Illinois*, 351 U.S. 12 (1956) (Harlan, J., dissenting); *Williams v. Illinois*, 399 U.S. 235 (1970) (Harlan, J., concurring)); *see also Reno v. Flores*, 507 U.S. 292, 301–302 (1993) (analyzing a due-process claim and citing to *Collins v. Harker Heights*, 503 U.S. 115, 125 (1992), an equal-protection case, for the "narrowly-tailored-to-serve-a-compelling-state-interest" test).

6. For an interesting explanation of how the sections of the Fourteenth Amendment developed, *see* Balkin, *Living Originalism*, 184–190. Discussing the differences between the February and April 1866 drafts of the Amendment, Balkin notes that "[t]he second half of the February draft[,] . . . [m]odeled on the Fifth Amendment's due process clause . . . gave Congress the power to guarantee 'to all persons in the several States equal protection in the rights to life, liberty, and property.' The reference to 'equal protection' was a gloss on the Fifth Amendment's due process clause . . . the Reconstruction Congress believed that the idea of due process of law included a guarantee of impartiality[.] . . . The new [April] language of section 1 divided this part of the February draft into two clauses, one tracking . . . the Fifth Amendment's due process clause . . . and one specifically guaranteeing equal protection." *Id.* at 189.

7. 410 U.S. 113 (1973).

8. *Id.* at 154.

9. *Id.*

10. *Id.*

11. *Id.* (citing *Palko*, 302 U.S. at 325).

12. *Id.*

13. *Id.* at 163–164.

14. *Id.* at 164.

15. *Id.* at 164–166.

16. *See, e.g., Moore v. City of East Cleveland*, 431 U.S. 494 (1977), discussed in chapter 7, *infra.*

17. *See*, respectively, *Bowers v. Hardwick*, 478 U.S. 186 (1986), discussed in chapter 8, *infra*; and *Washington v. Glucksberg*, 521 U.S. 702 (1997), discussed in chapters 11 and 12, *infra.*

18. *Corfield*, 6 F. Cas. at 551.

19. *Griswold*, 381 U.S. at 500 (Harlan, J., concurring).

20. *Hurtado*, 110 U.S. at 535 (quoting *Missouri v. Lewis*, 101 U.S. 22 (1879)).

21. *See, e.g., In re Oliver*, 333 U.S. 257 (1948) (incorporating the right to a public trial); *Mapp v. Ohio*, 367 U.S. 643 (1961) (incorporating the right against unreasonable searches and seizures and applying the federal court's "exclusionary rule" to the States); *Gideon v. Wainwright*, 372 U.S. 335 (1963) (incorporating the right to counsel); *Malloy v. Hogan*, 378 U.S. 1 (1964) (incorporating the right against self-incrimination); *Pointer v. Texas*, 380 U.S. 400 (1965) (incorporating the right to confront adverse witnesses); *Klopfer v. North Carolina*, 386 U.S. 213 (1967) (incorporating

the right to a speedy trial); *Washington v. Texas*, 388 U.S. 14 (1967) (incorporating the right to use compulsory process to obtain witness testimony).

22. 391 U.S. 145 (1968).
23. *Id.* at 146–147.
24. *Id.*
25. *Id.* at 146.
26. *Id.*
27. *Id.*
28. *Id.* at 147.
29. *Id.* at 149.
30. *Id.* at 148.
31. *Id.* at 149 footnote 14 (internal quotation marks omitted).
32. *Id.* at 154–155; *see also id.* at 154 ("We are aware of prior cases in this Court in which the prevailing opinion contains statements contrary to our holding today. . . . Louisiana relies especially on *Maxwell v. Dow*, 176 U.S. 581 (1900); *Palko v. Connecticut*, 302 U.S. 319 (1937); and *Snyder v. Massachusetts*, 291 U.S. 97 (1934).").
33. *Id.* at 149 footnote 14 (citing *Palko*, 302 U.S. at 325).
34. *Id.* (citing *Mapp v. Ohio*, 367 U.S. 643 (1961); *Griffin v. California*, 380 U.S. 609 (1965); *Robinson v. California*, 370 U.S. 660 (1962)).
35. *Id.*
36. *Id.* (citing *Maxwell v. Dow*, 176 U.S. 581 (1900)).
37. *Id.* at 162.
38. *Id.* at 151–162.
39. *Id.* at 149.
40. 391 U.S. at 176 (Harlan, J., dissenting).
41. Id. at 176–178.
42. *Id.* at 176.
43. *Id.* at 176–178.
44. *Id.* at 181.
45. *Id.* at 180–181.
46. *Id.* at 176–177 (quoting *Hurtado*, 110 U.S. at 529).

Chapter 7

Deeply Rooted in History and Tradition

Before *Duncan*, the ordered-liberty concept had survived a century of post-*Slaughterhouse* tribulation. The Fourteenth Amendment secured liberties basic to a free society—those belonging of right to persons living under free governments. The *Slaughterhouse* dissenters recognized, in the common-law tradition of arbitrariness review, how to analyze the claim to substantive liberty the Butchers' Benevolent Association raised. *Hurtado* likewise applied the common-law analysis to evaluate the fairness of California's criminal procedure. The concept survived for a century thereafter in opinions evaluating substantive and procedural legislation—in majority opinions (*Meyer*, *Pierce*, *West Coast Hotel*, *Palko*, and *Adamson*), concurrences (White and Harlan in *Griswold*), and dissents (Holmes and Harlan in *Lochner* and Harlan II in *Poe*). It survived the Court's forty-year flirtation with overseeing the States' economic policies and implementing an absolutist conception of liberty to contract. And it survived even the Court's gradual submission, over a thirty-year period, to the pragmatism of selective incorporation.

But *Duncan*'s procedural-substantive distinction, although aimed at the incoherence spreading across the post-*Griswold* jurisprudence, missed its intended target. As a consequence, the concept faced its most dangerous ordeal yet. The Court would never know if *Duncan*'s two-analysis solution might have been viable, because the problem prompting White's solution was also its undoing. In the fog of *Griswold*'s quasi-incorporation, distinguishing a procedural analysis from a substantive one would prove more difficult than White perhaps intended. In 1977, when the Court decided *Moore v. City of East Cleveland*,[1] it analyzed the infringement of an important substantive liberty, against the background of *Griswold*'s recourse to the Bill of Rights, using the new *Duncan* inquiry. This implied the Court should answer both procedural *and* substantive questions using the approach that Justice White had described in *Duncan.* And it created a unique opportunity for modern conservatism to infuse the words "history and tradition" with a new and radically altered meaning when analyzing substantive-due-process claims.

***

Inez Moore lived in East Cleveland with her son and two of her grandsons, only one of whom was her son's offspring.[2] A local zoning ordinance limited occupancy of residential dwellings to members of a single family. It "contain[ed] an unusual and complicated definitional section that recogniz[ed] as a 'family' only a few categories of related individuals[.]"[3] Because the boys living in Moore's home were first cousins instead of brothers, the City did not recognize the occupants as a family. It directed Moore to remove an offending boy.[4] She did not, and the City filed criminal charges against her.[5] She was convicted, the Ohio Court of Appeals affirmed, and the Ohio Supreme Court denied review.[6]

At the U.S. Supreme Court, the City argued that *Belle Terre v. Boraas*,[7] decided three years earlier, should control the Court's decision.[8] In *Belle Terre*, the Court rejected a challenge to a similar zoning ordinance in New York City.[9] The case was distinguishable, however, because while New York had likewise restricted occupancy to members of a single family, its definition of "family" included "unrelated persons, living and cooking together as a single housekeeping unit[.]"[10] Writing for a plurality in *Moore,* Justice Lewis Powell said the Court in *Belle Terre* had been "careful to note that [the ordinance] promoted . . . family values."[11] Unlike New York City, "East Cleveland . . . ha[d] chosen to regulate the occupancy of its housing by slicing deeply into the family itself."[12] Identifying *Meyer* and *Pierce* as their origin, Powell cited "a host of cases[,]" including *Roe*, Justices Goldberg's and White's *Griswold* concurrences, and Justice Harlan's *Poe* dissent, as "acknowledg[ing] a private realm of family life which the state cannot enter."[13] This statement epitomized the Court's post-*Griswold* approach to fundamental rights, recognizing only one aspect of the ordered-liberty concept. It obviously opposed Justice White's formulation of the concept in his *Griswold* concurrence, which acknowledged both: "[T]here is a realm of family life which the state cannot enter *without substantial justification*."[14]

Powell wrote, "[F]reedom of personal choice in matters of marriage and family life is one of the liberties protected by the Due Process Clause of the Fourteenth Amendment."[15] This conclusion might have followed from the first step in the common-law method. And the opinion appeared for a moment poised to consider the City's justification for infringing this liberty. "The family," Powell said, "is not beyond regulation."[16] Even so, "when the government intrudes on choices concerning family living arrangements, this

Court must examine carefully the importance of the governmental interests advanced and the extent to which they are served by the challenged regulation."[17] Powell predicted the ordinance could not survive such scrutiny, because in light of the City's justification for it—preventing overcrowding, minimizing traffic and parking congestion, and avoiding an undue financial burden on the school system—it "serve[d] them marginally, at best."[18] The ordinance, Justice Powell wrote, "has but a tenuous relation to alleviation of the conditions mentioned by the city."[19]

Despite this espousal of the common-law analysis, it was not the reason for *Moore*'s holding. The opinion's focus shifted to the City's argument that *Meyer*, *Pierce*, and their progeny were inapplicable because "none of them g[ave] grandmothers any fundamental rights with respect to grandsons."[20] This argument pointed in the direction *Griswold* was taking the Court—a departure from the tradition of reasoned judgment that Powell's own opinion embraced and amplified. According to Powell, and contrary to the City's position, the "force and rationale of the[] precedents" the City invoked derived from "the basic reasons why certain rights associated with the family have been accorded shelter under the Fourteenth Amendment's Due Process Clause[.]"[21] "Understanding those reasons," he said, "requires careful attention to this Court's function under [it.]"[22] He found the description of this function in passages from Justice Harlan's *Poe* dissent elaborating the concept of ordered liberty.[23]

But instead of working through the concept as Harlan had demonstrated, Powell alluded to *Griswold*'s quasi-incorporation. "There are risks[,]" he wrote, "when the judicial branch gives enhanced protection to certain substantive liberties without the guidance of the more specific provisions of the Bill of Rights."[24] Partially quoting Harlan's *Griswold* concurrence, Powell said, "Appropriate limits on substantive due process come from careful respect for the teachings of history (and), solid recognition of the basic values that underlie our society."[25] Considering what he was about to do, Powell not surprisingly omitted Harlan's third principle—"wise appreciation of the great roles that the doctrines of federalism and separation of powers have played in establishing and preserving American freedoms."[26]

Powell compared his stunted version of Harlan's "limits on substantive due process" to White's "new approach" to selective incorporation in *Duncan*. "A similar restraint marks our approach[,]" he explained, "to the question[] . . . whether or to what extent a guarantee in the Bill of Rights should be incorporated in the Due Process Clause because it is necessary to an Anglo-American regime of ordered liberty."[27] The due-process guarantee, Powell concluded, protected Moore against the ordinance. But *not* because, in pursuing its objective, the City employed means with an arbitrary collateral impact on her liberty. Instead, it protected Moore for the same reason that Duncan deserved a jury trial. The elevated status of the family in American social history, like that of the jury trial in American legal history, meant the Constitution protected it. "Our decisions establish," Powell explained, "that the Constitution protects the sanctity of the family precisely because the institution of the family is deeply rooted in this Nation's history and tradition."[28]

Here was the ground of opportunity in which modern conservatism would sow the seed of its political ideology, and attempt to raise a due-process guarantee protecting only those liberties already "deeply rooted in the Nation's history and tradition." Powell said that traditional respect for the family was not limited to the nuclear bonds uniting its members.[29] Like White had justified incorporating the federal jury-trial requirement with its importance and ubiquity in the American legal tradition, Powell emphasized "the accumulated wisdom . . . that support[ed] a larger conception of the family."[30] "Decisions concerning child rearing," implicated in prior due-process cases, "long ha[d] been shared with grandparents or other relatives who occup[ied] the same household[.]"[31] The fundamental right to "freedom of personal choice in matters of marriage and family life"[32] was not limited to members of a nuclear family. The liberty of the extended family was also in the fundamental-rights category.

The *Moore* opinion changed the jurisprudence in two inestimably profound respects. First, it equated whether a federal-procedural requirement was necessary to an Anglo-American criminal justice system with whether the Due Process Clause protected an unenumerated substantive liberty. But the effect here was far more significant than this simple equation, because *Moore* inverted and then collapsed White's bifurcation of the *Slauterhouse/Hurtado* insight. White had divided the insight into two conceptual analyses, one procedural and the other substantive. *Moore* recognized *one* of these two—the Court's "new approach to the incorporation debate"—for *both* procedural and substantive claims. Second, the opinion bolstered the post-*Griswold* fundamental-rights approach, omitting the second step in the common-law analysis. The Due Process Clause protected the liberty to live with one's family *because* the institution of family was deeply rooted in the Nation's history and tradition. This did not trigger strict scrutiny of the City's justification for infringing it. Instead, the Court found yet another right within the fundamental-rights category.

Justice White dissented. As in his *Griswold* concurrence, he pointed to Harlan's *Poe* example.[33] Now the lone voice on the Court advocating for Harlan's position—the sage had passed six years earlier, just after retiring from the bench—White briefly summarized the history of the Court's struggle with applying the liberty provision of the Due Process Clause. He insisted that Justice Harlan's view was "surely the preferred approach."[34] "[T]he statement of Mr. Justice Harlan in *Poe v. Ullman*," he argued, "most accurately reflects the thrust of prior decisions."[35]

> The term "liberty" is not, therefore, to be given a crabbed construction. I have no more difficulty than Mr. Justice Powell apparently does in concluding that appellant in this case properly asserts a liberty interest within the meaning of the Due Process Clause. The question is not one of liberty *vel non*. Rather, there being no procedural issue at stake, the issue is whether the precise interest involved . . . is entitled to such substantive protection under the Due Process Clause that this ordinance must be held invalid.[36]

Powell used the wrong analysis. There was no criminal-procedural question here like *Duncan*. White agreed that Inez Moore asserted a liberty interest implicating the due-process guarantee. The question was whether this liberty trumped the City's pursuit of its interest here, and the answer required the common-law judge's "particularly careful scrutiny of the [City's] needs asserted to justify the abridgment."[37] Powell made the same mistake as Justice Douglas in *Griswold*.[38] The importance of the liberty interest did not obviate the need to scrutinize the justification for impinging it—it was the very thing that required it.

But despite its nominal defense of Harlan's example, White's dissent illustrated his own capitulation to the fundamental-rights doctrine. First, unlike his *Griswold* concurrence, after pointing out Powell's mistake he did not perform the arbitrariness review the common-law tradition required. Instead, he asked whether the right that Moore asserted was "fundamental," concluded it was not, and ended the analysis there.[39] Second, his dissent further illuminated how the level of generality at which an asserted right was described might influence whether it was considered fundamental. White described Moore's interest as "the interest in having more than one set of grandchildren live in her home[.]"[40] He concluded that recognizing this interest as a personal right implicit in the concept of ordered liberty would "extend the limited substantive contours of the Due Process Clause beyond recognition."[41] Under the spell of *Griswold*'s spatial metaphor, White succumbed to the categorical simplicity of the fundamental-rights doctrine.

Answering White's criticism, Powell defended the *Duncan* method as a source of judicial restraint.

> Although he agrees that the Due Process Clause has substantive content, Mr. Justice White in dissent expresses fear that our recourse to history and tradition will "broaden enormously the horizons of the Clause." To the contrary, an approach grounded in history imposes limits on the judiciary that are more meaningful than any based on the abstract formula taken from *Palko v. Connecticut*, and apparently suggested as an alternative [in *Duncan*].[42]

White's dismissal of *Palko* had come back to haunt him. Despite the fact that *Duncan*, just like *Palko*, had involved a state-criminal procedure, White distinguished *Palko* as irrelevant because jury trial was not the specific issue. Powell thus accurately described, in *Moore,* White's *Duncan* opinion as "rejecting the *Palko* formula as the basis for deciding what procedural protections are required of a state, in favor of a historical approach based on the Anglo-American legal tradition."[43] Now, up against his own rejection of "the *Palko* formula," White hopelessly attempted to distinguish *Moore* from *Palko* while still invoking *Poe*.

Unlike *Moore*, White argued, "*Palko* was a criminal case, and the issue was thus not whether a protected liberty interest was at stake but what protective process was 'due' that interest."[44] *Moore* was, of course, a criminal case, too—Inez Moore had been criminally convicted. Justice White was emphasizing that *Palko* presented an issue of criminal *procedure*, and, therefore, unlike *Moore*, was not a case in which the Court's task was to decide whether a *substantive* liberty qualified as a fundamental right. Merely repeating this distinction did not explain how the Court was supposed to simultaneously disregard *Palko* and embrace *Poe*, in which Justice Harlan had undeniably elaborated *Palko*'s ordered-liberty concept. Justice White's tortured efforts to deal with *Palko* in both *Duncan* and *Moore* showed just how problematic was the artificial procedural-substantive distinction he had introduced.

Unpersuaded that the distinction should be maintained, Powell insisted that his analysis, like White's in *Duncan*, found meaningful judicial restraint in "the Nation's history and tradition."[45] Demonstrating a profound misunderstanding of Justice Harlan's example, Powell cited *Poe* for the conclusion that the institution of family was deeply rooted in history and tradition, and therefore the Due Process Clause protected it.

> Indeed, the passage [from Justice Harlan's *Poe* dissent] cited in Mr. Justice White's dissent as "most accurately [reflecting] the thrust of prior decisions" on substantive due process, expressly points to history and tradition as the source for "supplying . . . content to this Constitutional concept."[46]

Powell's "history and tradition" was not the common law's. It was not the history of a political tradition and its legal principles applied in discrete cases and controversies. This was not scrutiny of the balance struck between liberty and the demands of organized society, in a nation built upon postulates of respect for the individual.[47] As Justice Harlan demonstrated, basic values underlying American society were revealed in decisional law resolving the tension, in actual controversies, between contending majoritarian and counter-majoritarian concerns. For the common-law's evaluation of both aspects of the concept of ordered liberty, Powell substituted a statement of the family's status in American social history. "It is through the family[,]" he wrote, "that we inculcate and pass down many of our most cherished values, moral and cultural."[48]

***

Thus *Duncan* enabled *Moore*'s misinterpretation of Harlan's *Poe* dissent and *Griswold* concurrence. The words "history and tradition," in which Justice Harlan had so carefully enfolded the concept, were stripped of centuries of meaning. Their referent was the concept's lifeblood—the time-honored reasoned judgment of the common law. Here in *Moore*, "history and tradition" meant constitutional validation for a revered social institution.

NOTES

1. 431 U.S. 494 (1977).
2. *Id.* at 496–497.
3. *Id.* at 496.
4. *Id.* at 497.
5. *Id.*
6. *Id.* at 497–498.
7. 416 U.S. 1 (1974).
8. *Moore*, 431 U.S. at 498.
9. 416 U.S. at 7–8.
10. *Id.* at 2.
11. *Moore*, 431 U.S. at 498 (*quoting* 416 U.S. at 9) (internal quotation marks omitted).
12. *Id.*
13. *Id.* at 499.
14. *Griswold*, 381 U.S. at 502 (White., J., concurring) (*quoting Prince v. Massachusetts*, 321 U.S. 158, 166 (1944)) (internal quotation marks omitted; emphasis added).
15. *Moore*, 431 U.S. at 499 (*quoting Cleveland Board of Education v. Lafleur*, 414 U.S. 632 (1974)).
16. *Id.*
17. *Id.*
18. *Id.* at 499–500.
19. *Id.* at 500.
20. *Id.*
21. *Id.* at 501.
22. *Id.*
23. *Id.* at 501–503.
24. *Id.* at 502.

25. *Id.* at 503 (quoting *Griswold v. Connecticut*, 381 U.S. at 501 (Harlan, J., concurring)) (internal quotation marks omitted).
26. 381 U.S. at 501 (Harlan, J., concurring).
27. 341 U.S. at 503 footnote 10 (quoting *Duncan*, 391 U.S. at 149 footnote 14) (internal quotation marks omitted).
28. *Id.* at 503.
29. *Id.* at 504.
30. *Id.* at 505; *see also id.* at 504–505.
31. *Id.* at 505.
32. *Id.* at 499 (quoting *Cleveland v. Board of Education v. LaFleur*, 414 U.S. 632, 639–640 (1974)).
33. *Id.* at 542 (White, J., dissenting).
34. *Id.* at 542–544.
35. *Id.* at 545.
36. *Id.* at 547.
37. *Poe*, 367 U.S. at 543 (Harlan, J., dissenting).
38. *See* discussion of *Griswold v. Connecticut*, chapter 5, *supra.*
39. *See Moore*, 431 U.S. at 550–551 (White, J., dissenting).
40. 431 U.S. at 547 (White, J., dissenting).
41. *Id.* at 549 (quoting *Moore*, 431 U.S. 494, 537 (Stewart, J., dissenting)).
42. *Id.* at 504 footnote 12 (citing *id.* at 549–550 (White, J., dissenting)) (internal citations omitted).
43. *Id.* at 503 footnote 10.
44. *Id.* at 546 (White, J., dissenting).
45. *Id.* at 504 footnote 12.
46. *Id.* (citing *id.* at 545 (White, J., dissenting) (citing *Poe*, 367 U.S. at 542 (Harlan, J., dissenting))).
47. *See* discussion of *Poe v. Ullman*, chapter 4, *supra.*
48. 431 U.S. at 503–504.

Chapter 8

A Different Description of Fundamental Liberties

Georgia police arrested Michael Hardwick in 1982, in the bedroom of his home, for violating a criminal statute that made illegal all oral and anal sex in the State of Georgia.[1] The statute provided a penalty of up to twenty years in prison for any "person" convicted of "perform[ing] or submit[ting] to any sexual act involving the sex organs of one person and the mouth or anus of another."[2] The statute made no distinction between married and unmarried persons, or between heterosexual and homosexual conduct. It imposed a state-wide ban on specific sexual acts, and provided criminal penalties for anyone found engaging in them. After the district attorney decided not to present the case to a grand jury unless "further evidence" of the crime "developed," Hardwick brought suit in federal court, claiming that the statute under which he was arrested violated the Constitution.[3] The district court granted Georgia's motion to dismiss, but the Court of Appeals for the Eleventh Circuit reversed and remanded the case for trial.[4] Georgia appealed from the Eleventh Circuit's judgment to the U.S. Supreme Court.[5]

Notwithstanding Justice White's fidelity to the concept in *Griswold*, and his concern for its survival in *Moore*, he would betray it in *Bowers v. Hardwick*. White's opinion for the Court belied the extent to which the fundamental-rights doctrine, which had infiltrated his *Moore* dissent, was changing due-process jurisprudence. In *Bowers*, White disavowed completely *Palko*'s ordered-liberty analysis. He capitalized on the problem of how the level of generality at which a liberty interest was described could determine whether the Court considered it a fundamental right. And amplifying the asymmetry of post-*Griswold* personal-liberty jurisprudence, there was no consideration of any justification for the means the State chose to effectuate its objective.

The Eleventh Circuit had identified Hardwick's liberty interest at a level of generality reminiscent of *Griswold*'s right of privacy. His sexual activity was a "private and intimate association . . . beyond the reach of state regulation by reason of the Ninth Amendment and the Due Process Clause of the Fourteenth Amendment."[6] Justice White framed the issue differently, stating Hardwick's interest narrowly and within the framework of the fundamental-rights doctrine. "The issue presented," he wrote, "is whether the Federal Constitution confers a fundamental right upon homosexuals to engage in sodomy and hence invalidates the laws of the many States that still make such conduct illegal and have done so for a very long time."[7] This restatement of the issue showed just how far from the tradition of reasoned judgment the doctrine had taken the Court. This case was not about the particular controversy before it. Like *Roe*, and like procedural cases decided under the incorporation doctrine, the Court's decision here would categorically apply to every State in every prospective case. But oddly, this acknowledgment of the holding's breadth was juxtaposed against White's narrowing its substantive scope. Borrowing the as-applied limitation of arbitrariness review—not for the common law's purpose of honing the analysis using the details of the controversy—White explained that even though the statute was not directed at *homosexual* sodomy, Hardwick was a "practicing homosexual" and the Court would evaluate the statute in this regard only.[8]

According to White, the initial inquiry was whether the right asserted, as now characterized, was enough like other fundamental rights the Court had recognized to warrant inclusion in the category. The line of due-process precedent, from *Meyer* and *Pierce* to *Roe*, identified rights "connect[ed] [to] family, marriage, or procreation."[9] Because homosexual sodomy had nothing to do with family, marriage, or procreation, he distinguished the cases upon which the Eleventh Circuit had relied.[10] He concluded, "[W]e think it evident that none of the rights announced in those cases bears any resemblance to the claimed constitutional right of homosexuals to engage in acts of sodomy that is asserted in this case."[11] Having concluded the Court could not recognize a fundamental right to homosexual sodomy on the basis of such easily distinguishable precedent, White turned to a discussion of unenumerated rights.

"[D]espite the language of the Due Process Clauses of the Fifth and Fourteenth Amendments, which appear[ed] to focus only on the processes by which life, liberty, or property is taken," White noted that the clauses "ha[d] substantive content, subsuming rights that to a great extent are immune from federal or state regulation or proscription"[12] The Court had recognized such rights "that have little or no textual support in the constitutional language."[13] As his *Moore* dissent had foreshadowed, White was now committed to the doctrine and language of fundamental rights. The question for the Court was how to decide which rights were in the category: "Striving to assure itself and the public that announcing rights not readily identifiable in the Constitution's text involves much more than the imposition of the Justices' own choice of values on the States and the Federal Government, the Court has sought to identify the nature of the rights qualifying for heightened protection."[14]

White then adopted, in a brief paragraph and without explanation, Justice Powell's "history and tradition" analysis from *Moore*, against which he had argued in dissent. He abandoned not only his *Moore* position, but also *Palko*'s ordered-liberty concept, replacing it with Powell's criterion for determining whether an asserted liberty interest was in the fundamental-rights category.

> In *Palko* it was said that this category includes those fundamental liberties that are "implicit in the concept of ordered liberty" such that "neither liberty nor justice would exist if [they] were sacrificed." A different description of fundamental liberties appeared in *Moore*, where they are characterized as those liberties that are "deeply rooted in this Nation's history and tradition."[15]

Having repudiated the common law, White turned to the task of determining whether the right to engage in homosexual sodomy was fundamental because it was deeply rooted in America's history and tradition. Ignoring *Hurtado*'s warning, he pronounced, "Proscriptions against that conduct have ancient roots."[16] He pointed out, in two lengthy footnotes, that many of the States had enacted laws criminalizing homosexual conduct, both at the time of the founding and when the Fourteenth Amendment was ratified.[17] "Against this background," he concluded, "to claim that a right to engage in such conduct is 'deeply rooted in this Nation's history and tradition' or 'implicit in the concept of ordered liberty' is, at best, facetious."[18] This was self-evident, for there were many old statutes that criminalized exercising the "right to engage in homosexual sodomy." It was not deeply rooted in the Nation's history and tradition, and, therefore, not a fundamental right the Due Process Clause protected.

Hardwick argued also that the principle evident in *Stanley v. Georgia*[19] applied here. In *Stanley*, the Court invalidated a Georgia law making it a crime to possess and read obscene material in the privacy of one's home.[20] Like *Bowers*, the case had nothing to do with family, marriage, or procreation, and yet the Court had held that Georgia could not criminalize its citizens' choice to read and watch literature or films that the State deemed obscene. While Hardwick emphasized the residential-privacy implications of the case, White connected it to the incorporation aspect of the post-*Griswold* fundamental-rights doctrine. He distinguished *Stanley* as "firmly grounded in the First Amendment."[21] Because the right Hardwick asserted had "no similar support in the text of the Constitution," it did "not qualify for recognition under the prevailing principles for construing the Fourteenth Amendment."[22] He offered no explanation for why, if other provisions of the Constitution limited the due-process guarantee, the Court should look to the history of criminal statutes in the States to discover the scope of its protection.

Finally, White dismissed Hardwick's argument that even if the "conduct at issue [was] not a fundamental right . . . there must still be a rational basis for the law[,]" and here there was none other than the belief of a political majority "that homosexual sodomy [was] immoral and unacceptable."[23] Noting that laws often represented moral choices, he rejected the claim that "majority sentiments about the morality of homosexuality" was an inadequate justification for the law.[24]

In a dissenting opinion, Justice Blackmun, joined by Justices Brennan, Thurgood Marshall, and John Paul Stevens, accused the majority of improperly reframing the issue presented in its rush to reverse the Eleventh Circuit. The case was "no more about a fundamental right to engage in homosexual sodomy," the dissent argued, "than *Stanley v. Georgia* was about a fundamental right to watch obscene movies[.]"[25] Quoting Justice Brandeis's *Olmstead* dissent, Blackmun insisted the case was "about the most comprehensive of rights and the right most valued by civilized men, namely, the right to be let alone."[26] The dissent aptly criticized the level of specificity at which the majority framed the issue, thus situating it for exclusion from the "category of rights deemed to be fundamental."[27] But it also illustrated the problem that would continue to plague the fundamental-rights doctrine into the late-twentieth century, offering no explanation for why "the right to be let alone," obviously stated at a far greater level of generality, was an acceptable alternative.

Blackmun argued the Court's duty was to "analyze Hardwick's claim in the light of the values that underlie the constitutional right to privacy."[28] Like Justice White, Blackmun saw a category of fundamental rights, but his derived from a broader guarantee of personal privacy.[29] Like the "right to be let alone," no demonstration of how to understand its breadth accompanied this "right to privacy." Blackmun seemed to recognize, however, consistent with Harlan's *Poe* analysis, that because the State chose the full force of the criminal law to interfere with a basic liberty, it must have a compelling justification for choosing such onerous means. And Blackmun found mere moral disapproval unpersuasive.

> If that right means anything, it means that, before Georgia can prosecute its citizens for making choices about the most intimate aspects of their lives, it must do more than assert that the choice they have made is an abominable crime not fit to be named among Christians.[30]

And, echoing *Hurtado*'s warning that White had ignored, Blackmun quoted Justice Holmes.

> [I]t is revolting to have no better reason for a rule of law than that so it was laid down in the time of Henry IV. It is still more revolting if the grounds upon which it was laid down have vanished long since, and the rule simply persists from blind imitation of the past.[31]

In a dissenting opinion of his own, Justice Stevens seconded the argument that mere moral disapproval could not justify such intrusive means chosen to express it. "Our prior decisions make . . . abundantly clear[,]" Stevens wrote, "the fact that the governing majority in a State has traditionally viewed a particular practice as immoral is not a sufficient reason for upholding a law prohibiting [it.]"[32] The common-law analysis was perhaps implicit in the dissenters' suspicion of the moral opprobrium justifying such a severe intrusion into the privacy of the home and the details of the individual's intimate life within it. But with Harlan gone and White's about-face, there was no voice on the Court speaking for the tradition of reasoned judgment.

***

The *Bowers* opinion disregarded the common law's balancing of the State's interest in order against the individual's liberty, and changed the inquiry altogether to whether the Constitution conferred on a class of individuals a fundamental right to engage in a particular sexual practice. The dissents disagreed with such a narrow view of the right asserted, pointing to broader alternative formulations. In the wake of *Roe*, and now *Bowers*, the Court was embroiled in a full-blown culture war, and its jurisprudence reflected the social and political values of a divided nation. Two corresponding factions had emerged on the Court. A "liberal" camp found controversial substantive liberties within the fundamental-rights category, while a "conservative" one fought to keep them out.

And for the first time, the concept of ordered liberty was without a guardian. The great sage was gone. No longer allied with him, Justice White had split the concept in *Duncan*, failed to protect its history and tradition in *Moore*, and finally betrayed it here in *Bowers*. The mysterious spirit that *Griswold* had released into the jurisprudence worked its mischief. The union of two modern doctrines had paradoxically produced a partisan divide.

NOTES

1. *Bowers v. Hardwick*, 478 U.S. 186, 186 (1986).
2. *Id.* at 188 footnote 1 (citing Georgia Code Ann. §16-6-2 (1984)).
3. *Id.* at 188.

4. *Id.* at 188–189.
5. *Id.* at 189.
6. *Id.* (citing 760 F.2d 1202 (1985)).
7. *Id.* at 190.
8. *Id.* at 188 footnote 2.
9. *Id.* at 190.
10. *Id.* at 191.
11. *Id.* at 190–191.
12. *Id.* at 191.
13. *Id.*
14. *Id.*
15. *Id.* at 191–192 (quoting *Moore*, 431 U.S. at 503).
16. *Id.* at 192.
17. *See id.* at 192–193 footnotes 5 and 6.
18. *Id.* at 194.
19. 394 U.S. 557 (1969).
20. *Id.* at 568.
21. *Bowers*, 478 U.S. at 195.
22. *Id.*
23. *Id.* at 196.
24. *Id.*
25. *Id.* at 199 (Blackmun, J., dissenting) (citation omitted; internal quotation marks omitted).
26. *Id.* (quoting *Olmstead v. United States*, 277 U.S. 438, 478 (Brandies, J., dissenting)) (internal quotation marks omitted).
27. 478 U.S. at 195.
28. *Id.* at 199 (Blackmun, J., dissenting).
29. *Id.*
30. *Id.* at 199–200 (quoting *Herring v. State*, 119 Ga. 709, 721 (1904)) (internal quotation marks omitted).
31. *Id.* (citing Oliver Wendell Holmes, *The Path of Law*, 10 Harv. L. Rev. 457, 469 (1897)).
32. *Id.* at 216 (Stevens, J., dissenting).

Chapter 9

The Inquiry Thus Reduces

The same year the Court decided *Bowers*, Antonin Scalia joined the Court from the D.C. Circuit. He replaced associate Justice William Rehnquist, who became chief justice upon Chief Justice Burger's retiring. The liberal faction on the Court, still struggling with the Court's post-*Griswold* jurisprudence and how to identify the content of its fundamental-rights category, continued to argue that certain substantive liberties were within it. At the same time, as *Bowers* illustrated, a conservative faction reacted against this practice as the Court adjudicated controversial personal-liberty claims during the mid-twentieth century. In 1989, just three years after *Bowers* adopted *Moore*'s conflation of the *Duncan* distinction and its redefinition of "history and tradition," Justice Scalia authored the plurality opinion in *Michael H. v. Gerald D.*,[1] another case involving an issue of familial liberty. Using the developments of *Duncan*, *Moore*, and *Bowers*, Justice Scalia brought modern conservatism's majoritarian positivism into federal personal-liberty jurisprudence.

***

Gerald D. was married to an international model, Carole D. They lived together in California as husband and wife "when one or the other was not out of the country on business."[2] Carole had extramarital affairs, and one of them was with a neighbor, Michael H.[3] Carole and Michael had an on-and-off relationship, during which time Carole's daughter, Victoria, was born. Michael established a father-daughter relationship with Victoria,[4] and a paternity test revealed that Michael was Victoria's biological father.[5] Carole eventually ended the affair with Michael and reconciled with Gerald.[6] Michael filed an action in state court, seeking to establish his paternity and visitation rights as Victoria's natural father.[7] But because Gerald and Carole resided in California, and Victoria was born into their household while they lived together as husband and wife, an old California law provided that Gerald was presumptively Victoria's natural father.[8] The law provided that only the husband or wife of a marriage into which a child was born could challenge the presumption of paternity in favor of the husband.[9]

Michael claimed the law impermissibly infringed his freedom to have a relationship with his daughter.[10] The law prevented him from obtaining a hearing at which he might produce evidence to rebut the presumption that Gerald, Carole's husband, was Victoria's natural father.[11] The California Superior Court granted Gerald's summary-judgment motion, ruling that there were no disputed issues of material fact as to paternity—the law presumed Gerald was Victoria's father and denied Michael the opportunity to rebut the presumption.[12] The California Court of Appeal affirmed the judgment of the Superior Court and rejected Michael's assertion that he was denied due process.[13] The California Supreme Court let the Court of Appeal's decision stand, and Michael appealed to the U.S. Supreme Court.[14]

Writing for a plurality, Justice Scalia rejected Michael's claim. Following Justice White's example in *Bowers*, Scalia observed, "The California statute that is the subject of this litigation is, in substance, more than a century old."[15] Like *Bowers* had explicated laws criminalizing sodomy, Scalia presented a brief historical exegesis of the various forms the California statute had taken between 1872 and 1989.[16] And although offering an approach designed to limit the influence judges' personal predilections might have on the outcomes of difficult cases, Scalia introduced the opinion expressing distaste for the details of this one: "The facts of this case are, we must hope, extraordinary."[17] Michael was an "adulterous father" threatening the integrity of Gerald's marriage.[18]

Against the background of the *Duncan* distinction, Scalia characterized the case as requiring a "substantive-due-process" analysis. The Court need not consider Michael's "procedural" claim that before the State could "terminate his liberty interest in his relationship with his child" it must afford him a hearing at which he could "demonstrate his paternity."[19] The California law was a rule of evidence that "implement[ed] . . . a substantive rule of law."[20] Citing the California Court of Appeal, Scalia said the presumption of paternity was a "matter of overriding social policy," expressing the normative determination that "the integrity of the family unit should not be impugned."[21] The California law ostensibly furthered the State's "substantive policy" of preserving familial integrity.[22] Scalia observed that in prior cases where the Court had "struck down as illegitimate certain irrebuttable presumptions[,] [t]hose holdings did not . . . rest upon *procedural* due process."[23] "[O]ur 'irrebuttable presumption' cases[,]" he explained, "must ultimately be analyzed as calling into question not the adequacy of procedures but—like our cases involving classifications framed in other terms—the adequacy of the fit between the classification and the policy that the classification serves."[24]

Here again was something like a description of the common-law analysis—now characterized as a "substantive-due-process" analysis—which required testing the means the State had chosen, when impacting a basic liberty, for fitness with its objective. The analysis of Michael's claim should reveal whether, in light of the interest for which he sought vindication, the California law adequately fit the policy objective of protecting familial integrity. Michael's argument appealed to this very analysis: "[B]ecause he ha[d] established a parental relationship with Victoria, protection of Gerald's and Carole's marital union [was] an insufficient state interest to support termination of that relationship."[25] Despite Scalia's description of the analysis, and its applicability to the contending interests in this particular controversy, his opinion would not implement it. Like *Griswold*, *Moore*, and *Bowers*, the *Michael H.* opinion would focus on whether the substantive interest that Michael asserted was in the fundamental-rights category.

Michael's argument was predicated "on the assertion that Michael ha[d] a constitutionally protected liberty interest in his relationship with Victoria."[26] This was where a common-law judge would execute the first step in the analysis—determining whether the liberty interest triggered the requirement to strictly scrutinize the State's justification for abridging it. Instead, building on Justice White's reframing of the initial question in *Bowers*, Justice Scalia further customized the method for answering the now-ultimate question of whether the liberty interest Michael asserted was a fundamental right.

> In an attempt to limit and guide interpretation of the [Due Process] Clause, we have insisted not merely that the interest denominated as a "liberty" be "fundamental" . . . but also that it be an interest traditionally protected by our society. As we have put it, the Due Process Clause affords only those protections "so rooted in the traditions and conscience of our people as to be ranked as fundamental." Our cases reflect "continual insistence upon respect for the teachings of history [and] solid recognition of the basic values that underlie our society."[27]

This patchwork passage used *Bowers*'s adoption of *Moore*'s "history and tradition." In *Moore*, the family was deeply-rooted, and therefore constitutionally protected. Similarly, in this formulation, a fundamental liberty was one that American society "traditionally protected." Scalia misquoted Cardozo, equating his reference to "so-rooted" principles of justice with these "traditionally protected" liberties. And as authority for this equation, he co-opted "history" and "basic values" from Justice Harlan's *Griswold* concurrence. For modern conservatism, fundamental rights were those values so-historically rooted in American society that they were traditionally protected from government intrusion.[28] This new description of what the due-process guarantee required a judge to consider ignored the common-law tradition and reflected a profound misunderstanding of precedent.

Justice Cardozo had not said the Constitution afforded those *protections* "so rooted in the traditions and conscience of [the American] people as to be ranked as fundamental." Cardozo's statement, like his *Palko* analysis, accounted for both aspects—majoritarian and counter-majoritarian—of the concept of ordered liberty. Cardozo said, "The commonwealth of Massachusetts is free to regulate the procedure of its courts in accordance with its own conception of policy and fairness, unless in so doing it offends *some principle of justice* so rooted in the traditions and conscience of our people as to be ranked as fundamental."[29] The common law's question was whether the state policy allegedly interfering with an important liberty offended some "so-rooted" principle of justice—like the prohibition against arbitrary legislative infringements of basic liberties. The tradition counseled here to consider whether Michael asserted a basic liberty implicating the due-process guarantee's protection, and, if he did, whether the State of California could offer a non-arbitrary justification for the means it chose—denying him a hearing—to preserve familial integrity.

As *Palko* had taught, the ordered-liberty concept was the precise legal expression of a uniquely American theory of liberal democracy. Deeplyrooted principles of justice demarcated the boundaries within which majorities in the States established social order through democratic processes. These principles were enshrined in the text of the Constitution and in the American legal tradition, where they had been applied to resolve discrete cases and controversies. The due-process guarantee substantiated the so-rooted principle that a political majority, in choosing the means to effectuate its social policies, could not unreasonably interfere with a fellow citizen's basic liberty. States were free to enact their own laws, unless in applying them they violated a basic liberty without a reasonable (non-arbitrary) justification. But this conception of American law was directly contrary to the positivist position of modern conservatism.

Justice Scalia's version of the tradition bolstered Powell's misunderstanding of Harlan's "careful respect for the teachings of history[.]" Scalia characterized the cases from which Michael argued that natural parenthood was a basic liberty as "rest[ing] . . . upon the historic respect—indeed," he said, "sanctity would not be too strong a term—traditionally accorded to the relationships that develop within the *unitary* family."[30] Without explaining why the law valued relationships within the unitary family over natural parenthood, Scalia quoted *Moore*. "Our decisions," he observed, "establish that the Constitution protects the sanctity of the family precisely because the institution of family is deeply rooted in this Nation's history and tradition."[31] Michael's claim defeated itself.

> Thus, the legal issue in the present case reduces to whether the relationship between persons in the situation of Michael and Victoria has been treated as a protected family unit under the historic practices of our society, or whether on any other basis it has been accorded special protection. We think it impossible to find that it has. In fact, quite to the contrary, our traditions have protected the marital family . . . against the sort of claim Michael asserts.[32]

This was as far as the Court needed to look. "We have found nothing in the older sources," Scalia wrote, "nor in the older cases, addressing specifically the power of the natural father to assert parental rights over a child born into a woman's existing marriage with another man."[33] This focus on *Moore*'s and *Bowers*' redefining "history and tradition" further illustrated the Court's straying from the common-law tradition, even while pretending to invoke it. As Justice Harlan had demonstrated in *Poe*, the tradition allowed evaluating novel claims against state action arising within an ever-changing society like America's. The common-law method could analyze a challenge like Michael's—one to an old law enacted prior to the invention of reliable paternity testing and applied within a new social context that made possible determining paternity with a 98% probability of accuracy.[34] For Scalia, "respect for the teachings of history [and] solid recognition of the basic values that underlie our society"[35] required ignoring such changes.

But considering the line of cases on which *Moore* relied in finding a fundamental right to familial liberty—*Meyer*, *Pierce*, *Roe*, Justices Goldberg's and White's *Griswold* concurrences, and Justice Harlan's *Poe* dissent—Justice Scalia's method arrived at an untenable conclusion. Respect for the unitary family was deeply rooted in the Nation's history and tradition; respect for natural familial relationships was not. This problem dissolved, however, in Scalia's modern-conservative solution to it—prescribing the level of generality at which a liberty interest should be described. Aptly criticizing the liberal faction's preference for a fundamental-rights category populated with substantive liberties generally described, Scalia asked rhetorically, "Why should the relevant category not be even more general—perhaps 'family relationships'; or 'personal relationships', or even 'emotional attachments in general'?'"[36]

Under the modern-conservative method, Scalia explained, the "relevant category" should include no such general descriptions. "We refer to the most specific level at which a relevant tradition protecting, or denying protection to, the asserted right can be defined."[37] Because a liberty interest for which a litigant sought protection was evaluated against "the historic practices of our society[,]" evaluating it required first describing it as a social practice. Natural parenthood was too broad a formulation of the interest at stake here. The correct question was narrow—whether the Constitution conferred a fundamental right on Michael to threaten, via a claim to natural parenthood, the integrity of a unitary family to which he did not belong. And the answer in turn depended on whether the States already protected it.

> What counts is whether the States in fact award substantive parental rights to the natural father of a child conceived within, and born into, an extant marital union that wishes to embrace the child. We are not aware of a single case, old or new, that has done so. This is not the stuff of which fundamental rights . . . are made.[38]

This followed *Bowers*' describing the asserted interest as "the right of homosexuals to engage in sodomy."[39] Defining a liberty interest more broadly, Scalia explained, would thwart the Court's responsibility in due-process cases to "discern the society's views" and recognize only those social practices the States already protected.[40] This was ironic coming from a jurist who would later argue against non-originalist theories of judicial review as merely infusing the constitutional text with social values.[41]

As *Bowers*'s reliance on a long list of old state criminal statutes had taught, asking whether society already protected a liberty interest made unnecessary assessing it against the background of relevant constitutional principles applied throughout the tradition. Having reduced the inquiry to whether American society had "traditionally protected" the liberty to engage in a specific social practice, Scalia's examining the "historic practices of our society[,]" looking for protection for Michael's claim, included no citations to precedent.[42] This method required only a survey of American social traditions in the States to discover whether society already protected a social practice, or, had at least not outlawed it.

Society had not traditionally protected the "right" Michael asserted, so neither did the due-process guarantee. The guarantee protected a liberty interest, against the interference of a State's political majority, only where the States' political majorities already protected the interest. There was perhaps a temporal distinction. Scalia seemed to imply that the Court should look, like *Bowers* did, to the decisions of past majorities to determine limits on majoritarian power in the present. But this majoritarian-positivist ideology necessarily opposed the common-law tradition of arbitrariness review, which implemented a non-positivist conception of American law—the concept of ordered liberty. Scrutinizing the State's means for reasonable fitness with its ostensible objective specified the so-rooted principle that an arbitrary legislative act that infringes a basic liberty is *ultra vires.* Justice Scalia's approach eliminated this analysis altogether. When it came to questions of fundamental liberties held against majorities in the Sates, majorities in the States would provide the answers.

The hollow echo of the *Slaughterhouse* majority's holding resounded here. The Fourteenth Amendment protected rights already recognized before its ratification, and claims involving basic liberties were the States' to resolve.[43] Of course, no litigant would ever come before the Court seeking protection for a liberty the State already protected. Under this method, an individual challenging the State had already lost. The very fact that an individual sought protection in federal court meant that society had deemed the interest unworthy of protection. As Justice Scalia would later put it, "The mere novelty of . . . a claim [was] reason enough to doubt that 'substantive due process' sustain[ed] it[.]"[44]

Justice Brennan filed a dissenting opinion, joined by Justices Marshall and Blackmun, pointing to Scalia's contradiction. Noting its novelty, Brennan observed that had the Court in prior due-process cases used Justice Scalia's method, it would have in every case reached the opposite result with respect to the liberty interests it had recognized as deserving constitutional protection.[45] Understating the obvious, Brennan noted that the use of contraceptives, the freedom from corporal punishment in schools, and the right to raise one's natural children, to name a few, "were not 'interest[s] traditionally protected by . . . society', at the time of their consideration by th[e] Court."[46] Had the States already protected these interests, no one would need to seek shelter for them in federal court. Justice Brennan argued Scalia had "transform[ed] the protection afforded by the Due Process Clause in to [*sic*] a redundancy[,] mock[ing] those who, with care and purpose, wrote the Fourteenth Amendment."[47]

There was "no basis[,]" Scalia countered, "for the contention that th[e] methodology [was] nove[l]."[48] Three years earlier the Court had similarly decided *Bowers v. Hardwick*.[49] And despite the dissent's accurate criticism of the method, Scalia said he did not understand how "limiting the Due Process Clause to traditionally protected interests turn[ed it] into a redundancy."[50] The Clause's "purpose[,]" he insisted, was "to prevent future generations from lightly casting aside important traditional values."[51] Here, "important traditional values" did not refer to Justice Harlan's "basic values underlying our society" –values inherent to the American political experiment vivified in discrete cases throughout its legal tradition –but rather to social norms the States deemed sufficiently "traditional" to deserve federal-constitutional protection.

The incorporation doctrine had limited the States' criminal procedural options to those the federal government already adopted. *Griswold*'s penumbra metaphor merged incorporation with the doctrine of unenumerated rights, extending the protections of due process to liberty against unreasonable substantive legislation in the States. But after *Duncan*, *Moore*, *Bowers*, and now *Michael H.*, the due-process guarantee was no longer fixed to either the letter or penumbra of any Bill of Rights provision. It was now tethered to "traditional social practices" in the American States. In its modern-conservative manifestation, the doctrine now limited *federal* constitutional constraints on the States' substantive-legislative options to those the *States* already adopted. This was the intent of those who ratified the Fourteenth Amendment—to ensure that future generations of Americans maintained nineteenth-century social mores.

Here was a diabolical solution to the threat that liberty posed to modern-conservative social order. The purpose of the due-process guarantee was to prevent society from changing in ways a federal court decided that same society, either presently or in the past, would not abide. Reducing the inquiry to a study of traditional social practices in the American States, a judge wielding this new method might simply pick and choose those supporting a foregone conclusion. Perhaps the point was to abdicate judicial discretion altogether. Maybe the quest for meaningful restraint had led to its elimination, and Justice Harlan's most ominous prophecy had come to pass. The due-process guarantee could be used to restrict, rather than protect, individual liberty.[52]

***

Duncan had made possible *Moore*'s mistake. Building on *Bowers*'s adoption of the error, *Michael H.* turned upside down the elegant common-law theory that Justices Bradley, Field, Matthews, Holmes, Harlan, McReynolds, Cardozo, and Harlan II had, over the preceding 117 years, developed with care and attention to the unique history of the Anglo-American common-law tradition. They honored what modern conservatism ignored—the obligation to defer to the political will of majorities in the States, but also to identify, using reasoned judgment, discrete instances where the value of individual liberty required a federal court to invalidate arbitrary majoritarian action. Disregarding this feature of American federalism, Justice Scalia flattened the concept of ordered liberty, collapsing the distinction—and thereby eliminating the duty to resolve the tension—between its majoritarian and counter-majoritarian aspects. His method embodied the majoritarian positivism of modern-conservative politics. It advanced this positivist political theory despite the enduring recognition of the contrary and deeply-rooted common-law principle that an arbitrary legislative interference with a basic liberty, regardless of its democratic sanction, is not law, and the over 100 years of post-Reconstruction precedent demonstrating it.

But the reader should not despair, despite this hasty cutting up and reassembly of the concept, here at the nadir of the tale. For not long after this furtive reconfiguration of the tradition, an unassuming common-law judge sat before the Senate Judiciary Committee, nominated to fill the seat on the Court that Justice Brennan vacated. Here enters the quiet hero of the story, who will bring the redemption it requires, lest the tradition be irreversibly corrupted and the concept forever lost. A few words he offered during his confirmation hearing provide solace. As he deftly fielded a bevy of questions aimed at discovering his view of the fundamental-rights category, and, specifically, whether he saw the abortion decision in it, a thin ray of light pierced the darkness when the twentieth century's last incarnation of reasoned judgment invoked a category of a different sort.

> But I understand from your question, and I think it is unmistakable, that what you were concerned about is the principal basis for deriving a right of privacy, and specifically the kind of reasoning that I would go through to do so. And in response to that question . . . I would group myself in Justice Harlan's category.[53]

NOTES

1. 491 U.S. 110 (1989).
2. *Id.* at 113.
3. *Id.* at 113–114.
4. *Id.* at 114–115.
5. *Id.* at 114.
6. *Id.* at 115.
7. *Id.* at 114.
8. *Id.* at 115.
9. *Id.* at 113.
10. *Id.* at 121.
11. *Id.*
12. *Id.*
13. *Id.* at 116.
14. *Id.*
15. *Id.* at 117.
16. *Id.* at 117–118.
17. *Id.* at 113.
18. *Id.* at 130.
19. *Id.* at 119.
20. *Id.*
21. *Id.* at 119–120 (quoting 191 Cal.App.3d 995, 1005 (1987)).
22. *Id.* at 120.
23. *Id.* (internal citations omitted; emphasis in original).
24. *Id.* at 121.

25. *Id.*
26. *Id.*
27. *Id.* at 122–123 (citing *Snyder v. Massachusetts*, 291 U.S. 97, 105 (1934); *Griswold v. Connecticut*, 381 U.S. 479, 501 (1965) (Harlan, J., concurring)).
28. *Id.* at 122.
29. *Snyder v. Massachusetts*, 291 U.S. 97, 105 (1934) (citing *Twining v. New Jersey*, 211 U.S. 78, 106 (1908); *Rogers v. Peck*, 199 U.S. 425, 434 (1905); *Maxwell v. Dow*, 176 U.S. 581, 604 (1900); *Hurtado v. California*, 110 U.S. 516 (1884); *Frank v. Mangum*, 237 U.S. 309, 326 (1915); *Powell v. Alabama*, 287 U.S. 45, 67 (1932)) (emphasis added).
30. *Michael H.*, 491 U.S. at 123 (emphasis added).
31. *Id.* at 123–124.
32. *Id.* at 124.
33. *Id* at 125.
34. *Id.* at 114.
35. *Id.* at 122–123 (citing *Snyder v. Massachusetts*, 291 U.S. 97, 105 (1934); *Griswold v. Connecticut*, 381 U.S. 479, 501 (1965) (Harlan, J., concurring)).
36. *Id.* at 127.
37. *Id.* at 127 footnote 6.
38. *Id.* at 127.
39. *See Bowers*, 478 U.S. at 190.
40. *Michael H.*, 491 U.S. at 127 footnote 6.
41. *See, e.g.*, Justice Antonin Scalia, "Originalism, The Lesser Evil," in *Judges on Judging*, ed. David M. O'Brien (Thousand Oaks: CQ Press, 2004), 209–217. (characterizing non-originalist interpretive theories as "cast[ing] aside" the "original import of the constitution," and replacing it with "the fundamental values of the current society").
42. *See Michael H.*, 491 U.S. at 124–127.
43. *See* discussion of *Slaughterhouse Cases*, chapter 1, *supra*.
44. *See Reno v. Flores*, 507 U.S. 292, 303 (1993).
45. 491 U.S. at 139–140 (Brennan, J., dissenting).
46. *Id.* at 139.
47. *Id.* at 141.
48. *Id.* at 127 footnote 6.
49. *Id.*
50. 491 U.S. at 122 footnote 2.
51. *Id.*
52. *Griswold*, 381 U.S. at 500 (Harlan, J., concurring).
53. "Souter Confirmation Hearings," CSPAN.org, http://www.c-span.org/video/?13979-2/souter-confirmation-hearings, 22:40–23:03; "Hearings Before the Committee on the Judiciary, United States Senate, One Hundred First Congress, Second Session on the Nomination of David H. Souter to be Associate Justice of the Supreme Court of the United States," S.Hrg. 101-1263, Sep 13, 14, 17, 18, 19, 1990, Senate.gov, https://www.govinfo.gov/content/pkg/GPO-CHRG-SOUTER/pdf/GPO-CHRG-SOUTER.pdf, 54.

Part III

THE MODERN JUSTIFICATION FOR ARBITRARINESS REVIEW

[I]t is better not to go too far back into antiquity for the best securities for our 'ancient liberties.' It is more consonant to the true philosophy of our historical legal institutions to say that the spirit of personal liberty and individual right which they embodied was preserved and developed by a progressive growth and wise adaptation to new circumstances and situations of the forms and processes found fit to give, from time to time, new expression and greater effect to modern ideas of self-government.

—*Hurtado v. California* 110 U.S. 516, 530 (1884).

Chapter 10

The Dimension of Personal Liberty

Only Chief Justice Rehnquist joined Justice Scalia's *Michael H.* opinion in its entirety. Justice Sandra Day O'Connor filed a single-paragraph concurrence. She agreed with the plurality's disposition of the case, but was skeptical of the "mode of historical analysis" that Scalia argued should be "used when identifying liberty interests protected by the Due Process Clause."[1] She cited Harlan's point in *Poe* that the due-process guarantee derived from the peculiar purposes the Constitution served—the exercise of appropriately restrained reasoned judgment could not be reduced to any simple formula.[2] Focusing on the tactic of describing "relevant traditions protecting asserted rights" at "the most specific level available," she observed that "the prior imposition of a single mode of historical analysis" would "foreclose the unanticipated."[3]

This criticism exposed the method's radical departure from the common law. Because it tied the scope of the due-process guarantee to the historic practices of American society, any claim to liberty arising from novel circumstances in a changing society would fail. Only "social practices" recognized as "traditional"—or, already protected—when evaluated against the "historic practices" of American society were worthy of constitutional protection. Scalia's method was a version of his originalism.[4] It fixed the scope of constitutional protections in the present with reference to the protections society would have ostensibly recognized in the past. And like his originalism—and the incorporation doctrine that made this new method possible—it made a positivist claim. When considering in the present a challenge to a democratically enacted state law, the federal judiciary could limit its application only in ways a majority in the past had already sanctioned.

The method expressed a fundamental tenet of modern conservatism. In the absence of explicit constitutional text, a federal court had no authority to supplant the will of a democratic majority. Modern conservatism saw no such thing as common-law reasoning in due-process jurisprudence, and it necessarily denied centuries of history and tradition to the contrary.[5] The federal judiciary, in deciding personal-liberty cases in favor of individuals and against state majorities, had overstepped its bounds. As Judge Robert Bork, a paragon of modern conservatism and originalist ally of Justice Scalia, explained, "[I]t is the courts that are not merely endangering our freedoms but actually depriving us of them, particularly our most precious freedom, the freedom to govern ourselves democratically unless the Constitution actually says otherwise."[6]

Invoking *Moore*, *Bowers*, and *Michael H.*, Scalia applied his new method during the last decade of the twentieth century.[7] Chief Justice Rehnquist joined him, and together they held that the federal courts ought not to interfere with democratic policy making in the States, without explicit textual constitutional authority, unless a "right historically and traditionally protected against state interference" was at stake.[8] They touted the method's requirement, that "[s]ubstantive due-process analysis must begin with a careful description of the asserted right," as complying with the "doctrine of judicial self-restraint."[9] And they reinforced *Michael H.*'s misappropriation of Cardozo, asserting that social practices (and not, as Cardozo had said, "principles of justice") were either "so rooted in the traditions and conscience of our people as to be ranked as fundamental[,]" or, alternatively, were unworthy of constitutional protection.[10]

The absence of a clearly articulated alternative to this method magnified the problem of how broadly or narrowly the Court should construe the liberty interests upon which litigants based their claims. This aspect of the Court's discretion was crucial to the legitimacy of its decisions. As the modern-conservative method illustrated, describing a liberty interest as a social practice was outcome-dispositive. The point was to deny protection for "nontraditional" social practices and side-step the Court's obligation to exercise reasoned judgment in evaluating state interferences with individuals' liberties.

On the other hand, describing a liberty interest as "within the right of privacy," as *Griswold* and *Roe* had, while at the same time seeming to identify unenumerated rights at a more specific level—a "right to contraception" or a "right to abortion"—was inconsistent. And it presented the same problem, albeit inversely. Against the background of post-*Griswold* jurisprudence, the more broadly a litigant or the Court described a liberty interest, the more likely it would qualify for constitutional protection. Both the conservative and liberal factions would continue to emphasize the liberty aspect of the ordered-liberty concept. But neither offered any principled account of how to determine the level of generality at which to describe a liberty interest vying for status as a fundamental right. The modern conservatives repeated their "most-specific-level" requirement, while the liberal faction offered broader formulations of liberty without explaining why.

During the final decade of the twentieth century, two especially controversial cases arrived at the Supreme Court, involving state regulation of abortion and physician-assisted suicide, respectively. Both arose within an evolving medical profession, where technology was rapidly modernizing and the physician-patient relationship consequently changing. Three years after *Michael H.*, in the case of *Planned Parenthood of Southeastern Pennsylvania v. Casey* (1992) the Supreme Court reaffirmed *Roe v. Wade*'s central holding—the Due Process Clause protected, against undue state interference, a woman's decision to undergo a medically safe abortion and terminate a pregnancy in its early stages.[11] And in 1997, in *Washington v. Glucksberg*, the Court rejected a due-process challenge to a Washington State law criminalizing physician-assisted suicide.[12]

In each case, Chief Justice Rehnquist and Justice Scalia applied the modern-conservative method. Not surprisingly, neither abortion nor physician-assisted suicide were traditionally protected American social practices, and, according to those justices' opinions were not in the category of fundamental rights the Due Process Clause protected. A plurality in *Casey*—Justice O'Connor and two recent appointees, Justices Anthony Kennedy and David Souter—delivered the opinion of the Court, offering a startlingly broad formulation of liberty. But the opinion also seemed to lean at moments toward Justice Harlan's understanding of due process. Here was Justice Souter's influence appearing in the jurisprudence, as he subtly began the concept's resuscitation. In one especially telling section, *Casey* explained how the common-law tradition provided a consistent mode of reasoning for difficult controversies that significant social change generated. And in *Glucksberg*, in a separate opinion of astounding precision and clarity, Justice Souter would resurrect the concept of ordered liberty and complete the canonical triumvirate of common-law due-process precedent.

***

A challenge to *Roe v. Wade*'s central holding made its way to the Court after the State of Pennsylvania enacted legislation requiring a woman seeking an abortion to first meet certain conditions.[13] Prior to undergoing an abortive procedure, she must give informed consent (if a minor, a parent's informed consent); receive certain information; and, if married, sign a statement that she had notified her husband of her intended abortion.[14] The Court noted that "[t]he Court of Appeal found it necessary to follow an elaborate course of reasoning even to identify the first premise to use to determine whether the statute . . . meets constitutional standards,"[15] and that "19 years after our holding that the Constitution protects a woman's right to terminate her pregnancy within its early stages, that definition of liberty is still questioned."[16]

Reconsidering this most controversial right the due-process guarantee protected, the *Casey* opinion affirmed that "[c]onstitutional protection of the woman's decision to terminate her pregnancy derive[d] from the Due Process Clause of the Fourteenth Amendment."[17] "The controlling word in the cases before us," the opinion stated plainly, "is liberty."[18] The plurality quoted Harlan's *Poe* dissent; specifically, its quoting of *Hurtado*'s observation that the guarantees of due process originated in Magna Carta, and, through the common-law process had "in this country become bulwarks also against arbitrary legislation."[19] And like Harlan had in *Poe*, the plurality invoked Justice Brandeis, here quoting from his concurring opinion in *Whitney v. California*,[20] where he explained,

> despite arguments to the contrary . . . it is settled that the due process clause of the Fourteenth Amendment applies to matters of substantive law as well as to matters of procedure. Thus all fundamental rights comprised within the term liberty are protected by the Federal Constitution from invasion by the states.[21]

As invoked here, in the context of the post-*Griswold* fundamental-rights doctrine, this relatively early (1927) reference to "fundamental rights . . . within the term liberty" appealed to the modern Court's habitual absolutism. Its initial invocation of *Poe* notwithstanding, the *Casey* opinion illustrated the enduring influence of the categorical formalism *Griswold*'s penumbra metaphor had spawned, and boldly pronounced: "It is a promise of the Constitution that there is a realm of personal liberty which the government may not enter."[22] Like Justice Powell's statement in *Moore*, the second half that captured the ordered aspect of the concept—"without substantial justification"—was missing.[23] The Court explained that it had "vindicated this principle before[,]" citing precedent—including *Meyer*, *Pierce*, and *Griswold*—exemplifying unenumerated "aspect[s] of liberty protected against state interference by the substantive component of the Due Process Clause." [24]

Despite the apparently unqualified breadth of this liberty, the plurality acknowledged the ongoing challenge of adjudicating the limits of legislative power with authentic judicial restraint. The Court had long recognized that the Fourteenth Amendment protected some substantive liberties against certain state attempts to abridge them, but had declined, despite the advocacy of some to the contrary, to find the source of this protection in the incorporation doctrine.

> It is tempting, as a means of curbing the discretion of federal judges, to suppose that liberty encompasses no more than those rights already guaranteed to the

individual against federal interference by the express provisions of the first eight Amendments to the Constitution. But of course this Court has never accepted that view.[25]

And, like Justice O'Connor in her *Michael H.* concurrence, the plurality rejected the modern-conservative contradiction equating constitutionally protected liberties with social practices of which democratic majorities in the States generally approved.

> It is also tempting, for the same reason, to suppose that the Due Process Clause protects only those practices, defined at the most specific level, that were protected against government interference by other rules of law when the Fourteenth Amendment was ratified. But such a view would be inconsistent with our law.[26]

Driving the point home, the opinion concluded, "Neither the Bill of Rights nor the specific practices of the States at the time of the adoption of the Fourteenth Amendment marks the outer limits of the substantive sphere of liberty which the Fourteenth Amendment protects."[27]

The opinion described the extant jurisprudence as expressing the common-law theory of due process that Justice Harlan exemplified. It characterized *Griswold* as "adopting his position" four terms after *Poe*.[28] The plurality quoted at length from the *Poe* dissent's explanation of "the full scope of the liberty guaranteed by the Due Process Clause" as a "rational continuum which, broadly speaking, includes a freedom from all substantial arbitrary impositions and purposeless restraints."[29] It quoted Harlan's description of "a reasonable and sensitive judgment," which "recognizes . . . that certain interests require particularly careful scrutiny of the state needs asserted to justify their abridgement."[30] The Court's duty was to resolve claims to protected substantive liberties within the tradition of reasoned judgment.

> The inescapable fact is that adjudication of substantive due process claims may call upon the Court in interpreting the Constitution to exercise that same capacity which by tradition courts have always exercised: reasoned judgment. Its boundaries are not susceptible of expression as a simple rule. That does not mean we are free to invalidate state policy choices with which we disagree; yet neither does it permit us to shrink from the duties of our office.[31]

Perhaps this was, again, mere lip service to the tradition. Or, maybe a spark that Justice Souter threw down—one that would catch fire in his *Glucksberg* concurrence.

But as with all post-*Griswold* cases, the opinion did not follow Justice Harlan's example of the common-law analysis. The right identified in *Roe* was "an extension of th[e] . . . precedents . . . granting protection to substantive liberties of the person."[32] *Roe* had expanded the realm of personal liberty immune from government intrusion. Consistent with this theory, *Casey* offered an "explication of individual liberty" clarifying the "dimension of personal liberty *Roe* sought to protect."[33] This was consistent with the liberty-centric approach to fundamental rights that had so bewitched the Court over the previous decades and against which the modern conservatives reacted. The opinion ascended into lofty prose, likely attributable to Justice Kennedy and his emerging penchant for grandiloquence, which would flourish in his later personal-liberty opinions. Segueing into a discussion of "the heart of liberty" and "personal dignity and autonomy," the opinion spoke of "the right to define one's own concept of existence, of meaning, of the universe, and of the mystery of human life."[34] This "right," stated at such an extreme breadth of generality, exemplified the danger the hyper-liberal fundamental-rights doctrine represented to conservatives, and Justice Scalia would later refer to it sardonically as "the famed sweet mystery of life passage" in criticizing his liberal colleagues' judicial overreaching.[35]

The Court had "no doubt as to the correctness of" *Griswold* and its progeny. They "support[ed] the reasoning in *Roe* related to the woman's liberty[,] because they involve[d] personal decisions concerning . . . the meaning of procreation [and] human responsibility and respect for it."[36] According to the plurality, such matters were "[c]entral to the liberty protected by the Fourteenth Amendment"—those "involving the most intimate and personal choices a person may make in a lifetime, [and] choices central to personal dignity and autonomy[.]"[37] Even broader, such decisions were "central to the liberty" the due-process guarantee protected because "[b]eliefs about these matters could not define the attributes of personhood were they formed under compulsion of the state."[38] This "liberty" included "a person's most basic decisions," here, one "originat[ing] in the zone of conscience and belief."[39] It was this "dimension of personal liberty" that *Casey* reaffirmed.[40]

In his dissent, Justice Scalia aptly criticized the plurality. After claiming that it should proceed according to "reasoned judgment," it justified its conclusion that the "word liberty must include the right to" terminate a pregnancy by "rattl[ing] off a collection of adjectives."[41] After explicating the liberty at stake, the opinion discussed the suffering—"the anxieties, physical constraints, [and] pain"—peculiar to pregnancy, and concluded that society's view of the nobility of "these sacrifices . . . cannot alone be grounds for the State to insist [a woman] make" them.[42] This was so because "the liberty of the woman is at stake in a sense unique to the human condition and so unique to the law."[43] This liberty was protected against the State because "[t]he destiny of the woman must be shaped to a large extent on her own conception of her spiritual imperatives and her place in society."[44]

Even while affirming its holding, *Casey* rejected *Roe*'s "rigid trimester framework"[45]—the Court did "not consider [it] to be part of the essential holding of *Roe*"[46]—in favor of elaborating the viability threshold[47] and undue-burden standard.[48] The Court upheld the Court of Appeal's conclusion that all but the husband-notification provision of the Pennsylvania statute were constitutional,[49] but "refin[ed] the undue burden standard in accordance with the principles" it identified in reaffirming *Roe*'s central holding.[50] Here, as at other places, the opinion seemed to find momentary connections to the common-law method, finding within precedent the test of means for fitness with ostensible justifications, and overruling parts of two prior cases as "inconsistent with *Roe*'s statement that the State has a legitimate interest in promoting the life or potential life of the unborn."[51]

The opinion admitted, for example, the absolutist application of "liberty" to which the Court had succumbed post-*Griswold*: "As our jurisprudence relating to all liberties save perhaps abortion has recognized, not every law which makes a right more difficult to exercise is, *ipso facto*, an infringement of that right."[52] It described "a statute which, while furthering the interest in potential life or some other valid state interest, [that] has the effect of placing a substantial obstacle in the path of a woman's choice[,]" as beyond the "permissible means of serving its legitimate ends."[53] And it acknowledged, much like Justices Field and Bradley had over a century ago, that "the fact that a law which serves a valid purpose, one not designed to strike at the right itself, has the incidental effect of making it more difficult or more expensive to [exercise the right] cannot be enough to invalidate it."[54] The refined undue-burden analysis seemed an attempt, albeit a confusing one, to capture these expressions of the tradition—a state could not impose a burden, on the exercise of a fundamental right, that was *un*due those living under a free government.

Despite the common-law's influence, *Casey* did not address nor cure *Roe*'s basic problem—a holding that presented as a legislative answer to a complex social-policy question.[55] Indeed, the plurality admitted that arguments for overruling *Roe* and any "reservations" about "reaffirming [its] central holding" were simply "outweighed by the explication of liberty [it had] given combined with the force of *stare decisis*."[56] Accordingly, along with its explication of liberty, the opinion included a lengthy discussion of the doctrine,[57] perhaps compensating, as Scalia suggested,[58] for its questionable defense of the *Roe* decision. The opinion had opened, after all, with the declaration that "[l]iberty finds no refuge in a jurisprudence of doubt"[59]—yet another Kennedy-esque locution.

Section III B of this portion of the opinion, however, focused carefully on when and why the Court should overrule prior decisions. It explained two legal sea changes illustrative of "national controversies" comparable to the present one: *West Coast Hotel* and its ending the *Lochner* Era; and *Brown v. Board of Education*'s repudiating the separate-but-equal doctrine.[60] This section—undoubtedly Justice Souter's contribution—was more than a mere statement about what circumstances required overruling (or, maintaining) prior decisions. It explained the application of enduring legal principles to the exigencies of an evolving social context. It elaborated Justice O'Connor's point in *Michael H.* about "foreclos[ing] the unanticipated," and offered an answer to the question that Justice Scalia would rhetorically pose in defense of his originalist approach to fundamental rights: How could state proscriptions of certain conduct, thought acceptable for a hundred years, suddenly *become* "unconstitutional" in a later century?[61]

The *Lochner* Era's end and *Brown v. Board of Education*'s overruling *Plessy v. Ferguson* each exemplified appropriate repudiation of a prior interpretation of the Fourteenth Amendment. In *West Coast Hotel*, "The facts upon which the earlier case [*Adkins*] had premised a constitutional resolution of social controversy had proven to be untrue, and history's demonstration of their untruth not only justified but required the new choice of constitutional principle[.]"[62]

> [T]he interpretation of contractual freedom protected in *Adkins* rested on fundamentally false factual assumptions about the capacity of a relatively unregulated market to satisfy minimal levels of human welfare.
>
> [T]he clear demonstration that the facts of economic life were different from those previously assumed warranted the repudiation of the old law.[63]

Likewise, by the time the Court decided *Brown*, "Society's understanding of the facts upon which a constitutional ruling was sought in 1954 [*Brown*] was . . . fundamentally different from the basis claimed for the decision in 1896 [*Plessy*]."[64]

> *West Coast Hotel* and *Brown* each rested on facts, or an understanding of facts, changed from those which furnished the claimed justifications for the earlier constitutional resolutions. Each case was comprehensible as the Court's response to facts that the country could understand, or had come to understand already, but which the Court of an earlier day, as its own declarations disclosed, had not been able to perceive. As the decisions were thus comprehensible, they were also defensible, not merely as the victories of one doctrinal school over another . . . but as applications of constitutional principle to facts as they had not been seen by the Court before.[65]

These cases showed that overruling precedent was justified, even required, in light of evidence that social circumstances, in which a once-reasonable resolution of contending interests had been struck, had since changed. A new and different understanding of *what facts meant* could require striking the balance among complementary constitutional principles—like democratically established order and federally-protected individual liberty—differently than a prior understanding of the facts demanded. "In constitutional adjudication as elsewhere in life, changed circumstances may impose new obligations, and the thoughtful part of the Nation could accept each decision to overrule a prior case as a response to the Court's constitutional duty."[66] Because the cases before the Court here presented "no such occasion[,]" overruling *Roe* would be to "pretend to be reexamining the prior law" for some other reason than "a present doctrinal disposition to come out differently from the Court of 1973."[67] This would "run counter to the view repeated in . . . cases, that a decision to overrule should rest on some special reason over and above the belief that a prior case was wrongly decided."[68] This section of the opinion argued for the common-law's restraint, moderation, and caution in the face of a national controversy—ironic as this might have sounded to conservatives in the context of the debate over *Roe*.

The modern-conservative justices argued for overruling *Roe*, using their new version of the fundamental-rights doctrine. In his dissenting opinion, Chief Justice Rehnquist cited to *Michael H.* as authority for the modern-conservative restatement of Cardozo's "so-rooted-in-the-traditions-and-conscience-of-our-people" language.[69] For Rehnquist, neither the category of fundamental rights that the Court had recognized nor "the historical traditions of the American people" revealed a right to terminate one's pregnancy.[70] Justice Scalia offered similar reasons for dissenting, concluding, consistent with *Bowers* and *Michael H.*, that the "right to an abortion" was not "in" the Constitution, and society had not traditionally protected a woman's decision to terminate a pregnancy.

> The issue is whether [the power of a woman to abort her unborn child] is a liberty protected by the Constitution of the United States. I am sure it is not. I reach that conclusion not because of anything so exalted as my views concerning the "concept of existence, of meaning, of the universe, and of the mystery of human life." Rather, I reach it . . . because of two simple facts: (1) the Constitution says absolutely nothing about it, and (2) the longstanding traditions of American society have permitted it to be legally proscribed.[71]

In his concurring opinion, Justice Blackmun, who had authored the *Roe* opinion twenty years earlier, disapproved of the modern-conservative interpretation of the Court's due-process cases. It "establish[ed] only a laundry list of particular rights," which Blackmun called a "constricted view . . . reinforced by . . . exclusive reliance on tradition as a source of fundamental rights."[72]

Blackmun would find "a right to terminate [a] pregnancy in its early stages"[73] within the category of rights the Court had deemed fundamental. But he would construe the category more broadly than modern-conservative "tradition" allowed.[74] He criticized the modern-conservative failure to construe the Court's "personal-liberty cases" as establishing a "principled account of how these particular rights [were] grounded in a more general right of privacy."[75] Despite his accurate description of modern conservatism's restrictive view of basic liberties, Blackmun's argument belied his own reliance on the Court's fundamental-rights doctrine, and its "list of rights"—rights different than those modern conservatives would have the Constitution protect, to be sure, but a list nonetheless. Justice Blackmun clarified what the modern-liberal and modern-conservative fundamental-rights doctrines offered: dueling laundry lists of fundamental rights—one of varying specifications of a more general liberty interest, and another of already-protected social practices.

NOTES

1. *Michael H.*, 491 U.S. at 132 (O'Connor, J., concurring).
2. *Id.* (citing *Poe*, 367 U.S. at 542, 544 (Harlan, J., dissenting)).
3. *Id.*
4. *See* Justice Antonin Scalia, "Originalism, The Lesser Evil," in *Judges on Judging*, ed. David M. O'Brien (Thousand Oaks: CQ Press, 2004), 209–217.
5. *See* Bruce Ledewitz, "Justice Harlan's Law and Democracy," *Journal of Law & Politics* 373, no. 20 (Summer 2004): 426. Ledewitz compares Harlan the II's and Scalia's approaches to law and democracy, noting that "Justice Scalia implies that trying to do the best thing is the 'common-law method' of judging and that it is an illegitimate approach."
6. Robert H. Bork, *Slouching towards Gomorrah* (New York: HarperCollins, 1996), 117.
7. *See, e.g.*, *Cruzan v. Director, Missouri Dept. of Health*, 497 U.S. 261, 294 (1990) (Scalia, J., concurring); *see also Reno v. Flores*, 507 U.S. 292 (1993).
8. *See Cruzan*, 497 U.S. at 294 (1990) (Scalia, J., concurring).
9. *Flores*, 507 U.S. at 302 (citing *Bowers v. Hardwick*, 478 U. S. 186, 191 (1986); quoting *Collins v. Harker Heights*, 503 U.S. 115, 125 (1992) (internal quotation marks omitted)).
10. *Id.* at 303.
11. 505 U.S. 833 (1992).
12. 521 U.S. 702 (1997).
13. 505 U.S. at 844
14. *Id.*
15. *Id.* at 845.
16. *Id.* at 844.
17. *Id.* at 846.

18. *Id.*
19. *Id.* at 847 (internal quotation marks omitted).
20. 274 U.S. 357 (1927) (Brandeis, J., concurring).
21. *Id.* at 373.
22. 505 U.S. at 847.
23. *See* 381 U.S. at 502 (White, J., concurring) (citing *Prince v. Massachusetts*, 321 U.S. 158, 166 (1944)).
24. 505 U.S. at 847–848 (*citing Loving v. Virginia*, 388 U.S. 1, 12 (1967); *Turner v. Safley*, 482 U.S. 78, 94–99 (1987); *Carey v. Population Services International*, 431 U.S. 678, 684–686 (1977); *Griswold v. Connecticut*, 381 U.S. 479, 481–482 (1965); *Pierce v. Society of Sisters*, 268 U.S. 510, 534–535 (1925); *Meyer v. Nebraska*, 262 U.S. 390, 399–403 (1923)).
25. *Id.* at 847 (citing *Adamson v. California*, 332 U.S. 46, 68–92 (1947) (Black, J., dissenting)).
26. *Id.* (citing *Michael H.*, 491 U.S. at 127–128).
27. *Id.* at 848.
28. *Id.* at 849.
29. *Id.* at 848–849 (quoting *Poe*, 367 U.S. at 548 (Harlan, J., dissenting)).
30. *Id.*
31. *Id.* at 849.
32. *Id.* at 853.
33. *Id.* at 853.
34. *Id.* at 851.
35. *See Lawrence v. Texas*, 539 U.S. 558, 588 (2003) (Scalia, J., dissenting).
36. *Casey*, 505 U.S.at 852–853.
37. *Id.* at 851.
38. *Id.*
39. *Id.* at 852.
40. *Id.* at 853.
41. *Id.* at 983 (Scalia. J., dissenting).
42. *Casey*, 505 U.S. at 852.
43. *Id.*
44. *Id.*
45. *Id.* at 878.
46. *Id.* at 873.
47. *Id.* at 870–873.
48. *Id.* at 877–879.
49. *Id.* at 879.
50. *Id.*
51. *Id.* at 870 ("Although we must overrule those parts of [*Thornburgh v. American College of Obstetricians and Gynecologists*], 476 U.S. 747 (1986) and [*Akron v. Akron Center for Reproductive Health, Inc.*, 462 U.S. 416 (1983) (*Akron I*)] which, in our view, are inconsistent with *Roe*'s statement that the State has a legitimate interest in promoting the life or potential life of the unborn, *see infra*, at 882–883, the central premise of those cases represents an unbroken commitment by this Court to the essential holding of *Roe*. It is that premise which we reaffirm today.").

52. *Id.* at 873–874 (*citing Anderson v. Celebrezze*, 460 U.S. 780, 788 (1983); *Norman v. Reed*, 502 U.S. 279 (1992) (involving state ballot regulations and the right to vote)).

53. *Id.* at 877.

54. *Id.* at 874; *see Slaughterhouse*, 83 U.S. at 114 (Bradley, J., dissenting) ("The right of a State to regulate the conduct of its citizens is undoubtedly a very broad and extensive one, and not to be lightly restricted. But there are certain fundamental rights which this right of regulation cannot infringe. It may prescribe the manner of their exercise, but it cannot subvert the rights themselves.").

55. *Id.* at 878–879.

56. *Id.* at 853.

57. *Id.* at 854–869.

58. *Id.* at 982 (Scalia, J., dissenting).

59. *Id.* at 844.

60. *Id.* at 861–864.

61. *See, e.g., Hollingsworth v. Perry*, No. 12-144, March 26, 2013, 37:23-41:23 (during oral argument, Justice Scalia suggested that he could not decide the case unless counsel could tell him "the date when the Constitution changes[.]"); *see* Jennifer Senior, "In Conversation: Antonin Scalia," https://nymag.com/news/features/antonin-scalia-2013-10/ (Answering a question about his commitment to originalism as a philosophy, Scalia said, "I don't know when I came to that view. I've always had it, as far as I know. Words have meaning. And their meaning doesn't change. I mean, the notion that the Constitution should simply, by decree of the Court, mean something that it didn't mean when the people voted for it—frankly, you should ask the other side the question! How did they *ever* get there?").

62. 505 U.S. at 862.

63. *Id.* at 861–862.

64. *Id.* at 863.

65. *Id.* at 863–864.

66. *Id.* at 864.

67. *Id.*

68. *Id.*

69. *Id.* at 952 (Rehnquist, J., dissenting).

70. *Id.* at 951–953.

71. *Id.* at 980 (Scalia, J., dissenting).

72. *Id.* at 940 (Blackmun, J., concurring).

73. *Id.* at 844.

74. *Id.* at 923–924 (Blackmun, J., concurring).

75. *Id.* at 940.

Chapter 11

The Guideposts of History, Tradition, and Practice

Five years later, in *Glucksberg v. Washington*, the Court answered the question "whether [the State of] Washington's prohibition against 'causing' or 'aiding' a suicide offend[ed] the Fourteenth Amendment to the United States Constitution."[1] Chief Justice Rehnquist authored the Court's opinion and applied the modern-conservative method. Repeating *Michael H.*'s misquotation of Cardozo and citing to *Palko*, Rehnquist described the method's reliance on "so-rooted" social practices as the Court's "established method of substantive-due-process analysis[.]"[2] He explained its "two primary features."[3] "First," he claimed, "[W]e have regularly observed that the Due Process Clause specially protects those fundamental rights and liberties which are, objectively, deeply rooted in this Nation's history and tradition[.]"[4] Second, the Court "required in substantive-due-process cases a careful description of the asserted fundamental liberty interest."[5] The "Nation's history, legal traditions, and practices thus provide[d] the crucial guideposts for responsible decision making" about the status of these carefully described interests.[6]

This approach to fundamental rights, Rehnquist said, "tends to rein in the subjective elements that are necessarily present in due process judicial review."[7] "[E]stablishing a threshold requirement—that a challenged state action implicate a fundamental right—before requiring more than a reasonable relation to a legitimate state interest to justify it . . . avoids the need for complex balancing of competing interests in every case."[8] And, as in *Bowers* and *Michael H.*, whether an asserted liberty interest met the "threshold requirement" depended on its status when evaluated "[a]gainst th[e] backdrop of history, tradition, and practice[.]"[9] This required a survey of the States' historical treatment of the crime of suicide and assistance in committing it.[10]

Like Justice White had done in *Bowers* and Scalia in *Michael H.*, Rehnquist began with an exegesis of laws in the American States pertaining to suicide. "We begin," Rehnquist cited to *Moore*, "as we do in all due process cases, by examining our Nation's history, legal traditions, and practices."[11] Echoing *Bowers*'s and *Michael H.*'s emphasis on the age of the challenged law, the opinion noted, "It has always been a crime to assist a suicide in the State of Washington."[12] For eight pages, it explored the history of the prohibition against assisting suicide in thirteenth-century English common law and in early American colonial laws, the first American state and territorial prohibitions,[13] and "recent" reexaminations and reaffirmations of the States' "deeply rooted . . . assisted suicide bans[.]"[14] "[I]n almost every State," the opinion observed, "it is a crime to assist a suicide."[15]

The level of generality at which to describe the liberty interest was again critical. The court from which the appeal was taken had analyzed whether "there [was] a liberty interest in determining the timing and manner of one's death."[16] In the case before the Court, "respondents assert[ed] a 'liberty to choose how to die' and a right to 'control of one's final days[.]'"[17] Against the backdrop of history, tradition, and practice, Rehnquist invoked the modern-conservative requirement that Scalia had introduced in *Michael H.*—what Rehnquist called the Court's "tradition of carefully formulating the interest at stake in substantive-due-process cases."[18] Noting that the "Washington statute at issue in this case prohibit[ed] 'aid[ing] another person to attempt suicide'," and following *Bowers*'s example, Rehnquist concluded, "[T]hus, the question before us is whether the 'liberty' specially protected by the Due Process Clause includes a right to commit suicide which itself includes a right to assistance in doing so."[19]

With the asserted "right" thus construed, the opinion answered easily whether it was included in the fundamental-rights category, or, as Rehnquist put it in modern-conservative terms, "whether this asserted right has any place in our Nation's traditions."[20] "[W]e are confronted," he wrote, "with a consistent and almost universal tradition that has long rejected the asserted right, and continues explicitly to reject it today[.]"[21] Rehnquist punctuated this conclusion with Scalia's observation. "The mere novelty of such a claim[,]" he said, "is reason enough to doubt that substantive due process sustains it."[22] Laws against assisting suicide were old and plentiful; therefore, Washington State's regulation of individuals' choices, made within the doctor-patient relationship, regarding the circumstances and timing of their own impending deaths, did not implicate the due-process guarantee. And, consistent with the Court's habit of disregarding as a source of restraint the details of the discrete controversy before it, Rehnquist saw a potential victory for the respondents in this case not as a defeat for the State of Washington, but rather for almost all of the States at once. "To hold for respondents," he warned, "we would have to reverse centuries of legal doctrine and practice, and strike down the considered policy choice of almost every State."[23]

The application of the modern-conservative method in *Glucksberg* left the same glaring analytic deficiency that it did in *Michael H.* and the *Casey* dissents. The old law at issue in *Michael H.* was enacted prior to the existence of reliable paternity testing. Similarly, by the time of *Casey*, developments in medical technology and treatment arguably made abortive procedures at least as safe as other regularly performed medical procedures. *Glucksberg*, too, presented an issue arising within the doctor-patient relationship, influenced by modern medical technology and reflecting a developing ethos within the medical profession. Foreclosing the unanticipated, the modern-conservative method ignored these issues, and reduced the tradition of reasoned judgment to "rules fixed in the past . . . deny[ing] every quality of the law but its age . . . render[ing] it incapable of progress or improvement."[24] Except, of course, through democratic processes in the States—a quintessentially modern conservative position. The federal constitution afforded those protections against the States to which a federal court determined the States were willing to accede.

The respondents invoked the Court's liberty-centric fundamental-rights cases, but Rehnquist easily dismissed their reliance on this precedent.[25] They argued that it "reflect[ed] a general tradition of self-sovereignty" in the Court's Fourteenth Amendment jurisprudence.[26] Rehnquist acknowledged "the broad, individualistic principles" that the Court's "liberty jurisprudence" reflected. But he insisted—contrary to Justice Kennedy's approach that had shone in *Casey* and would soon dominate the jurisprudence—the rights the Court had recognized as fundamental were "not simply deduced from abstract concepts of personal autonomy."[27] The capacious language of *Casey*'s mystery-of-human-life passage, he explained, was an apt description of liberties in the fundamental-rights category, but it was not the reason for their inclusion.[28] As *Michael H.* had taught, discerning whether a social practice was "deeply rooted" and, therefore, in the fundamental-rights category required only a survey of the States' laws pertaining to the asserted interest described as a social practice.

> That many of the rights and liberties protected by the Due Process Clause sound in personal autonomy does not warrant the sweeping conclusion that any and all important, intimate, and personal decisions are so protected[.] . . . The history of the law's treatment of assisted suicide in this country has been and continues to be one of the rejection of nearly all efforts to permit it. That being the case, our decisions lead us to conclude that the asserted 'right' to assistance in committing suicide is not a fundamental liberty interest protected by the Due Process Clause.[29]

***

The "substantive sphere of liberty"[30] was not so permeable as to allow to pass into it any and every "right" derived from personal autonomy. This was a legitimate and important conclusion. As the great sage had taught, the common-law tradition counseled moderate and cautious developments in due-process cases. Attention to the details defining the contending interests a case presented, and careful and critical analyses of the justifications offered to vindicate them, circumscribed these developments. The trajectory of the twentieth-century liberty-centric cases, however, showed that modern liberalism had abandoned the tradition. It began with penumbras emanating from Bill of Rights provisions, became a category of fundamental rights, expanded into a realm of personal liberty which the government may not enter, and reached its apex recognizing within this realm those decisions and actions implicating personal autonomy and dignity, originating in the zone of conscience and belief, and shaping one's own conception of one's spiritual imperatives and place in society. The modern-conservative version of the Nation's history and tradition supplied the check on claims of such breadth.

But it was merely a reaction to the overreach—a desperate attempt to salvage some vestige of restraint in an institution wading deeper each decade into a rising tide of social controversies and playing an inappropriate role in implementing responsive policies. This was a *political* contest with much at stake, and at the Court a polarization had occurred during the second half of the twentieth century. At one end, liberals championed freedom, autonomy, and dignity; at the other, conservatives defended against federal interference the States' rights to adopt and enforce social policies aimed at preserving a traditional way of life. The former's disregard for the constraints inherent to the tradition of reasoned judgment made its overreach possible, while the latter's wholesale rejection of the tradition took the form of a bald and dishonest co-option of it. When modern conservatism invoked "our Nation's history and tradition," it referred to a collection of sovereign States free of the obligation to honor the values the post-Reconstruction federal Union enshrined in the Fourteenth Amendment. This was not respect for the basic values *underlying* American society, but rather maintenance of, and rejection of challenges to, the values *of* society in the States where claims to liberty against government originated.

As broken from the tradition as its liberal counterpart, this method was as suspect as the ever-expanding and increasingly inclusive zone of substantive liberties. It used *Bowers*'s reframing of the liberty interest a litigant presented; exploited *Moore*'s conflation of the *Duncan* distinction; adopted *Moore*'s stunted conception of Harlan's history and tradition; and then co-opted Harlan's *Griswold* concurrence to legitimize it. Repeatedly misquoting Cardozo, it conflated his description of principles of justice validating federal judicial review of state legislation ". . . with deeply rooted social practices."

Michael H. formalized the *Bowers* inquiry, insisting that a liberty interest asserted as worthy of constitutional protection be carefully and specifically described as a social practice. The method ended up here, in *Glucksberg*, evaluating a carefully described social practice against the historic guideposts of American society, portraying itself as the guardian of tradition and defender of democracy.[31]

NOTES

1. *Glucksberg v. Washington*, 521 U.S. 702, 705–706 (1997).
2. *Id.*
3. *Id.*
4. *Id.* at 720–721 (internal quotation marks omitted).
5. *Id.* at 721 (internal quotation marks omitted).
6. *Id.* (internal quotation marks omitted).
7. *Id.* at 722.
8. *Id.*
9. *Id.* at 719.
10. *Id.*
11. *Id.* at 710.
12. *Id.* at 706.
13. *Id.* at 711–719.
14. *Id.* at 716.
15. *Id.* at 710.
16. *Id.* at 722.
17. *Id.*
18. *Id.* at 722.
19. *Id.* at 723.
20. *Id.*
21. *Id.*
22. *Id.* (citing *Reno v. Flores*, 507 U.S. 292, 303 (1993)) (internal quotation marks omitted).
23. *Id.*
24. *Hurtado*, 110 U.S. at 529.
25. 521 U.S. at 724.
26. *Id.* at 724–725 (internal quotation marks omitted). The respondents pointed to *Cruzan v. Director, Missouri Dept. of Health*, 497 U.S. 261 (1990), where the Court "assume[d] . . . a competent person['s] . . . right to refuse lifesaving hydration and nutrition." They urged the Court to recognize that "the principle behind recognizing the patient's liberty" in *Cruzan* "applie[d] at least as strongly" to the issue in *Glucksberg*.
27. *Id.* at 725.
28. *Id.* at 726–727.
29. *Id.* at 727–728.

30. See *Casey*, 505 U.S. at 848.

31. *See* 521 U.S. at 735 ("Throughout the Nation, Americans are engaged in an earnest and profound debate about the morality, legality, and practicality of physician-assisted suicide. Our holding permits this debate to continue, as it should in a democratic society.").

Chapter 12

The Tradition Is a Living Thing

Writing separately in *Glucksberg*, Justice Souter began, "My understanding of unenumerated rights . . . avoids the absolutist failing of many older cases without embracing the opposite pole of equating reasonableness with past practice described at a very specific level."[1] He dismissed both the modern-liberal fundamental-rights doctrine and the modern-conservative reaction to it. These were recent innovations, disconnected from the Court's "sustained" post-Reconstruction "enterprise" of "interpretation of the word[] 'liberty' . . . as used in Due Process Clauses."[2]

He invoked the concept.

"That understanding begins with a concept of ordered liberty comprising a continuum of rights to be free from arbitrary impositions and purposeless restraints[.]"[3] Evaluating claims to liberty along this continuum, the "Court generally describ[ed] the due process criterion in converse terms of reasonableness or arbitrariness."[4] This "standard," Souter observed, was "fairly traceable to Justice Bradley's dissent in the *Slaughterhouse Cases*, in which he said that a person's right to choose a calling was an element of liberty . . . and declared that the liberty . . . protected by due process was not truly recognized if [it] may be arbitrarily assailed."[5]

He acknowledged the concept's origins.

> Before ratification of the Fourteenth Amendment, substantive constitutional review resting on a theory of unenumerated rights occurred largely in the state courts applying state constitutions that commonly contained either due process clauses like that of the Fifth Amendment (and later the Fourteenth) or the textual antecedents of such clauses, repeating Magna Carta's guarantee of "the law of the land." On the basis of such clauses, or of general principles untethered to

> specific constitutional language, state courts evaluated the constitutionality of a wide range of statutes.[6]

He traced the concept's genealogy.

He gave examples of antebellum state cases that applied it, and then turned to antebellum federal jurisprudence, where the "Court anticipated the developments that would presage both the Civil War and the ratification of the Fourteenth Amendment."[7] In these cases, the court "ma[de] it clear on several occasions that it too had no doubt of the judiciary's power to strike down legislation that conflicted with important but unenumerated principles of American government."[8] Here was the concept's lifeblood, evident in early-American federal jurisprudence, and in state jurisprudence long before *Hurtado.*

The tradition counseled that with this judicial power came the obligation to exercise meaningful restraint. For even while declaring its confidence that the judicial power could "invalidate what it might find inconsistent with rights of liberty and property," the Supreme Court "[i]n most such instances, after declaring [this] power . . . nevertheless went on to uphold the legislative Acts under review."[9] But, still a half century before the War, "the Court went further."[10] In *Fletcher v. Peck*,[11] it struck down a State's unreasonable interference with property. "[T]he Georgia Legislature [had] . . . rescind[ed] . . . a sale of public land . . . reclaim[ing] title for the State, and . . . depriv[ing] subsequent, good-faith purchasers of property conveyed by the original grantees."[12] Chief Justice John Marshall "rested the invalidation" of the statute "on alternative sources of authority[,]" including "general principles which are common to our free institutions[.]"[13] By this, Souter explained, "Chief Justice Marshall meant that a simple deprivation of property by the State could not be an authentically 'legislative' Act."[14] This was, of course, the same justice who had brought into jurisprudential consciousness, earlier in the same decade, the institutional prerogative of federal-judicial review of Congressional legislation.[15] Not every legislative act was legitimate law.

"The most telling early example of such review" by the Nation's highest court, Souter explained, was one that no justice on the *Slaughterhouse* Court had mentioned—"the case that the [Fourteenth] Amendment would in due course overturn, *Dred Scott v. Sanford*[.]"[16] The decision was "textually based on a Due Process Clause (in the Fifth Amendment, applicable to the federal government) and it was in reliance on that Clause's protection of property that the Court invalidated the Missouri Compromise."[17] As for the legitimacy of *Dred Scott*'s "substantive protection of an owner's property in a slave taken to the territories[,]" Souter said, "[t]he ensuing judgment of history needs no recounting here."[18] Following the ratification of the Fourteenth Amendment and Justice Bradley's *Slaughterhouse* analysis, "opinions comparable to those that preceded *Dred Scott* expressed willingness to review legislative action for consistency with the Due Process Clause even as they upheld the laws in question."[19] *Dred Scott* had disrupted an otherwise consistent development of the common-law due-process tradition in federal jurisprudence, and the Fourteenth Amendment exposed and corrected the mistake. He recounted the concept's twentieth-century history.

When *Allgeyer* initiated the *Lochner* Era, the due-process "theory became serious . . . offer[ing] a substantive interpretation of 'liberty,' that in the aftermath of the . . . Era ha[d] been scaled back in some respects, expanded in others, and never repudiated in principle."[20] The *Lochner*-Era Court invalidated state legislation interfering with "Fourteenth Amendment liberty to contract," concluding that the Amendment protected "the right of the citizen to be free . . . to pursue any livelihood or avocation . . . and for that purpose to enter into all contracts which may be proper, necessary and essential[.]"[21] The court in *Allgeyer* had articulated what Souter called an "unobjectionable principle"—that "[w]hen and how far [the State's police] power may be legitimately exercised with regard to these subjects must be left for determination to each case as it arises."[22] Despite the court's perfunctory invocation of the principle, "what followed for a season was, in the realm of economic legislation, the echo of *Dred Scott*."[23] "[F]amous now for striking down as arbitrary various sorts of economic regulations that post-New Deal courts have uniformly thought constitutionally sound," the *Lochner* Era was suspect because "while the cases . . . routinely invoked a correct standard of constitutional arbitrariness review, they harbored the spirit of *Dred Scott* in their absolutist implementation of the standard they espoused."[24] One might level this very criticism at the Court's post-*Griswold* liberty-centric cases, notwithstanding Justice Douglas's declining in *Griswold* the invitation to follow *Lochner*.[25]

Even before the cases that characterized the *Lochner* Era "had been repudiated, . . . the more durable precursors of modern substantive due process[,]" *Meyer* and *Pierce*, "were reaffirming this Court's obligation to conduct arbitrariness review."[26] In these cases, "the Court invoked precedent from the *Slaughterhouse Cases* through *Adkins* . . . without referring to any specific guarantee of the Bill of Rights."[27] This was the point that Justice Douglas had ignored, when in *Griswold* he mischaracterized both *Meyer* and *Pierce* as identifying rights within the penumbral emanation of the First Amendment.[28] Like Justice Harlan, Souter saw that *Meyer* and *Pierce* illustrated common-law arbitrariness review, effectuating the principle that Cardozo articulated in *Palko*: "[E]ven in the field of substantive rights and duties the legislative judgment, if oppressive and arbitrary, may be overridden by the courts."[29] *Meyer* and *Pierce* thus connected the pre-*Lochner* federal judiciary's obligation to conduct arbitrariness review to its post-*Lochner* redemption, despite the forty-year interposition of "the deviant economic due process cases."[30]

With *Meyer* and *Pierce* making this connection, "two further opinions took the major steps . . . lead[ing] to the" concept's modern manifestation.[31] The first, *Skinner v. Oklahoma*,[32] although "about equal protection," was significant for the Court's emphasis on the "'fundamental' nature of individual choice about procreation."[33] This "foreshadowed not only the later prominence of procreation as a subject of liberty protection, but [also] the corresponding standard of 'strict scrutiny,' in th[e] Court's Fourteenth Amendment law."[34] *Skinner* had "suggested, as a gloss on [the] standard of arbitrariness, a judicial obligation to scrutinize any impingement on such an important interest with heightened care."[35] "In so doing, it suggested a point that Justice Harlan would develop [in] . . . [t]he second major opinion leading to the modern doctrine[,]" *Poe v. Ullman*.[36] Harlan's reasoned judgment in *Poe* exemplified "that the kind and degree of justification a sensitive judge would demand of a State would depend on the importance of the interest being asserted by the individual."[37] "In the face of [an] interest in liberty sufficiently important to be judged 'fundamental,'" *Poe* taught, "a State may not rest on threshold rationality or a presumption of constitutionality, but may prevail only on the ground of an interest sufficiently compelling to place within the realm of the reasonable a refusal to recognize the individual right asserted."[38]

Although the claims at issue here in *Glucksberg* "arouse[d] the skepticism of those who [found] the Due Process Clause an unduly vague or oxymoronic warrant for judicial review of substantive state law," this two-hundred-year tradition revealed "the persistence of substantive due process review in [the Court's] cases" and "point[ed] to the legitimacy of the modern justification for such judicial review found in Harlan's dissent in *Poe*[.]"[39]

> For two centuries American courts, and for much of that time this Court, have thought it necessary to provide some degree of review over the substantive content of legislation under constitutional claims of textual breadth. The obligation was understood before *Dred Scott* and has continued after the repudiation of *Lochner*'s progeny[.][40]

> This enduring tradition of American constitutional practice is . . . nothing more than what is required by the judicial authority and obligation to construe constitutional text and review legislation for conformity to that text.[41]

> The text of the Due Process Clause . . . imposes nothing less than an obligation to give substantive content to the words "liberty" and "due process of law."[42]

***

Souter focused on Harlan's *Poe* example, which offered three lessons "point[ing] to [the Court's] responsibilities today."[43] "Respect for the tradition of substantive due process review itself" was the first. The obligation to perform constitutional arbitrariness review was "deeply rooted in reason and in the compelling traditions of the legal profession."[44] The tradition imposed "limits" on judicial discretion "derived from considerations that are fused in the whole nature of [the] judicial process."[45] Here, in *Glucksberg*, the duty arose to scrutinize with particular care the State's justification for infringing the respondents' liberty, only if the value to which their claim appealed was "truly deserving [of] constitutional stature[.]"[46] The common-law judge "was bound to confine the values . . . recogniz[ed] to . . . those exemplified by the traditions from which [the Nation] developed, or revealed by contrast with the traditions from which it broke."[47] Where such values were at stake, "the State's asserted interest . . . was not immune to distinctions turning (at least potentially) on the precise purpose being pursued and the collateral consequences of the means chosen[.]"[48] The liberty-centric and modern-conservative approaches to fundamental rights mistakenly treated as the sole and dispositive question what was properly the initial inquiry in the common-law tradition of arbitrariness review.

Poe's second lesson was the restraint that Harlan demonstrated—a "reminder that the business of such review is not the identification of extratextual absolutes[,] but a scrutiny of a legislative resolution (perhaps unconscious) of clashing principles, each quite possibly worthy in and of itself, but each to be weighed within the history of our values as a people."[49] This point "implicitly addressed those cases . . . that are now condemned with virtual unanimity as disastrous mistakes of substantive due process review."[50] The "judicial task" of arbitrariness review was not to determine which liberty interests, although unenumerated, were nevertheless fundamental constitutional rights. It was "not a deduction from some first premise[,] . . . [but] a comparison of the relative strengths of opposing claims[,]" informed by the concept of ordered liberty.[51] "Thus informed, judicial review . . . ha[d] no warrant to substitute one reasonable resolution of the contending positions for another, but authority to supplant the balance already struck between the contenders when it falls outside the realm of the reasonable."[52] After all, Souter observed, "constitutional review, not judicial lawmaking, is a court's business here."[53] This illuminated just how wrong were both the Court's statutory holding in *Roe* and the modern-conservative practice of identifying social norms the Court should prevent society from "lightly casting aside."[54]

The due-process guarantee was a bulwark against arbitrary legislation. "Only if this standard point[ed] against the statute c[ould] the individual claimant be said to have a constitutional right."[55] The fundamental-rights doctrine—both the modern-liberal and conservative versions—focused not on the rights of individual claimants, but on unenumerated rights as abstract propositions. Whether described as aspects of a general interest in privacy or specified as historic social practices, the category of fundamental rights—the zone, realm, substantive sphere, or dimension of personal liberty—contained reifications of discrete claims that litigants brought to the Court, estranged from their factual context and without regard to the state interests ostensibly justifying their impingement.[56] "Precision in terminology," Souter counseled, "favors reserving the label 'right' for instances in which the individual's liberty interest actually trumps the government's countervailing interests; only then does the individual have anything legally enforceable as against the state's attempt at regulation."[57] Contrary to the Court's post-*Griswold* absolutist enterprise of identifying (or, in its modern-conservative manifestation, denying) unenumerated fundamental rights, the common-law due-process tradition was an as-applied endeavor, reserved for discrete cases and controversies and limited to review for arbitrariness.

Poe's third lesson was instructive for its "explicit attention to detail that is no less essential to the intellectual discipline of substantive due process review than an understanding of the basic need to account for the two sides in the controversy and to respect legislation within the zone of reasonableness."[58] "This approach," Souter explained, "calls for a court to assess the relative 'weights' or dignities of the contending interests."[59] *Poe* "reminds us," he said, "more by its example than by any particular statement of constitutional method . . . that the process of substantive review by reasoned judgment is one of close criticism going to the details of the opposing interests and to their relationships with the historically recognized principles that lend them weight or value."[60]

"The same insistence on exactitude[,]" he continued, "lies behind questions, in current terminology, about the proper level of generality at which to analyze claims and counterclaims[.]"[61] "For here," he said, "we are faced with an individual claim *not* to a right on the part of just *anyone* to help *anyone else* commit suicide under *any* circumstances[.]"[62] This case was no more about "a right to commit suicide with another's assistance" than *Poe* was about the "right to use birth control." It was about the concept of ordered liberty. The Court was "faced with an individual claim . . . to the right of a narrow class under a set of limited circumstances."[63] And this claim to liberty was met, on the ordered side of the concept, with "the state's assertion" that recognizing the "rights of such narrow scope" for which the respondents sought protection would "jeopard[ize] . . . individuals whom the state may concededly protect through its regulations."[64]

> When identifying and assessing the competing interests of liberty and authority . . . the breadth of expression that a litigant or a judge selects in stating

the competing principles will have much to do with the outcome and may be dispositive.[65]

> Just as the results in substantive due process cases are tied to the selections of statements of the competing interests, the acceptability of the results is a function of the good reasons for the selections made.[66]

Poe again provided the example, where Justice Harlan "viewed it as essential to the plaintiffs' claimed right to use contraceptives that they sought to do so within the privacy of the martial bedroom."[67] This attention to the details of the context in which the claim arose "rescued [it] from a breadth that would have threatened all state regulation of contraception or intimate relations."[68] This constrained Harlan's judgment, and so the "right [he] . . . recognized in that case" pertained to married couples.[69] This was not because rights pertaining to extramarital intimacy were unimportant, nor because the Court would never recognize them. It was because liberties pertaining to nonmarital relations were not at issue in *Poe.* The litigants were married couples wanting to use contraception within this relationship who claimed the State inadequately justified its intruding into their marriage.

At the same time, this detail served a "complementary function . . . allow[ing] the interest to be valued as an aspect of a broader liberty to be free from all unreasonable intrusions into the privacy of the home and the family life within it[.]"[70] Framed this way, the weight of the individual claim became apparent, not in light of the historic practices of society or of reifications belonging to a category labeled "fundamental," but against the background of "constitutional provisions such as the Third and Fourth Amendments, in prior decisions of the Court involving unreasonable intrusions into the home and family life, and in the then-prevailing status of marriage as the sole lawful locus of intimate relations."[71] The claim to liberty in *Poe* rested at the interface between fact and law, where its weight was "at its peak" because it was narrow enough to constrain the common-law judge to recognizing only a right to which the facts in the record of the case pointed, and simultaneously broad enough to appeal to "basic values that underlie our society."[72]

The claim in *Poe* was neither that the State interfered with an abstract fundamental right to personal autonomy, nor that the social practice of using contraception was an unenumerated right the Constitution protected. Juxtaposed against these deviant approaches to due-process review, the value of *Poe*'s third lesson was unambiguously clear.

> [T]he usual thinking of the common law is suspicious of the all or nothing analysis that tends to produce legal petrification instead of an evolving boundary between the domains of old principles. Common-law method tends to

> pay respect . . . to detail, seeking to understand old principles afresh by new examples and new counterexamples. The tradition is a living thing, albeit one that moves by moderate steps carefully taken.[73]

Here, at the cutting edge of the American legal tradition, with the parties' claims properly presented for arbitrariness review, Justice Souter would evaluate Washington State's resolution of the clashing principles of order and liberty as specified in this particular controversy.

***

He began with the liberty side of the analysis. "[T]he argument supporting respondents' position[,]" he said, "progresses through three steps of increasing forcefulness."[74] First, the respondents' argument "emphasize[d] the decriminalization of suicide" in the State of Washington.[75] Contrary to Rehnquist's opinion, Justice Souter did "not understand [respondents'] argument to rest on any assumption that rights either to suicide or to assistance in committing it are historically based as such."[76] Instead, the "[r]espondents . . . acknowledge[d] the prohibition of each historically, but rel[ied] on the fact that to a substantial extent the State ha[d] repudiated that history."[77] Citing to *Poe*, Souter explained, "Reliance on this fact is sanctioned under the standard that looks not only to the tradition retained, but to society's occasional choices to reject traditions of the legal past."[78]

The fact of decriminalization was in no way dispositive of how the Court should weight the respondents' claim to liberty. "Decriminalization" did not "imply the existence of a constitutional liberty interest in suicide[.]"[79] The reasons for it, "after all, may have had more to do with difficulties of law enforcement than with a shift in the value ascribed to life in various circumstances or in the perceived legitimacy of taking one's own."[80] The fact of decriminalization, instead, "open[ed] the door to claims . . . to be accorded one of the options open to those with different, traditionally cognizable claims to autonomy in deciding how their bodies and minds should be treated."[81] History was relevant to the inquiry, but its "principal significance . . . in the State of Washington [was] its repudiation of the old tradition to the extent of eliminating criminal suicide prohibitions."[82] This left "the criminality of [assisting suicide] open to questioning[.]"[83]

"The second step in the argument," he continued, "is to emphasize that the State's own act of decriminalization gives a freedom of choice much like the individual's option in recognized instances of bodily autonomy."[84] The respondents' argument picked up weight against the background of twentieth-century precedent in which a liberty interest in bodily integrity appeared. Nodding to Field and Bradley's reliance on state cases illustrating the tradition, and to the now-legendary common-law giant, Souter found a general description of this liberty interest in a 1914 New York State opinion of "then-Judge Cardozo," which said, "Every human being of adult years and sound mind has a right to determine what shall be done with his own body in relation to his medical needs."[85] Examples of this interest, specified as a right in discrete federal cases, "derive[d] from the common law of battery and include[d] the right to be free from medical invasions into the body."[86] Here at the end of the twentieth century, it was "settled now . . . that the Constitution place[d] limits on a State's right to interfere with a person's most basic decisions about . . . bodily integrity."[87] The Court had applied this principle in the contexts of "marital privacy and contraception, abortion, and personal control of medical treatment."[88] Recently, the Court had recognized the interest in "bodily integrity as underl[ying] the assumed right, good against the State, to require physicians to terminate artificial life support[.]"[89]

This appeal to the interest in bodily integrity intersected with the twentieth-century Court's awareness of the doctor-patient relationship as the locus of important personal decisions implicating it. Here, the abortion cases were "most telling[,]" as they recognized "the importance of bodily integrity and the concomitant tradition of medical assistance[.]"[90] There was no "fundamental right to abortion" as an aspect of a general "right to personal autonomy" with which States may not interfere, for the "State has a legitimate interest in discouraging abortion."[91] Even so, "the Court recognized a woman's right to a physician's counsel and care[,]" and this influenced the analysis of "the decision to abort potential life[,]" which might otherwise, like the decision at issue in *Glucksberg*, "be made irresponsibly and under the influence of others[.]"[92] Indeed, "Without physician assistance in abortion, the woman's right would have too often amounted to nothing more than a right to self-mutilation[;]" analogously, "without a physician to assist in the suicide of the dying, the patient's right will often be confined to crude methods of causing death, most shocking and painful to the decedent's survivors."[93]

The abortion cases were "only the most obvious illustration of [a] further point" placing the respondents' claim "within the accepted tradition of medical care in our society."[94] The Court had recognized, even before the abortion cases, "that the good physician is not just a mechanic of the human body whose services have no bearing on a person's moral choices, but one who does more than treat symptoms, one who ministers to the patient."[95] In *Griswold*, for example, it was significant that the law challenged there "operate[ed] directly on an intimate relation of husband and wife and their physician's role in one aspect of that relation[.]"[96] Making the point that Justice Douglas glossed over, Souter observed this was because of the "high value traditionally placed on the medical relationship[,]" in which the "physician . . . serv[ed] the whole person," a value "surely as apparent here as in the abortion cases[.]"[97] The patients here, Souter noted, claimed that "when the end is imminent, . . . the decision to end life is closest to decisions that are generally accepted as proper instances of exercising autonomy over one's own body."[98]

The resonance of their claim with these examples was evident not only in federal-constitutional law, but also in the "State's own law[.]"[99] Washington law "authorize[d] physicians to withdraw life-sustaining medical treatment and artificially delivered food and water" when a patient requested, even when doing so would "hasten death."[100] Physicians in Washington were allowed to "administer medication" to "alleviate anxiety and discomfort" associated with withdrawing such care, even when it would "hasten death even further."[101] And, Washington physicians "administered medication to patients in terminal conditions" for palliative purposes, "even when the medication [wa]s so powerful as to hasten death and the patient cho[se] to receive it with that understanding."[102] Together with federal-constitutional recognition of decisions pertaining to bodily integrity and autonomy, made within the physician-patient relationship, these aspects of the State's own laws placed respondents claim among those "instances in which the help of physicians is accepted as falling within the traditional norm."[103] The "moral judgment" underlying the claim "was implied by the State's . . . recognition[,]" in its own laws, "of the legitimacy of medical procedures necessarily hastening the moment of impending death."[104]

The third step in the argument emphasized that the claim respondents presented, narrowed by the details of the factual context in which the contending interests clashed, did not depend on "some broad principle" mutually exclusive with the State's countervailing interest "in discouraging suicide."[105] A common-law judge would be skeptical of such a broad claim, as it "would be subject to exceptions" if the State's interest "were to be recognized at all."[106] The claim here, however, was "that a patient facing imminent death, who anticipates physical suffering and indignity, and is capable of responsible and voluntary choice, should have a right to a physician's assistance in providing counsel and drugs to be administered by the patient to end life promptly."[107] It was based on the "traditional right to medical care and counsel, subject to . . . limiting conditions that support a strong analogy to rights of care in other situations in which medical counsel and assistance have been available as a matter of course."[108] The respondents' asserted interest was, like the claim in *Poe,* "broad enough to cover the claim at hand without being so broad as to be shot-through by exceptions."[109]

"The importance of the individual interest here," Souter concluded, "as within that class of certain interests demanding careful scrutiny of the State's contrary claim, cannot be gainsaid."[110] He turned to the ordered aspect of the analysis and the interests the State "ha[d] put forward to justify the

Washington law[.]"[111] The State asserted its interest in "protecting life generally, discouraging suicide even if knowing and voluntary, and protecting terminally ill patients from involuntary suicide and euthanasia, both voluntary and involuntary."[112]

Souter distinguished the first two "claims of justification[,]" which "oppose[d respondents'] claim . . . with a moral judgment[,]" from the third.[113] As Harlan taught in *Poe*, a controversial moral question suggested that the Court was no more qualified than the State in choosing among opposing views.[114] Similarly, the common-law analysis here need not "discuss the exact strengths of the first two claims of justification[,]" for the State's third claim "addresse[d] specific features of respondents'[,]" and was, therefore, useful to evaluating for arbitrariness the particular balance the State had struck between order and liberty, as applied here in *Glucksberg*.[115] This claim opposed the respondents' "with a recognized state interest in the protection of nonresponsible individuals and those who do not stand in relation either to death or to their physicians as do the patients whom respondents describe."[116]

Recognizing the respondents' interest as a right here, the State argued, would prevent it from exercising its undisputed authority to protect individuals without capacity to make knowing and responsible end-of-life decisions. The State asserted a legitimate interest in preventing mistakes about, and coercion of, individuals not similarly situatedto the respondents. Even "leaving aside" the difficulty "in coming to a clear concept of imminent death," mistakes might "result from inadequate palliative care or a terminal prognosis that turn[ed] out to be error[.]"[117] Moreover, "coercion or abuse [might] stem from the large medical bills that family members [could not] bear or unreimbursed hospitals decline[d] to shoulder."[118] Of equal concern, "doctors and perhaps others would abuse a limited freedom to aid suicides by yielding to the impulse to end another's suffering under conditions going beyond the narrow limits the respondents propose[d]."[119] Voluntary and involuntary instances of euthanasia might "result once doctors [were] authorized to prescribe lethal medication[,]" as "they might find it pointless to distinguish between patients who administer their own fatal drugs and those who wish not to[.]"[120] In light of these considerations, the State argued "that a progression would occur, obscuring the line between the ill and the dying, and between the responsible and the unduly influenced."[121]

The point of "restricting any right of assistance to physicians[,]" Justice Souter observed, was "to condition the right on an exercise of judgment by someone qualified to assess the patient's responsible capacity and detect the influence of those outside the medical relationship."[122] The State argued that for two reasons "dependence on the vigilance of physicians w[ould] not be enough."[123] First, the requirement implicit in the respondents' claim, that a physician to a dying patient ensure that the patient's end-of-life decision was "knowing and voluntary[,]" would be more difficult to meet than workable limits with respect to "other recently recognized due process rights" in the physician-patient context.[124] The State offered *Poe* as one example, where it was significant to Harlan's recognition of the right claimed that it "posed no threat to the State's capacity to regulate contraceptives in other ways that were assumed at the time of *Poe* to be legitimate."[125] The State pointed also to the "trimester measurements of *Roe* and the viability determination in *Casey*" as far more certain than the "knowing and responsible mind" of a patient facing imminent death, which was "much harder to assess."[126] Second, the difficulty of assessing a patient's state of mind "could become greater" if "physicians simply [were] not . . . assiduous to preserve the line" between qualified and unqualified patients.[127] This was "within the realm of plausibility," for doctors "have compassion, and those who would be willing to assist in suicide at all might be the most susceptible to the wishes of a patient, whether the patient was technically quite responsible or not."[128] This compassion "for those who suffer [might] obscure the distinction between those who ask for death and those . . . unable to request it."[129]

The State's argument thus cast doubt, not on the respondents' claim that they asserted an important liberty interest, but on the consequences of the Court recognizing the interest as a right enforceable against the State in this controversy. "The case for the slippery slope," Justice Souter said, "is fairly made out here[.]"[130] The State presented "a plausible case that the right claimed would not be readily containable by reference to facts about the mind that are matters of difficult judgment, or by gatekeepers who are subject to temptation, noble or not."[131] The State argued, persuasively, "that respondents' claim is not as narrow as it sounds, simply because no recognition of the interest they assert could be limited to vindicating those interests and affecting no others."[132] Recognizing the respondents' claim as a right against the State "would entail consequences that the State could, without doubt legitimately act to prevent."[133] The means the State chose here impacted the respondents' liberty, but did so in pursuit of a legitimate end involving other persons "the State could concededly protect through its regulations"—individuals actually without capacity to make responsible and knowing choices to end their lives and yet susceptible to plausible errors in judgment that those charged with their care and assistance might make. "The legitimacy of [the State's] action," Souter concluded, "to deny a physician the option to aid any but the knowing and responsible is beyond question."[134]

This did not end the inquiry, however, for the "[r]espondents propose[d] an answer to all this[.]"[135] The State, they argued, could adopt means that would accomplish its ends without infringing the liberty they sought to exercise within the physician-patient relationship. Here was the "narrowly-tailored test," presented not as an unapplied abstraction, but as an aspect of the respondents' argument. The State might reasonably accomplish its ends, for example, if its regulation of physician-assisted suicide followed "[l]egislation proposed in several States . . . authoriz[ing] physician-assisted suicide but requir[ing] two qualified physicians to confirm the patient's diagnosis, prognosis, and competence; . . . mandat[ing] that the patient make repeated requests witnessed by at least two others over a specified timespan; and . . . impos[ing] reporting requirements and criminal penalties for various acts of coercion."[136] The collateral consequences of the State's chosen means here, the respondents argued, were not a necessary condition to it accomplishing its legitimate end—protecting those outside the class to which they belonged. The State could address its legitimate concerns regarding certainty about end-of-life decisions through means other than criminalizing the act of assisting a suicide as broadly as it did here.

"[T]here are reasons for caution," Justice Souter warned, "in predicting the effectiveness" of the regulatory framework that the respondents offered as a less intrusive means to the State's legitimate ends.[137] The support for it came from "the Netherlands, the only place where the experience with physician-assisted suicide and euthanasia ha[d] yielded empirical evidence about how such regulations might affect actual practice."[138] But "[s]ome commentators," he explained, "marshall[ed] evidence that the Dutch guidelines ha[d] in practice failed to protect patients from involuntary euthanasia and ha[d] been violated with impunity."[139] "Th[e] evidence [was] contested," raising the concern that "whichever way the Court might rule . . . , events could overtake its assumptions . . . about progression from assisted suicide to euthanasia."[140] The judicial power could not supplant a reasonable legislative judgment, and the "facts necessary to resolve the controversy [were] not readily ascertainable through the judicial process."[141]

> It is not, of course, that any controversy about the factual predicate of a due process claim disqualifies a court from resolving it. Courts can recognize captiousness, and most factual issues can be settled in a trial court. At this point, however, the factual issue at the heart of this case does not appear to be one of those . . . I question whether an independent front-line investigation into the facts of a foreign country's legal administration can be soundly undertaken through American courtroom litigation.[142]

> Legislatures, on the other hand, . . . have flexible mechanisms for factfinding . . . includ[ing] the power to experiment, moving forward and pulling back as facts emerge within their jurisdictions.[143]

"The day may come," Souter surmised, "when we can say with some assurance which side is right, but for now it is the substantiality of the factual disagreement, and the alternatives for resolving it, that matter. They are, for me, dispositive of the due process claim at this time."[144] Whether the liberty interest for which the respondents sought protection "might in some circumstances, or at some time, be seen as 'fundamental' to the degree entitled to prevail," he explained, "is not . . . a conclusion that I need draw here[.]"[145] "The basic concept of judicial review," which undoubtedly included the possible "displacement of legislative judgment[,]" at the same time "bar[red] any finding that a legislature has acted arbitrarily when . . . there is a serious factual controversy over the feasibility of recognizing the claimed right without at the same time making it impossible for the State to engage in an undoubtedly legitimate exercise of power."[146] The "factual controversy" here was "not open to a judicial resolution with any substantial degree of assurance at this time," and so Justice Souter was "satisfied that the State's interests . . . [were] sufficiently serious to defeat the present claim that its law is arbitrary or purposeless."[147]

> It is no justification for judicial intervention merely to identify a reasonable resolution of contending values that differs from the terms of the legislation under review. It is only when the legislation's justifying principle, critically valued, is so far from being commensurate with the individual interest as to be arbitrarily or pointlessly applied that the statute must give way.[148]

Certainty about the relationship between the liberty interest and the State's justification for impinging it depended upon a factual question the Court was not institutionally positioned to resolve. Justice Souter could not conclude, therefore, that the application of Washington's statute was in this instance arbitrary. This did not foreclose potential judicial intervention in the future, for example, in response to "legislative foot dragging in ascertaining the facts going to the State's argument that the right in question could not be confined as claimed."[149] But for now, the "examination of legislative reasonableness should consider the fact that the Legislature of the State of Washington is no more obviously at fault than this Court is in being uncertain" about the consequences "if respondents prevailed today."[150] "The experimentation that should be out of the question in constitutional adjudication displacing legislative judgments is entirely proper, as well as highly desirable, when the legislative power addresses an emerging issue like assisted suicide."[151] "While I do not decide for all time," he concluded, "that respondents' claim should not be recognized, I acknowledge the legislative institutional competence as the better one to deal with that claim at this time."[152]

Here was authentic conservative deference to institutional process, not modern-conservative lip service to democracy. This was "respect for the teachings of history,"[153] not the abrogation of responsible judging in favor of equating federal constitutional protections with accepted social practices. There was no federal-judicial maintenance of the American States' social values here, but "solid recognition of the basic values" underlying American civil society.[154] Justice Souter's conclusion that the Court "should . . . stay its hand to allow reasonable legislative consideration"[155] demonstrated "wise appreciation of the great roles that the doctrines of federalism and separation of powers ha[d] played in establishing and preserving American freedoms."[156] This was a far cry from the modern-conservative denial of post-Reconstruction federalism and of the federal judiciary's corresponding "obligation to give substantive content to the words 'liberty' and 'due process of law.'"[157]

Justice Souter's fidelity to the tradition exposed the Court's fixation on only half of the ordered-liberty concept, and its neglect of "the basic need to account for the two sides in the controversy."[158] While recognizing the importance of the liberty interest in *Glucksberg*, Souter did not intimate any "extension" of a totalizing "realm of personal liberty" immune from government entry. Even had he concluded "the statute must give way," the opinion would not have contributed to this liberty-centrism, which in the twenty-first century would become more extreme, opening the sphere of substantive liberties to just what modern conservatism reacted against—any interest sounding in personal autonomy, or, just as broad and at least as vague, a right to dignity.[159] These were surely unobjectionable values, but the approach to them was without a principled account of the breadth of expression at which an "unenumerated right" specifying them was stated. It was hyper-focused on the liberty inquiry, and ignored the ordered side of the analysis—the careful consideration of the State's objectives and their ostensible fit with the means chosen to pursue them—which Souter exemplified in *Glucksberg*, like Harlan had in *Poe*.

"We may . . . classify Justice Harlan's example of proper analysis[,]" Justice Souter said, "as applying concepts of normal critical reasoning, as pointing to the need to attend to the level of generality at which countervailing interests are stated, or as examining the concrete application of principles for fitness with their own ostensible justifications."[160] Like the *Poe* dissent, Justice Souter's *Glucksberg* opinion did all three, following and elaborating further the common-law tradition of arbitrariness review. It integrated a century and a half of due-process precedent. And it fit with the very cases it identified in explaining the tradition, taking its place among those opinions in which the Court, while confident of its own power to "invalidate what it might find inconsistent with rights of liberty . . . nevertheless went on to uphold the legislative Acts under review."[161] There was no doubt here of the federal courts' obligation to protect individuals from arbitrary state legislation—a role sanctioned under the Due Process Clause of the Fourteenth Amendment.

At the close of the twentieth century, Justice Souter's *Glucksberg* concurrence stood, like Harlan's *Poe* dissent in the mid-twentieth, as a monument to the common-law tradition. This was the middle way between two modern extremes. It was conservative in its caution toward supplanting the legislative judgment; precise in evaluating the asserted right's resonance with liberal principles applied in precedent; constrained by the factual record and cognizant of its details; willing to scrutinize the State's justification for its choices; and deferential to institutional proficiency. Justice Souter had completed the canon of twentieth-century due-process precedent. *Palko*, *Poe*, and *Glucksberg* now contained and illuminated the common-law tradition of arbitrariness review. *Palko* presented the moral philosophy and named the concept of ordered liberty. *Poe* provided the first modern example, explaining and elaborating the analysis. And *Glucksberg* demonstrated that attention to the details of each particular controversy informed the proper juxtaposition of contending claims, in turn calibrating their levels of generality and driving the analysis to a conclusion via authentic judicial restraint—one born of a deep and abiding respect for institutional integrity. It had taken over a century, but the lineage of common-law judges had refined the once rough-hewn gemstone of the *Slaughterhouse* dissents into an adamantine jewel of legal reasoning. The last of three exceptional luminaries, Justice Souter had completed the work of his predecessors.

***

One might imagine that Justice Souter's colleagues, confronted with the inescapable force and acuity of this opinion, would at least consider its invitation to rediscover common-law reasoning. Such a hope, however, would underestimate the power of ideological recalcitrance. In his opinion, Justice Rehnquist easily dismissed Souter's. "In [it]," said Rehnquist, "Justice Harlan's *Poe* dissent supplies the 'modern justification' for substantive-due process review. But although Justice Harlan's opinion has often been cited in due-process cases, we have never abandoned our fundamental-rights-based analytical method."[162] Rehnquist scolded Souter for his dismissing the modern-conservative "restrained methodology" to "instead ask whether [Washington's] statute sets up one of those arbitrary impositions or purposeless restraints at odds with the" due-process guarantee.[163]

And at least as powerful as the modern-conservative impulse to halt it—and as dangerous to the Court's integrity—was the concretization of *Griswold*'s penumbral emanations. Through thirty years of reification, the once ethereal metaphor had gradually materialized into a foundation upon which the Court's liberal faction raised a doctrine of rights qualifying for heightened protection. Throughout this period, *Griswold*'s mischievous spirit continued its unrelenting quest for corporeality. But as the twenty-first century approached, this hypostatization of the zone of substantive liberties into an edifice of fundamental rights was like a gravitational collapse that precedes a super nova—the precondition for an explosion into a nebulous manifestation of colossal scale. Modern liberalism would soon undergo its most significant transformation since *Griswold*. Now almost half a century out from its break with the tradition of reasoned judgment, it would take its fixation on one aspect of the ordered-liberty concept to new heights, leaving modern conservatism to exaggerate the other with corresponding zeal.

NOTES

1. *Glucksberg*, 521 U.S. at 765 (Souter, J., concurring).
2. *Id.* at 759.
3. *Id.* at 765 (internal quotation marks omitted).
4. *Id.*
5. *Id.* (citing *Slaughterhouse Cases*, 16 Wall. 36, 116 (1873) (Bradley, J. dissenting)).
6. *Id.* at 756–757.
7. *Id.* at 757 (citing *Goshen v. Stonington*, 4 Conn. 209, 225–226 (1822); *Bank of the State v. Cooper*, 10 Tenn. 599, 602–608 (1831) (opinion of Green, J.); *Wynehamer v. People*, 13 N.Y. 378, 486–487 (1856); *Wilkinson v. Leland*, 2 Pet. 627 656–661 (1829); *Calder v. Bull*, 3 Dall. 386, 386–395 (1798); *Corfield v. Coryell*, 6 F. Cas. 546, 550–552 (1823); *Fletcher v. Peck*, 6 Cranch 87 (1810)).
8. *Id.* at 757–758 (citing Corwin, *Liberty Against Government*, 58–115 (discussing substantive due process in the state courts before the Civil War); *see also* Corwin, *Liberty Against Government*, 63 (discussing the renowned positions of Justices Iredell and Chase in *Calder v. Bull*, 3 Dall. 386 (1798), regarding the nature of legislative power, Corwin notes, "The answer to this question [To which of these positions has history awarded the palm of victory?] . . . is that while Iredell's view has enjoyed in the final upshot a formal triumph, the substance of victory has gone to Chase in what . . . became in due course the most important field of American constitutional law."), *see Id.* at 66 ("The truth is that Iredell's tenet that courts were not to appeal to natural rights and the social compact as furnishing a basis for constitutional decisions was disregarded at one time or other by all of the leading judges and advocates of the initial period of our constitutional history, an era which closes about 1830.").
9. *Id.* at 758 (citing *Wilkinson v. Leland*, 2 Pet. 627 656 661 (1829); *Calder v. Bull*, 3 Dall. 386, 386–395 (1798)).
10. *Id.*
11. 6 Cranch 87 (1810).
12. 521 U.S. at 758 (Souter, J., concurring).
13. *Id.* (citing *Fletcher*, 6 Cranch at 135–139; quoting *Fletcher*, 6 Cranch at 140) (internal quotation marks omitted).
14. *Id.*

15. *See Marbury v. Madison*, 1 Cranch 137 (1803).
16. 521 U.S. at 758 (Souter, J., concurring) (citing 19 How. 393 (1857)).
17. *Id.* (citing 19 How. at 449–452).
18. *Id.* at 759.
19. *Id.* (citing *Bartemeyer v. Iowa*, 18 Wall. 129, 133–135 (1874); *Munn v. Illinois*, 94 U.S. 113, 123–135 (1877); *Railroad Comm'n Cases*, 116 U.S. 307, 331 (1886); *Mugler v. Kansas*, 123 U.S. 623, 659–670 (1887)).
20. *Id.* at 760.
21. *Id.* (quoting *Allgeyer v. Louisiana*, 165 U.S. 578, 589 (1897)) (internal quotation marks omitted).
22. *Id.* (quoting *Allgeyer,* 165 U.S. at 590) (internal quotation marks omitted).
23. *Id.*
24. *Id.* at 760–761.
25. *See* discussion of *Griswold v. Connecticut*, chapter 5, *supra*; *see Griswold*, 381 U.S. at 481–482.
26. 521 U.S. at 761 (Souter, J., concurring).
27. *Id.*
28. *See* discussion of *Griswold v. Connecticut*, chapter 5, *supra*; *see Griswold*, 381 U.S. at 482–483.
29. 521 U.S. at 762 (Souter, J., concurring) (quoting *Palko*, 302 U.S. at 327–328).
30. *Id.* at 761.
31. *Id.* at 762.
32. 316 U.S. 535 (1942).
33. 521 U.S. at 762 (Souter, J., concurring).
34. *Id.*
35. *Id.*
36. *Id.*
37. *Id.* (*citing Poe*, 367 U.S. at 543).
38. *Id.* at 767 (*citing Poe*, 367 U.S. at 548).
39. *Id.* at 756.
40. *Id.* at 763.
41. *Id.*
42. *Id.* at 764.
43. *Id.* at 762–763.
44. *Id.* at 768.
45. *Id.* at 767–768.
46. *Id.* at 767.
47. *Id.* (quoting *Poe*, 367 U.S. at 542) (internal quotation marks omitted).
48. *Id.* at 772 (citing *Poe*, 367 U.S. 547–548).
49. *Id.* at 764.
50. *Id.*
51. *Id.*
52. *Id.*
53. *Id.* at 768.
54. *See Roe*, 410 U.S. at 164–165; *Michael H.*, 491 U.S. at 122 footnote 2.

55. 521 U.S. at 768 footnote 10 (Souter, J., concurring).

56. Well before *Glucksberg*, the Court's due-process jurisprudence—and arguably much of its jurisprudence more broadly—exhibited this habit of scientific materialism and vestige of enlightenment rationalism that Alfred North Whitehead called "the fallacy of misplaced concreteness." *See* A.N. Whitehead, *Science and the Modern World* (New York: Free Press, 1925), 51 ("[T]his spatialisation is the expression of more concrete facts under the guise of very abstract logical constructions. There is an error, but it is merely the accidental error of mistaking the abstract for the concrete. . . . This fallacy is the occasion of great confusion in philosophy."). Much of this story's criticism of both the modern-liberal and modern-conservative fundamental-rights doctrines is aimed at their treatment of fundamental rights as reifications of liberties asserted in discrete controversies, somehow existing beyond the actual experiences of the litigants who assert them as recounted in the records of the lawsuits describing those experiences. Inducing abstract generalizations from discrete instances is indeed an integral feature of western legal thought (as an aspect of western thought generally), but so too is habitually treating those generalizations as if they are phenomena more concrete than the actual experiences from which they were induced. This point, and what it illuminates about what process is, and what process is due those living under free governments, is worthy of significant further development.

57. 521 U.S. at 768 (Souter, J., concurring).

58. *Id.* at 765.

59. *Id.* at 767.

60. *Id.* at 769.

61. *Id.* at 772.

62. *Id.* at 773 (emphasis added).

63. *Id.*

64. *Id.*

65. *Id.* at 769–770.

66. *Id.* at 770; *see* A.N. Whitehead, *Science and the Modern World*, 18 ("But observation is selection. Accordingly, it is difficult to transcend a scheme of abstraction whose success is sufficiently wide.").

67. *Id.*

68. *Id.* at 771.

69. *Id.*

70. *Id.*

71. *Id.*

72. *Griswold*, 381 U.S. at 501 (Harlan, J. concurring).

73. 521 U.S. at 770 (Souter, J., concurring) (internal quotation marks omitted).

74. *Id.* at 781.

75. *Id.*

76. *Id.* at 773.

77. *Id.*

78. *Id.* at 781.

79. *Id.* at 777.

80. *Id.* at 776–777.
81. *Id.* at 773–774.
82. *Id.* at 775–776.
83. *Id.* at 781.
84. *Id.* at 781.
85. *Id.* at 777 (quoting *Schloendorff v. Society of New York Hospital*, 211 N.Y. 125, 129 (1914)) (internal quotation marks omitted).
86. *Id.*
87. *Id.* (quoting *Casey*, 505 U.S. at 849) (internal quotation marks omitted).
88. *Id.* at 763 (citing *Carey v. Population Services Int'l*, 431 U.S. 678, 684–691 (1977); *Griswold*, 381 U.S. at 481–486; *Casey*, 505 U.S. at 869–879; *Roe v. Wade*, 410 U.S. 113, 152–166 (1973); *Cruzan v. Director, Mo. Dept. of Health*, 497 U.S. 261, 287-289 (1990) (O'Connor, J., concurring); 497 U.S. at 302 (Brennan, J., dissenting); 497 U.S. at 331 (Stevens, J., dissenting); 497 U.S. at 278 (majority opinion)).
89. *Id.* at 778 (citing *Cruzan*, 497 U.S. at 279).
90. *Id.* at 778.
91. *Id.*
92. *Id.*
93. *Id.*
94. *Id.* at 779.
95. *Id.*
96. *Id.* (citing *Griswold*, 382 U.S. at 482).
97. *Id.*
98. *Id.*
99. *Id.*
100. *Id.* at 780.
101. *Id.*
102. *Id.*
103. *Id.* at 779.
104. *Id.* at 781.
105. *Id.*
106. *Id.*
107. *Id.* at 773.
108. *Id.* at 781.
109. *Id.* at 771.
110. *Id.* at 782 (internal quotation marks omitted).
111. *Id.*
112. *Id.*
113. *Id.*
114. *See* discussion of *Poe*, chapter 4, *supra*.
115. 521 U.S. at 782 (Souter, J., concurring).
116. *Id.*
117. *Id.*
118. *Id.* at 782–783.
119. *Id.* at 783.

120. *Id.*
121. *Id.*
122. *Id.*
123. *Id.*
124. *Id.* at 783–784.
125. *Id.* at 784.
126. *Id.*
127. *Id.*
128. *Id.*
129. *Id.* at 783.
130. *Id.* at 785.
131. *Id.*
132. *Id.* at 783.
133. *Id.*
134. *Id.* at 787.
135. *Id.* at 785.
136. *Id.*
137. *Id.*
138. *Id.*
139. *Id.* at 786.
140. *Id.* at 787.
141. *Id.* at 786–787.
142. *Id.* at 787.
143. *Id.* at 789.
144. *Id.* at 786.
145. *Id.* at 782.
146. *Id.* at 786.
147. *Id.* at 787, 782.
148. *Id.* at 768.
149. *Id.* at 788.
150. *Id.*
151. *Id.* at 789.
152. *Id.*
153. *Griswold*, 381 U.S. at 501 (Harlan, J., concurring).
154. *Id.*
155. 521 U.S. at 764 (Souter, J., concurring).
156. *Griswold*, 381 U.S. at 501 (Harlan, J., concurring).
157. 521 U.S. at 764 (Souter, J., concurring).
158. *Id.* at 765.
159. *See* discussions of *Lawrence v. Texas* and *United States v. Windsor*, Part IV, *infra*.
160. 521 U.S. at 772–773 (Souter, J., concurring).
161. *Id.* at 758.
162. 521 U.S. at 721 note 17.
163. *Id.* at 721 (internal quotation marks omitted).

Part IV

A MORE TRANSCENDENT LIBERTY

To practice the requisite detachment and to achieve sufficient objectivity no doubt demands of judges the habit of self-discipline and self-criticism, incertitude that one's own views are incontestable and alert tolerance toward views not shared. But these are precisely the presuppositions of our judicial process.

—*Rochin v. California*, 342 U.S. 165, 171–172 (1952).

Chapter 13

Certain Actions Are Prohibited

The century turned, and the Court continued to hear and decide contentious personal-liberty cases. The rights of homosexual persons became an especially salient issue, and Justice Kennedy secured the swing-vote position as cases involving it reached the Supreme Court. Some accordingly saw Kennedy as the most important man in America. Others saw him as "the most dangerous."[1] As the most senior justice when voting with the liberal faction, he assigned to himself the task of drafting the Court's opinions in the most controversial cases. In them he presided over the realm of personal liberty, which under his dominion would "extend" far "beyond" mere "spatial bounds" and into a new and uncharted dimension.[2] His opinions were often subject to conservative criticism as examples of judicial power run amok.[3] And as Kennedy played the role of liberty's champion, Justice Scalia became the foil—a surly and increasingly bitter dissenter from such an arrogant and self-aggrandizing judgment. Both justices became caricatures of politicized judges sitting on the highest court of a polarized nation.

Justice Souter would soon leave the Court, perhaps unable to watch from so close a vantage point as the institution he had served with such distinction disintegrated into a theater of the absurd. And the ordered-liberty concept, despite its revival in Souter's *Glucksberg* concurrence, would suffer the worst fate of all. This would be no mere misunderstanding. Nor deliberate misuse. It would not be another betrayal or surreptitious reconfiguration. In the twenty-first century, each side of the partisan divide would pledge absolute fealty to only one of the concept's complementary aspects. It was thus cleft in two and simply forgotten. During the first decade of the new millennium, retirements and appointments changed the Court's membership. And as it issued personal-liberty decisions of a new and unfamiliar sort, its majority opinions and dissents from them shared one glaring commonality. Both begged for the restraint, caution, and moderation of the common-law due-process tradition.

***

Six years after *Glucksberg*, the issue of criminal homosexual conduct arrived again at the Court. In the case of *Lawrence v. Texas*,[4] the people of the State had expressed their view that homosexuality is immoral with a statute providing criminal punishment for engaging in deviate sexual conduct.[5] The police arrested both petitioners in one's home.[6] The Texas Court of Appeals affirmed their convictions, and the U.S. Supreme Court granted the petitioners' request for review. They asked the Court to reverse the judgment of the Court of Appeals and to overrule *Bowers*.[7] The State offered as its sole justification for the statute the morality of its majority.[8] With the proper approach to such a controversial question so clearly presented in Justice Souter's *Glucksberg* concurrence, *Lawrence* presented the perfect opportunity to apply it—one the Court, ever under the spell of its post-*Griswold* jurisprudence, would miss.

***

During oral argument, counsel for the petitioners aimed initially at the modern-liberal approach to fundamental rights. The claim to liberty here, he argued, was "among the fundamental rights that are implicit in the concept of ordered liberty[.]"[9] This echoed Justice Blackmun's mistake in *Roe*, where he suggested, contrary to Cardozo's explanation, that implicit in the concept was a list of fundamental rights.[10] The *Bowers* Court, counsel argued, erred in framing the right too narrowly. It must be seen in "general terms[,] which is the right of everyone to decide for themselves about consensual private sexual intimacy."[11] Describing the right more broadly would compel a different result.

The first voice from the bench was that of Chief Justice Rehnquist. "[C]ertainly, the kind of conduct we're talking about here has been banned for a long time. . . . I think our case is like *Glucksberg* . . . if you're talking about a right that is going to be sustained, it has to have been recognized for a long time."[12]

But counsel was prepared to argue from the modern-conservative doctrine of fundamental rights, too. Not only had the Court in *Bowers* framed the fundamental right too narrowly, but it had also misunderstood the history of laws against homosexual sodomy. It incorrectly assumed the States' proscriptions against the conduct were longstanding. Counsel argued that their "roots" were not so "ancient" as Justice White had proclaimed.[13] Laws regulating sexual conduct were old, but they were not aimed at homosexuals. They targeted public sexual conduct, coercive sexual conduct, and sexual conduct involving children.[14] And they applied to conduct within heterosexual, as well as homosexual, relationships.[15]

"If you are going to suggest that the state of the law on the books in the 19th century is the touchstone," counsel argued, "you have to take into account that in the 19th century . . . married couples were regulated in terms of their forms of sexual intimacy[.]"[16] Seventeen years ago the people of Georgia, where *Bowers* originated, had repudiated this law. Therefore, counsel insisted, nineteenth-century law could not be the "deciding factor" today.[17] The modern-conservative touchstone for determining fundamental rights—the people of the State—had "conceded . . . that married couples cannot be regulated . . . in their personal sexual expression in the home[.]"[18]

"They conceded it[,]" Justice Scalia retorted. "I haven't[.]"[19] Regardless of who else the law targeted historically, all that mattered to Scalia was that the particular sexual act had been proscribed for same-sex couples, too. "What more do you need than that?" he asked. "It was prohibited."[20] The very law the petitioners challenged meant their challenge should fail.

Determined nevertheless to undermine *Bowers*'s reliance on the history and tradition of laws against sodomy, counsel pointed to a general trend among the States to decriminalize it.[21] In response, Justice Scalia posed a hypothetical: "[S]uppose all the States had laws against flagpole sitting at one time, you know, there was a time when it was a popular thing and probably annoyed a lot of communities, and then almost all of them repealed those laws."[22] He asked, "Does that make flagpole sitting a fundamental right?"[23] He made the same point during the State's argument, when he asked the District Attorney arguing for Texas, "Might there be a difference between the people's willingness to prosecute something criminally and the people's embracing of that as a fundamental right?"[24]

Counsel for Texas eagerly agreed. "[J]ust because someone has decriminalized sodomy doesn't mean that they embraced that practice as something that ought to be taught in the schools[.]"[25]

All missed the point that Justice Souter made in *Glucksberg*, where the decriminalization of suicide did not "imply the existence of a constitutional liberty interest[,]" but merely "open[ed] the door to" claims resonant with "traditionally cognizable" ones.[26] The arguments in *Lawrence* showed just the sort of "all or nothing analysis" that Justice Souter warned "tends to produce legal petrification instead of an evolving boundary between the domains of old principles."[27]

The decision of three quarters of the States to no longer regulate homosexual intimacy, the petitioners' counsel claimed, was "based on a recognition that it's not consistent with our basic American values" regarding "the relationship between the individual and the state."[28] Here, counsel played to the modern-conservative position that Harlan's "basic values" were not principles of justice inherent to American democracies and "underlying our society,"[29] but were instead products of democratic processes in the States.

For Justice Scalia, this argument did not go far enough. "Well," he responded, "it depends on what you mean by our basic American values."[30]

> Really what's at issue in this case is whether we're going to adhere to . . . what we said . . . in *Glucksberg*, . . . that before we find a substantive due process right, a fundamental liberty, we have to assure ourselves that that liberty was, *objectively*, deeply rooted in this Nation's history and tradition. That's what we said in *Glucksberg* and we've said it in other cases.[31]

The only other option, in Scalia's view, was to "depart from" *Glucksberg* "and go to the approach that we've adopted with regard to the Eighth Amendment, which is it evolves[,] and changes . . . in social values will justify a new perception."[32] For modern conservatism, fundamental rights were either limited to practices already accepted in the States, or, there was no limit. Hence the need for deference to traditional social mores—basic American values—as the only available objective constraint when considering fundamental-rights claims.

"Don't you think," asked Scalia, leading counsel for Texas, "that what laws a State may constitutionally pass has a lot to do with what laws it has always been thought that a State can constitutionally pass[?]"[33]

Again, counsel agreed.[34]

Scalia explained. "[T]he presumption is that the State is within the bounds of . . . the Constitution to pass that law in . . . declaring what it has proscribed as *contra bonos mores* . . . as against good morals[.]"[35] "[I]f you have a two-hundred-year tradition of" prohibiting conduct based on a State's moral judgment, this justified the prohibition.[36] What conduct a State could legally proscribe was "determined pretty much on the basis of what kind of laws the State ha[d] traditionally been allowed to pass[.]"[37]

One of the few times Justice Souter spoke, he laid bare the absurdity of Scalia's position. "[E]ven if you take the narrowest view of *Glucksberg*[,]" he said, "and even if you say there's got to be a positive historical sanction, . . . in fact there is . . . no substantial historical evidence . . . because . . . the sodomy laws . . . were not aimed at homosexual as opposed to sodomy in general[.]"[38] "Is that your historical point?" he asked counsel for the petitioners. "[Y]ou say[:] even if I accept your argument, I should win?"[39]

And he asked counsel for Texas, "[W]hen did Texas select homosexual sodomy as . . . a subject of specific criminal prohibition?"[40]

Counsel dodged the question. "[S]odomy . . . has a longstanding tradition [in] the history of Texas of . . . being against the law[.]"[41] Here, the State's interest in social order benefitted from characterizing the prohibited conduct broadly—sodomy generally, and not homosexual sodomy. This of course violated the modern-conservative requirement that the Court "refer to the most specific level at which a relevant tradition . . . denying protection to[] the asserted right can be defined."[42]

Souter pressed. "When . . . was the first statute passed? I think two-hundred years was mentioned. Was there a law on the books in 1803?"[43]

"No," counsel answered, "I don't think Texas was a State back then."[44] But, he countered, laws prohibiting certain sexual acts were old. "[C]ertainly . . . in the 1854 Penal Code, . . . the kinds of activity that . . . were classified now as sodomy were against the law."[45]

"When did . . . they single out *homosexual* sodomy?"[46] "[D]id they pass it at the . . . first meeting of the legislature?"[47]

Counsel conceded the point. "In 1973, in the passage of the 1974 Penal Code."[48]

With the historical pedigree of Texas's moral judgment in doubt, the arguments turned to whether there was some other justification for the law. Counsel for Texas tried to connect the State's interest to "marriage, families, and the procreation of children."[49] He suggested that the Court, in determining what conduct the States could prohibit, "may draw the line at the bedroom door of the heterosexual married couple because of the interest" in preserving these institutions.[50] He quickly retreated, however, when Justice Ruth Bader Ginsburg asked if Texas allowed same-sex couples to adopt children or be foster parents, which it did.[51] "We're not saying," he clarified, "that they can't be proper guardians and we can't say that they can't raise children. . . . [T]hat's not the issue."[52] "We're penalizing . . . only the particular activity that those unmarried couples may have with respect to whether they have sexual intimacies."[53]

This played right into the petitioners' argument. "[T]he real issue here," their counsel insisted, "is whether th[e] fundamental right" to "personal sexual expression in the home[,]" which he argued the jurisprudence recognized as protected for married couples, "extends outside the marital context into other unmarried couples . . . for whom sexual intimacy plays an equally important role in their lives."[54] The petitioners were asking the Court to draw a line different than the one Texas had drawn—to substitute one resolution of the contending interests in order and liberty for another. Invoking *Casey*, counsel reminded the justices that "[t]he Court has said that it's going to use reasoned judgment to identify a realm of personal liberty that involves matters . . . central and core to how a person defines their own lives and relates to other key people."[55] "[T]he Court shouldn't[,]" he insisted, "draw distinctions between gay couples and other couples."[56]

Doing his best to cull together an argument appealing to both the modern-liberal and modern-conservative approaches, the petitioners' counsel argued that the Court in *Bowers* had described the right at issue too narrowly before finding no historical support for recognizing it as fundamental. If, contrary to *Bowers*, the Court would "look at the issue in general terms[,]"[57] and use a different version of the history and tradition of relevant laws in the American States, it would see a "more complicated picture"[58]—one compelling a result the opposite of *Bowers*.

And the State of Texas argued that the people's moral disapproval of the practice for which the petitioners sought protection validated the law. In the end, counsel simply stated, "I think Texas has the right to prohibit certain conduct."[59] And, "I think as a matter of public policy, the State can . . . have preferences[.]"[60]

Justice Scalia seemed to think the petitioners were asserting the inverse proposition—claiming that the law was unconstitutional *because* it was based on a moral judgment. "[T]hese are laws dealing with public morality[,]"[61] he complained. "They've always been on the book, nobody has ever told them they're unconstitutional simply because there are moral perceptions behind them."[62] "Any law," he insisted, "stops people from doing what they really want to do."[63]

For Scalia, the State's objective—expressing its people's moral judgment—was alone sufficient to sustain the law. But now this was not even because the specific practice it prohibited had been legally proscribed in the past. Justice Souter's query to counsel undermined this contention. Nor was it because most (or even a majority) of the States shared Texas' values. They didn't.[64] For Justice Scalia, now the law's rationality derived from the mere fact that the people of Texas authorized it.

This became clear when Justice Breyer asked counsel for Texas to offer something in addition to the moral opprobrium ostensibly justifying the law. "[W]hat can you add to what you're saying, other than simply asserting its morality?"[65] he asked. "Because I don't think [that] you think . . . the State could pass *anything* in the name of morality?"[66]

"Certainly not," conceded counsel. "But . . . any law that would pass would have to have some rational basis[.]"[67]

"You've not given a rational basis," said Breyer, "except to repeat the word morality."[68]

Justice Scalia tried to help. "Is the rational basis . . . that the State thinks it immoral[?]"[69]

From the modern-conservative perspective, the law's moral basis *was* its rational basis. The law's rationality had nothing to do with the means the State chose to express its moral judgment, or with any relevant tradition reflecting it. The law was a moral judgment expressed through democratic process. This alone validated it, and meant that the practice it proscribed was not a fundamental right.

Neither side juxtaposed the parties' claims to hone their levels of generality. There was no discussion of how the means the State chose fit with its proffered objective. There was no argument, made against the background of precedent, for why the liberty the petitioners asserted was basic to a free society. There was simply an extant fundamental right that should be "extend[ed,]" and a countervailing assertion that the State could criminalize conduct it deemed immoral.[70] And, once again, this case was not about these petitioners. They were stand-ins for "gay families [where] family relationships are established[,]" for "hundreds of thousands of people registered in the 2000 census who have formed gay families, gay partnerships, many of them raising children[.]"[71] No one pointed out that the petitioners did not claim to be a family or a partnership, and were not raising children.[72]

Petitioner's counsel implored the Court: "There's a jagged piece missing from the edifice of this Court's fundamental rights jurisprudence!"—the fundamental right to sexual expression for homosexuals.[73]

***

Although he had not spoken much during oral arguments, Justice Kennedy authored the Court's opinion. It would give the petitioners a victory, but it would do much more than find the missing right for which they asked. The *Lawrence* opinion would not expressly announce a fundamental right, nor extend the boundaries of an existing one. Kennedy would unveil a more ambitious agenda. On the way to overruling *Bowers*, he would transport the jurisprudence into what he called the "more transcendent dimension" of personal liberty.[74] There he would not find a categorically protected substantive right, but encounter his first vision of the due-process guarantee enforcing "the Constitution['s] promise[] of liberty to all within its reach."[75]

The parties had argued about both the equal-protection and due-process guarantees.[76] Kennedy clarified which would control the Court's decision. This was a due-process inquiry, and resolving the case required considering only the interest asserted as worthy of constitutional protection.

> We conclude the case should be resolved by determining whether the petitioners were free as adults to engage in the private conduct in the exercise of their liberty under the Due process Clause of the Fourteenth Amendment to the Constitution. For this inquiry we deem it necessary to reconsider the holding in *Bowers v. Hardwick*.[77]

There were "broad statements of the substantive reach of liberty[,]" Kennedy said, "in earlier cases" like *Meyer* and *Pierce*. He did not discuss these cases nor cite any particular passage from them.[78] Having established the breadth of the substantive liberty the Constitution protected, he identified "as the most pertinent beginning point" the Court's decision in *Griswold*.[79] Much like the *Slaughterhouse* holding had resounded in Justice Scalia's *Michael H.* opinion, Kennedy's *Lawrence* opinion would take its place as the twenty-first-century echo of Douglas's mid-twentieth-century opinion. But here the zone of substantive liberties was neither penumbrally tethered to the Bill of Rights nor populated with social practices the American States considered fundamental. In its "more transcendent dimension[,]. . . freedom extend[ed] beyond spatial bounds[,]" and "[l]iberty presume[d] an autonomy of self that includ[ed] freedom of thought, belief, expression, and certain intimate conduct."[80]

Kennedy explained that *Griswold* identified the "protected interest" at issue in that case as "a right to privacy[,]" emphasizing the "marriage relation and the protected space of the marital bedroom."[81] But not long thereafter, the Court recognized that "the right to make certain decisions regarding sexual conduct extends beyond the marriage relationship."[82] In *Eisenstadt v. Baird*, an equal-protection case, the Court invalidated a statute limiting the use of contraceptives to married persons.[83] The significance of *Eisenstadt*, Kennedy explained, was its recognition that "[i]f the right of privacy means anything, it is the right of the *individual*, married or single, to be free from unwarranted government intrusion into matters so fundamentally affecting a person[.]"[84]

Eisenstadt and *Griswold* "were part of the background for the decision in *Roe v. Wade*," in which the Court "recognized the right of a woman to make certain fundamental decisions affecting her destiny[.]"[85] This "confirmed once more that the protection of liberty under the Due Process Clause has a substantive dimension of fundamental significance in defining the rights of the person."[86] Then, in *Carey v. Population Services Int'l*,[87] the Court recognized that the right to use contraception could not be legislatively limited to persons over the age of sixteen.[88] Together, *Eisenstadt*, *Roe*, and *Carey* "confirmed that the reasoning of *Griswold* could not be confined to the protection of rights of married adults."[89]

"This was the state of the law with respect to some of the most relevant cases[,]" Kennedy said, "when the Court considered *Bowers v. Hardwick*."[90] While the law challenged in *Bowers* "purport[ed] to do no more than prohibit a particular sexual act[,]" its "penalties and purposes[,]" like the law here in *Lawrence*, "ha[d] more far-reaching consequences[.]"[91] These laws "[t]ouch[ed] upon the most private human conduct . . . and in the most private of places . . . seek[ing] to control a personal relationship that . . . is within the liberty of persons to choose without being punished as criminals."[92] Kennedy said that this "general rule . . . counsel[ed] against the State, or a court, . . . defin[ing] the meaning of the relationship or . . . set[ting] its boundaries absent injury to a person or abuse of an institution the law protects."[93]

This sudden invocation of the "harm principle" seemed to imply that a demonstrable harm might justify a State's defining the meaning of the relationship or setting its boundaries. But Kennedy left this fleeting reference to the principle unconnected to any precedent, and he did not apply it. He would just as fleetingly invoke the principle in his post-*Lawrence* opinions, likewise without citation to legal authority or connection to their holdings, leaving unclear whether proof of harm might be a limiting principle to his broad conception of liberty's promise.[94] This reference to "abuse of an institution the law protects" more likely preemptively addressed an argument intertwined with the issue in *Lawrence* and destined for the Court—if the Constitution required the States to allow same-sex couples to marry, this would harm a time-honored and revered social institution.

Having reviewed the pertinent cases, Kennedy connected the liberty they recognized to the value of personal dignity. "It suffices for us to acknowledge," he wrote, "that adults may choose to enter upon this relationship . . . and still retain their dignity as free persons."[95] "The liberty protected by the Constitution," he concluded, allowed a homosexual person, like other persons, the right to choose to form a "personal bond" with another, in which "sexuality finds overt expression in intimate conduct."[96] In light of the selection of precedents he had just explained, these statements appeared to vindicate the petitioners' claim and justify overruling *Bowers*—the liberty the due-process guarantee protected included the choice of unmarried homosexual persons to have intimate sexual relationships.

But *Lawrence* did not so hold. Although he seemed to have found the "jagged piece" the petitioners claimed was missing from the Court's fundamental-rights edifice, Kennedy did not identify a right to sexual expression for homosexuals. To the contrary, he explained: "To say that the issue in *Bowers* was simply the right to engage in certain sexual conduct demeans the claim the individual put forward."[97] And so Justice White's formulation of the issue in *Bowers* "disclose[d] the Court's own failure to appreciate the extent of the liberty at stake."[98] Kennedy's conclusions here about the liberty the Constitution protected showed that the *Bowers* Court had "misapprehended the claim . . . there presented to it."[99] Kennedy would not make the same mistake. His presentation of the Court's personal-liberty cases was just an introduction. Because for *Lawrence* and its progeny, accounting for "history and tradition" would be as central to their analyses as it was to the case that *Lawrence* would overrule.

***

Having undervalued the liberty at stake in *Bowers*, the Court had said that "[p]roscriptions against that conduct have ancient roots."[100] But "[t]here is no longstanding history," Kennedy clarified, "in this country of laws directed at homosexual conduct as a distinct matter."[101] The American colonies had laws against sodomy, derived from early English laws, but they were not aimed at homosexuals. They proscribed sodomy within heterosexual relationships, too.[102] This "may be explained in part by noting[,]" Kennedy suggested, "that according to some scholars the concept of the homosexual as a distinct category of person did not emerge until the late 19th century."[103] As counsel for the petitioners had argued, prosecutions for sodomy historically involved coercion and predatory acts against minors or other non-consenting victims.[104]

"It was not until the 1970's," he continued, "that any State singled out same-sex relations for criminal prosecution, and only nine States ha[d] done so."[105] Even after *Bowers*, some were lax in enforcing these laws, and some had "moved toward abolishing them."[106] There was a pattern of nonenforcement with respect to "consenting adults acting in private."[107] Even the "State of Texas admitted in 1994 that as of that date it had not prosecuted anyone under those circumstances."[108] Kennedy nevertheless acknowledged "that the Court in *Bowers* was making the broader point that for centuries there have been powerful voices to condemn homosexual conduct as immoral."[109] But "[i]n all events," he concluded, without explaining why, "we think that our laws and traditions in the past half century are of most relevance here."[110]

***

Quoting his own concurring opinion in *County of Sacramento v. Lewis*,[111] which the Court had decided one term after *Glucksberg*, Kennedy wrote, "History and tradition are the starting point, but not in all cases the ending point of the substantive due process inquiry."[112] Here in *Lawrence*, his *Lewis* opinion took on a significance unnoticed when he authored it in 1998. In *Lewis*, the Court considered whether a police officer's deliberate or reckless indifference to life, during a high-speed chase of a motorcyclist resulting in the death of his passenger, violated substantive due process.[113] Unlike more familiar substantive-due-process claims challenging legislative acts, this one challenged executive action as violative of the guarantee.[114] As a measure of arbitrariness, the Court applied the "shocks-the-conscience" standard to the actions of the police officer.[115] Justice Scalia argued in his concurrence that the *Glucksberg* test should apply in this context just at it did when evaluating legislative action.[116] "I would ask[,]" Scalia had said, "whether our Nation has traditionally protected the right" that the representatives for the estate of Lewis asserted.[117]

Kennedy partially agreed. The due-process inquiry should ask, he said, whether "the objective character of certain conduct is consistent with our traditions, precedents, and historical understanding of the Constitution and its meaning."[118] He had joined Justice O'Connor's *Michael H.* concurrence disagreeing with Scalia's "single mode of historical analysis[,]"[119] and in *Lewis* he wrote separately to explain the proper approach.[120] His concurrence evinced a significant deviation from Scalia's method that would show in *Lawrence* and its progeny. With history and tradition as the "starting point," the Court should also consider the "present needs" of the government officials accused of violating the due-process guarantee.[121] The object of Kennedy's inquiry was not the liberty interest asserted as worthy of special protection. Instead, the "certain conduct" evaluated for "consisten[cy]" with the Nation's history and tradition was the government action allegedly violative of due process.[122]

Here in *Lawrence*, this pivot fit easily within post-*Griswold* fundamental-rights doctrine. The practice was now one of naming categorical fundamental rights. Scrutinizing countervailing interests in social order was so deemphasized that a State's role in the analysis was reduced to providing a perfunctory corollary—an impermissible state action—to the fundamental right with which it interfered. In *Lewis*, after citing *Glucksberg*, *Michael H.*, and *Casey* for the proposition that "due process has a substantive component as well" as a procedural one, Kennedy had observed, "As a consequence, certain actions are prohibited *no matter what procedures attend them*."[123] *Lawrence* and its progeny would make clear that for Kennedy, this was not an expression of the common-law prohibition against *arbitrary* government action. Kennedy would complete the turn his *Lewis* opinion foreshadowed. Under this history-and-tradition analysis, the Court could declare certain government policies categorically invalid, regardless of the means adopted to implement them.

***

The most recent fifty years, Kennedy explained, "show[ed] an emerging awareness that liberty gives substantial protection to adult persons in deciding how to conduct their private lives in matters pertaining to sex."[124] In 1955, the American Law Institute's Model Penal Code, which several States had followed, recommended not criminalizing private and consensual sexual relations.[125] In 1957, the repeal of such laws began in England.[126] "Of even more importance," five years before *Bowers*, the European Court of Human Rights "held that the laws proscribing the conduct were invalid under the European Convention on Human Rights."[127] This "emerging recognition," which "should have been apparent when *Bowers* was decided[,]"[128] pointed toward the opposite of its holding, even at the time the Court had invoked history and tradition to justify it. And in the years following it, the trend toward decriminalization or nonenforcement in the American States made *Bowers*' deficiencies "even more apparent."[129]

In the "laws and traditions in the past half century . . . [t]wo principal cases decided after *Bowers* cast its holding into even more doubt."[130] In *Casey*, the mystery-of-human-life passage—surely Kennedy's contribution—emphasized "the respect the Constitution demands for the autonomy of the person in making . . . the most intimate choices a person may make in a lifetime, choices central to personal dignity and autonomy[.]"[131] "The decision in *Bowers*[,]" Kennedy wrote, "would deny" homosexual persons "this right."[132] "The second post-*Bowers* case of principal relevance," he explained, was *Romer v. Evans*, in which the Court invalidated "class-based legislation directed at homosexuals" as violative of the equal-protection guarantee.[133] *Romer*, which Kennedy had authored, held that the law "was born of animosity toward the class of persons affected and further that it had no rational relation to a legitimate governmental purpose."[134]

The *Lawrence* petitioners had argued that *Romer*'s principle was a reason to overrule *Bowers* and invalidate the Texas statute.[135] But even while declining to decide the case on equal-protection grounds, Kennedy emphasized that like the law challenged in *Romer*, the criminal statute in *Lawrence* imposed a serious stigma on a class of persons.[136] He noted the Court's recent rejection of challenges to "state laws requiring the registration of sex offenders[,]" and that four States would require adults convicted under the Texas statute to register if they entered those jurisdictions.[137] A conviction under the Texas statute carried with it "other collateral consequences," like the requirement to disclose it on a job application.[138] This underscored the "state-sponsored condemnation attendant to the criminal prohibition."[139]

This stigmatizing effect on a class of persons implicated the substantive protections for liberty that due process afforded. "If protected conduct is made criminal," Kennedy said, "and the law which does so remains unexamined for its substantive validity, its stigma might remain even if it were not enforceable as drawn for equal protection reasons."[140] In one respect, this echoed Justice Harlan II's observation in *Poe* that due process was not "merely a procedural safeguard" guaranteeing impartial treatment for individuals whom a government might deprive of liberty.[141] As Harlan had taught, even "the fairest possible procedure in application to individuals" could "nevertheless destroy the enjoyment of" a basic liberty.[142] But as Kennedy's subsequent personal-liberty opinions would reveal, the point here was to import *Romer*'s emphasis—there under an equal-protection analysis—on the demeaning *effect* of challenged legislation, into a new doctrine of substantive liberty under the due-process guarantee. Liberty's more transcendent dimension would prohibit demeaning government action, regardless of whether the guarantee of equal protection did.

Kennedy concluded that *Casey* and *Romer* had "seriously" eroded "the foundations of *Bowers*."[143] "When . . . precedent has been thus weakened," he explained, "criticism from other sources is of greater significance."[144] He cited two works of legal scholarship criticizing *Bowers*, and the decisions of "the courts of five different States[.]"[145] Each court had "declined to follow [*Bowers*] in interpreting provisions in their own State constitutions parallel to the Due Process Clause of the Fourteenth Amendment."[146] Other nations had rejected the "reasoning and holding" of *Bowers*, too.[147] "In many other countries," Kennedy said, "[t]he right the petitioners seek in this case has been accepted as an integral part of human freedom[.]"[148] And, alluding to *Lewis*, he observed that "[t]here has been no showing" that in the United States the present needs of government were "somehow more legitimate or urgent" and required "circumscribing personal choice[.]"[149]

Comparing *Bowers* to democratic trends around the world revealed its holding was behind the times. Allowing it to "continu[e] as precedent" would "demean[] the lives of homosexual persons."[150] And, its holding had "not induced detrimental reliance"—a justification on which the *Casey* plurality had relied in reaffirming *Roe.* The doctrine of *stare decisis* thus presented no countervailing reason to resist overruling it.[151] Kennedy concluded that Justice Stevens' dissenting opinion in *Bowers* "should have been controlling . . . and should control" the Court's decision in *Lawrence.*[152]

***

Here was the introduction of a consequentialist jurisprudence as novel in its patchwork as the one Justice Scalia invented in *Michael H.* Its conception of liberty originated in *Griswold*'s right to privacy. Like the modern-conservative method, a survey of history and tradition revealed what mattered: an "emerging awareness" during the past fifty years within the "traditions, precedents, and historical understanding of the Constitution and its meaning"[153] that liberty protected persons from government interference with their sexual practices.[154] In light of *Casey*'s right to determine one's own destiny, and *Romer*'s protection against demeaning legislation, this more transcendent substantive liberty shielded the rights of autonomy and dignity from government invasion.

> The petitioners are entitled to respect for their private lives. The State cannot demean their existence or control their destiny by making their private sexual conduct a crime. Their right to liberty under the Due Process Clause gives them the full right to engage in their conduct without intervention of the government. It is a promise of the Constitution that there is a realm of personal liberty which the government may not enter.[155]

A State could not demean its citizens or control their destinies. The laws challenged in *Bowers* and *Lawrence* did. According to Kennedy, the

American Constitution prohibited such a basic affront to human freedom. "[C]ertain actions [were] prohibited, no matter what procedures attend[ed] them."[156] Although Kennedy's conclusion referred to the criminal prohibitions challenged in *Bowers* and *Lawrence*, the "certain action" prohibited here was not the criminalization of intimate homosexual conduct. The State's means did not matter. Nor did its objective. What mattered was the law's *consequences* for autonomy and dignity. Like Scalia's dismissal during oral argument of the need for any rational inquiry, this was not about testing the means the State chose to express its moral disapproval of homosexual conduct, and whether those means unreasonably impacted the basic liberties of these petitioners. The effect of the laws in *Bowers* and *Lawrence* was to control the destiny of a class of persons and demean them.[157] This the Constitution forbade.

Telling was the evolution in *Lawrence* of the issue presented. Kennedy initially stated it, somewhat modestly, as "whether petitioners' criminal convictions for adult consensual sexual intimacy in the home violate their vital interests in liberty and privacy protected by the Due Process Clause of the Fourteenth Amendment."[158] This formulation included the individual litigants and the means the State chose to interfere with their liberty, as well as significant details of the controversy. Like Justice Harlan's observation in *Poe* that "the State is asserting the right to enforce its moral judgment by intruding upon the most intimate details of the marital relation with the full power of the criminal law[,]"[159] Kennedy's initial version could have accommodated arbitrariness review. In the midst of preparing to overrule *Bowers*, however, the question became "whether the majority may use the power of the State to enforce [religious and moral] views [condemning homosexuality] *on the whole society* through operation of the criminal law."[160] Like all post-*Griswold* personal-liberty cases, this one was not about these litigants, nor about this controversy. The Court was announcing a categorical social-policy limitation on state legislation.

In his dissent, Justice Scalia offered an equally extreme interpretation of the due-process guarantee. Despite the plain language of the Due Process Clause, it was not a prohibition against governmental interference. It rather gave *permission* to the States to invade the liberty of individuals, requiring only that they do so through legislated process. "[T]here is no right to liberty under the Due Process Clause," he insisted, "though today's opinion repeatedly makes that claim."[161] "The Fourteenth Amendment *expressly allows* States to deprive their citizens of liberty," he emphasized, "*so long as due process of law is provided*."[162] Citing *Moore*, *Michael H.*, and *Glucksberg*, Scalia reminded the Court that the *Lawrence* opinion did not (and, under Scalia's method, could not) identify a fundamental right—a social practice "deeply rooted in this Nation's history and tradition,"[163] or "so rooted in the traditions and conscience of our people,"[164] or "traditionally protected by our society"[165]—and that "[a]ll other liberty interests may be abridged pursuant to a validly enacted state law" with a rational basis.[166] But as his comments during oral arguments indicated, a law's rationality had nothing to do with how its means related to its end.[167]

Just like Kennedy, to Scalia the means the State chose were irrelevant.[168] All that mattered was that the State pursued a legitimate objective, and "the promotion of majoritarian sexual morality" easily qualified.[169] And for Kennedy the law's objective—like the means chosen to pursue it—was irrelevant. What mattered was the law's effect. Unlike *Romer*, where Kennedy had looked behind the law and emphasized that it was "born of animosity" toward homosexuals,[170] there was no scrutiny in *Lawrence* of Texas's motive in maintaining the criminal prohibition against same-sex sodomy. Regardless of the motive, the law's negative impact on the autonomy and dignity of homosexuals meant that it was unconstitutional. This implied a point that Kennedy's subsequent opinions would make explicit—where a law had the prohibited effect, the Court would presume this was its purpose.

"The Texas statute furthers no legitimate state interest[,]" Kennedy concluded, "which can justify its intrusion into the personal and private life of the individual."[171] Implicit in this statement was the common-law analysis of fit between means and ends. Surely the State could promote majoritarian sexual morality through other means—ones without such a substantial imposition on personal liberty. But this was just another routine nod to the vestigial remnants of common-law reasoning strewn throughout post-*Griswold* fundamental-rights opinions. It was not that Texas failed to proffer a compelling-enough justification for interfering with an important personal liberty. The question was whether the right claimed was found within the transcendent realm of personal liberty which the government *may not enter*. Kennedy's post-*Lawrence* personal-liberty opinions would make clear the obvious answer—there was presumptively no justification for a law that assailed such a right.

Justice Scalia accused Kennedy of "apply[ing] an unheard-of form of rational-basis review that will have far-reaching implications beyond this case."[172] He railed against the "bald, unreasoned disclaimer" that "the present case does not involve whether the government must give formal recognition to any relationship that homosexual persons seek to enter."[173] "Do not believe it," he warned.[174] Kennedy's "progression of thought" in noting the "constitutional protections afforded to personal decisions relating to *marriage* . . . [and] family relationships" belied his real agenda.[175] According to Scalia, Kennedy "laid waste the foundations of our rational basis jurisprudence[,]" preparing for the "judicial imposition of homosexual marriage[.]"[176] But there was obvious irony in Scalia's criticism. It ignored his own inclination to abrogate any judicial scrutiny and find the law's rational basis in the mere fact that the Texas legislature passed it.

How *Lawrence* fit with precedent was anything but clear. In one sense it tracked the petitioners' argument for a broad conception of their liberty interest. It did not expressly say so, but maybe the law was invalid because the liberty at stake was fundamental and trumped the State's regulation of homosexual sodomy. But it also willingly stepped onto the modern conservatives' ground, arguing from the Nation's history and tradition. Perhaps the law was invalid because there was no relevant tradition in the American States targeting homosexual conduct for legal proscription. Kennedy explained that the conduct here, unlike traditionally prohibited sexual conduct, did "not involve minors[,]" or "persons who might be injured or who are situated in relationships where consent might not easily be refused[,]" or "public conduct or prostitution."[177] Like the petitioners' oral argument, the *Lawrence* opinion appealed to a fundamental-rights doctrine that emphasized history and tradition.

But like "society's views" informed the modern-conservative method in *Michael H.* and *Glucksberg*, current attitudes toward homosexual conduct played a prominent role in the *Lawrence* opinion.[178] Further imitating the modern-conservative opinions, Kennedy emphasized some of the States' own laws.[179] But he looked even farther, beyond the American States, to consider "the values we share with a wider civilization," noting that the "reasoning and holding of *Bowers* ha[d] been rejected elsewhere."[180] This was at least in part because *Bowers* had invoked the "Judeo-Christian moral and ethical standards" in "the history of Western civilization."[181] But in its reliance on a selection of non-constitutional-law sources to identify constitutional values, this refutation of *Bowers* eerily resembled it, *Michael H.*, and *Glucksberg*. Kennedy's *Lawrence* opinion exemplified what modern conservatism feared—the judicial social-policy arbitrating that Scalia's method was supposed to stop—even while echoing its hypocrisy and resorting to social values to answer difficult constitutional questions.

Here were two diametrically extreme positions. For Kennedy, there was no rational basis for the law because it infringed autonomy and dignity. The due-process guarantee offered totalizing protection for a special dimension of substantive freedom. For modern liberalism, there was no justification for interfering with a transcendent personal liberty. And for modern conservatism, the law was rational because the State passed it. The State's democratic pursuit of social order was justification enough. The guarantee was a perfunctory procedural requirement—a low hurdle to clear—before depriving persons of liberty. Two modern perspectives on the due-process guarantee each sought an outcome mutually exclusive with the other's. Both were blind to any scrutiny of *how* the State justified pursuing its objective, and each relied on a hodgepodge selection of source material from the past fifty years.

Broken from the tradition, both were wrong.

***

Thirty-five years earlier, *Duncan* had extricated two analyses from the penumbral incorporation of unenumerated rights, attempting to resolve the perturbation within the jurisprudence that *Griswold*'s break from the tradition left behind. Then, in the twenty 15.5short years between *Moore* and *Glucksberg*, mistakes and opportunistic misappropriation had spawned a dialectic of opposed political ideologies. A complete servility to democracy reacted against the judicial pronouncement of categorical fundamental rights. And now, just six years after *Glucksberg*, a more transcendent constitutional law of liberty responded in turn. Throughout this brief jurisprudential trajectory, each ideology denied the common-law tradition as it opposed the other. Both ignored the ordered-liberty concept's paradoxically situated yet integrated complements that together implemented a basic value underlying American society. And each found its twenty-first-century identity in an all-consuming obsession with only one of the concept's two aspects.

"The Court's obligation," Justice Kennedy proclaimed, "is to define the liberty of all[.]"[182]

"What a massive disruption," Justice Scalia lamented, "of the current social order . . . the overruling of *Bowers* entails."[183]

***

In *Michael H.*, Justice Scalia stole "history and values" to equate constitutional liberty with the States' interest in maintaining a "traditional" social order. In *Lawrence*, Justice Kennedy used "history and tradition" to support a new constitutional regime in which liberty categorically prohibited impacting a basic human right. Justice Souter had offered in *Glucksberg* the common-law alternative to the modern-conservative method. He offered no alternative to Kennedy's. The modern conservatives had summarily dismissed him,[184] and his liberal colleagues seemed not to notice his *Glucksberg* concurrence. Perhaps there was no point in once again demonstrating a judge's carefully restrained role in the political life of the Nation. This was, after all, the same Court that had baldly inserted itself into the American electoral process to decide a presidential election just three years earlier.[185] It might have seemed, at this point, a futile endeavor to again exemplify the reasoned judgment of the common law. Justice Souter quietly retired from the bench shortly after *Lawrence*, leaving his *Glucksberg* opinion to speak for the concept of ordered liberty—and to fall on deaf ears.

NOTES

1. *See, e.g.*, Jeffrey Toobin, "Swing Shift: How Anthony Kennedy's passion for foreign law could change the Supreme Court," https://www.newyorker.com/magazine/2005/09/12/swing-shift ("In 2003, James Dobson, the founder and director of the influential evangelical group, Focus on the Family, called Kennedy 'the most dangerous man in America.'").
2. *Lawrence v. Texas,* 539 U.S. 558, 562 (2003).
3. *Id.* at 602 (Scalia, J., dissenting) ("It is clear from this that the Court has taken sides in the culture war, departing from its role of assuring, as neutral observer, that the democratic rules of engagement are observed.").
4. 539 U.S. 558 (2003).
5. *Id.* at 563.
6. *Id.* at 563–564.
7. *Id.* at 564.
8. *Lawrence v. Texas*, No. 02-102, 46:6–7; 47:6–8.
9. Tr. at 4:3–8.
10. *See* discussion of *Roe*, chapter 6, *supra.*
11. *Lawrence v. Texas*, No. 02-102, Tr. at 5:4–6.
12. Tr. at 4:14–22.
13. *Bowers*, 478 U.S. at 192.
14. *Lawrence v. Texas*, No. 02-102, Tr. at 8:3–5.
15. Tr. at 5:19–25.
16. Tr. at 5:20–25.
17. Tr. at 6:16–18.
18. Tr. at 6:11–16.
19. Tr. at 6:19–20.
20. Tr. at 6:4–6.
21. Tr. at 8:13–17.
22. Tr. at 9:10–14.
23. Tr. at 9:15–16.
24. Tr. at 32:16–18.
25. Tr. at 32:19–22.
26. 521 U.S. at 773–774, 777.
27. *Id.* at 770.
28. *Lawrence v. Texas*, No. 02-102, Tr. at 8:13–17.
29. *Griswold*, 381 U.S. at 501 (Harlan, J., concurring).
30. Tr. at 8:18–19.
31. Tr. at 8:20–9:4.
32. Tr. at 9:4–7.
33. Tr. at 39:5–8.
34. Tr. at 39:19.
35. Tr. at 39:11–15.
36. Tr. at 39:8–18.

37. Tr. at 39:16–18.
38. Tr. at 11:15–21.
39. Tr. at 11:23–24.
40. Tr. at 40:17–19.
41. Tr. at 41:2–4.
42. *Michael H.*, 491 U.S. at 127 footnote 6.
43. *Lawrence v. Texas*, No. 02-102, Tr. at 41:5–7.
44. Tr. at 41:8–9.
45. Tr. at 41:20–22.
46. Tr. at 41:24–25.
47. Tr. at 41:17–19 (emphasis added).
48. Tr. at 42:1–2.
49. Tr. at 35:6–13.
50. *Id.*
51. Tr. at 35:14–16.
52. Tr. at 36:9–12.
53. Tr. at 36:18–20.
54. Tr. at 6:24–7:3.
55. Tr. at 10:2–6.
56. Tr. at 24:15–19.
57. Tr. at 5:3–4.
58. Tr. at 5:6–7.
59. Tr. at 46:6–7.
60. Tr. at 47:6–8.
61. Tr. at 17:10–11.
62. Tr. at 17:11–13
63. Tr. at 9:25–10:1.
64. *See* 539 U.S. at 570.
65. *Lawrence v. Texas*, No. 02-102, Tr. at 43:6–7.
66. Tr. at 43:8–9 (emphasis added).
67. Tr. at 43:10–12.
68. Tr. at 43:13–14.
69. Tr. at 43:15–16.
70. Tr. at 6:25–7:1.
71. Tr. at 23:10–18.
72. *See*, *e.g.*, Dale Carpenter, *Flagrant Conduct* (New York: W.W. Norton & Company, 2012), 41–45. In chapter 3 (The Defendants and the Troublemaker) Carpenter provides insight into the lives of the men who were arrested and became the petitioners at the Supreme Court in *Lawrence*.
73. *Lawrence v. Texas*, No. 02-102, Tr. at 11:3–5.
74. 539 U.S. at 562.
75. *Obergefell v. Hodges*, 135 S.Ct. 2584, 2593 (2015).
76. 539 U.S. at 564.
77. *Id.*
78. *Id.*

79. *Id.*
80. *Id.* at 562.
81. *Id.* at 564–565.
82. *Id.* at 565.
83. *Id.*
84. *Id.* (emphasis in original).
85. *Id.*
86. *Id.*
87. 431 U.S. 678 (1977).
88. 539 U.S. at 566.
89. *Id.*
90. *Id.*
91. *Id.* at 567.
92. *Id.*
93. *Id.*
94. *See, e.g.*, *Obergefell v. Hodges*, 135 S.Ct. 2584, 2606–2607 (2015), discussed in chapter 15, *infra*.
95. 539 U.S. at 567.
96. *Id.*
97. *Id.*
98. *Id.*
99. *Id.*
100. *Id.* (quoting *Bowers*, 478 U.S. at 192).
101. *Id.* at 568.
102. *Id.*
103. *Id.*
104. *Id.*
105. *Id.* at 570.
106. *Id.*
107. *Id.* at 569.
108. *Id.* at 573.
109. *Id.* at 571.
110. *Id.* at 571–572.
111. 523 U.S. 833 (1998).
112. *Id.* at 857 (Kennedy, J., concurring).
113. 523 U.S. at 836.
114. *Id.* at 840.
115. *Id.* at 836.
116. *Id.* at 862 (Scalia, J., concurring).
117. *Id.* In contrast, Justice Souter's opinion for the majority captured the traditional analysis applied in the context of qualified immunity: "[I]n such circumstances only a purpose to cause harm unrelated to the legitimate object of arrest will satisfy the element of arbitrary conduct shocking to the conscience, necessary for a due process violation." *Id.* at 836.
118. *Id.* at 857 (Kennedy, J., concurring).

119. *Michael H.*, 491 U.S. at 132 (O'Connor, J., concurring).
120. 523 U.S. at 856 (Kennedy, J., concurring).
121. *Id.* at 857–858.
122. *Id.* at 857. Kennedy's personal-liberty jurisprudence would amplify this shift, echoing *Moore*'s application of *Duncan*, where the Court applied a "procedural" analysis to a "substantive" question. The object of *Duncan*'s history-and-tradition inquiry was state action—procedures that due process required the government to implement. The object of Kennedy's history-and-tradition inquiry was likewise the government action allegedly violating due process. While the *Duncan/Moore* influence on "substantive due process" jurisprudence developed in the early twenty-first century via Justice Kennedy, *Duncan*'s influence on procedural analyses persisted in the Court's jurisprudence. During the Supreme Court's 2019 term, for example, it heard oral arguments in *Kahler v. Kansas*, in which the petitioner challenged Kansas' abolishing the insanity defense to the mens rea element of a criminal offense—the claim that one is unable to tell right from wrong—as violative of due process. 140 S.Ct. 1021, 1024–1025. During oral argument, counsel for the petitioner argued that Kansas violated due process because in abolishing the defense it "uproot[ed] the deeply rooted by eliminating any mechanism to assess whether a defendant's capacity for moral judgment was intact or was irretrievably compromised by mental illness." Counsel for the respondent began his argument answering this contention: "The first thing I'd like to talk about is that it's not deeply rooted. The right versus wrong test is of relatively recent vintage." *See Kahler v. Kansas*, No. 18-6135, 4:4–8; 29:20–21. The Court held that due process did not compel the State to allow the defense. 140 S.Ct. at 1025. Writing for the Court, Justice Elena Kagan's explanation of the proper "procedural" analysis echoed the modern conservative approach to substantive due process, but, like Kennedy's jurisprudence and contra the modern-conservative method, the object of inquiry was not any liberty interest, but rather state action: "Under well-settled precedent, a state rule about criminal liability—laying out either the elements of or the defenses to a crime—violates due process only if it 'offends some principle of justice so rooted in the traditions and conscience of our people as to be ranked as fundamental.' *Leland v. Oregon*, 343 U.S. 790, 798 (1952) (internal quotation marks omitted). Our primary guide in applying that standard is 'historical practice.' *Montana v. Egelhoff*, 518 U.S. 37, 43 (1996) (plurality opinion)." 140 S.Ct. at 1027. The Court's inquiry was "whether a rule of criminal responsibility is so old and venerable—so entrenched in the central values of our legal system—as to prevent a State from ever choosing another." *Id.* at 1028.
123. *Id.* at 856 (emphasis added).
124. 539 U.S. at 572.
125. *Id.*
126. *Id.* at 572–573.
127. *Id.* at 573.
128. *Id.* at 572.
129. *Id.* at 573.
130. *Id.* at 571–572; 573.

131. *Id.* at 574 (quoting *Casey*, 505 U.S. at 851) (internal quotation marks omitted).

132. *Id.*

133. *Id.* at 574 (citing 517 U.S. 620 (1996)).

134. *Id.* (quoting 517 U.S. at 634) (internal quotation marks omitted).

135. *See Lawrence v. Texas*, No. 02-102, Tr. at 18:18–19:13.

136. 539 U.S. at 574.

137. *Id.*

138. *Id.* at 576.

139. *Id.*

140. *Id.* at 575.

141. 367 U.S. at 541 (Harlan, J. dissenting).

142. *Id.*

143. 539 U.S. at 575.

144. *Id.*

145. *Id.* (citing *Jegley v. Picado*, 349 Ark. 600, 80 S.W.3d 332 (2002); *Powell v. State*, 270 Ga. 327, 510 S.E.2d 18, 24 (1998); *Gryczan v. State*, 283 Mont. 433, 942 P.2d 112 (1997); *Campbell v. Sundquist*, 926 S.W.2d 250 (Tenn. App. 1996); *Commonwealth v. Wasson*, 842 S.W.2d 487 (Ky. 1992)).

146. *Id.*

147. *Id.*

148. *Id.* at 577.

149. *Id.*

150. *Id.* at 575; 578.

151. *Id.*

152. *Id.* at 578. *See* discussion of *Bowers v. Hardwick*, chapter 8, *supra.*

153. 523 U.S. at 857 (Kennedy, J., concurring).

154. 539 U.S. at 572.

155. *Id.* (quoting *Casey*, 505 U.S. at 847).

156. 523 U.S. at 856 (Kennedy, J., concurring).

157. 539 U.S. at 578.

158. *Id.* at 564.

159. *Poe*, 367 U.S. at 548 (Harlan, J., dissenting).

160. 539 U.S. at 571 (emphasis added).

161. *Id.* at 592 (Scalia, J., dissenting).

162. *Id.* (emphasis in original).

163. *Id.* at 593 (citing *Glucksberg*, 521 U.S. at 721).

164. *Id.* (citing *Flores*, 507 U.S. at 303).

165. *Id.* (citing *Michael H.*, 491 U.S. at 122).

166. *Id.*

167. *Lawrence v. Texas*, No. 02-102, 43:15–16.

168. *See Lawrence*, 539 U.S. at 599 (Scalia, J., dissenting) (including in his analysis of the Texas law's rational basis a consideration of the State's objective—promoting majoritarian sexual morality—but no mention of the means chosen or how they related to it).

169. *Id.*
170. 539 U.S. at 574 (quoting *Romer*, 517 U.S. at 620).
171. *Id.* at 578.
172. 539 U.S. at 586 (Scalia, J., dissenting).
173. *Id.* at 604 (quoting *Lawrence*, 539 U.S at 578) (internal quotation marks omitted).
174. *Id.*
175. *Id.* (emphasis in original; internal quotation marks omitted).
176. *Id.*
177. *Id.* at 578.
178. *See* 491 U.S. at 127 footnote 6; *see also* discussion of *Michael H.*, chapter 9, *supra*, and discussion of *Glucksberg*, chapter 11, *supra*.
179. 539 U.S. at 576.
180. *Id.* at 576–577.
181. *Id.* at 571.
182. *Id.*
183. *Id.* at 591 (Scalia, J., dissenting).
184. *See Lewis*, 523 U.S. at 860 (Scalia, J., dissenting) ("Just last term, in *Washington v. Glucksberg*, . . . the Court specifically rejected the method of substantive-due-process analysis employed by Justice Souter in his concurrence in that case[.]").
185. *See Bush v. Gore*, 531 U.S. 98 (2000). Justices Souter and Breyer filed concurring opinions, agreeing that there was an equal-protection violation but arguing that the Court should send the case back to the State of Florida rather than decide the election's outcome. In *The Nine*, Jeffrey Toobin explained Justice Souter's reaction to the Court's decision: "Souter seriously considered resigning. For many months, it was not at all clear whether he would remain as a justice." Jeffrey Toobin, *The Nine* (New York: Knopf Doubleday Publishing Group, 2008), 208.

Chapter 14

A Prudential Exercise of the Judicial Power

Any doubts about the direction of Justice Kennedy's jurisprudence were laid to rest in the same-sex marriage cases that *Lawrence* anticipated. The first came ten years later, when in *United States v. Windsor*[1] the Court invalidated section 3 of the federal Defense of Marriage Act ("DOMA") as violative of the Fifth Amendment's due-process guarantee. Writing for the Court, Kennedy sketched out in greater detail the doctrine that *Lawrence* had introduced. But *Windsor* was significant for an even more compelling feature than the opportunity it gave Kennedy to develop and apply his new doctrine. Renouncing the respect for institutional integrity that Justice Souter had demonstrated in *Glucksberg*, the Court in *Windsor* wielded the judicial power and ruled on the most controversial social-policy issue in half a century, in a case it appeared to have no authority to decide.

***

In 1996, seven years before *Lawrence*, amid the sharpening national debate over whether same-sex couples should be allowed to marry, Congress amended the Dictionary Act of the U.S. Code.[2] The amendment defined "marriage" and "spouse" for the purpose of "determining the meaning of any Act of Congress, or of any ruling, regulation, or interpretation of the various administrative bureaus and agencies of the United States[,]"[3] A "marriage" was "only a legal union between one man and one woman as husband and wife," and a "spouse" was "a person of the opposite sex who [was] a husband or a wife."[4] While the Act had no effect on whether same-sex couples could marry, it "control[led] over 1,000 federal laws in which marital or spousal status [was] addressed as a matter of federal law."[5]

Long-term same-sex partners Edith Windsor and Thea Spyer wed in 2007, in Canada. The State of New York, where they resided, recognized theirs as a valid marriage. When Spyer died two years later and left her estate to Windsor, DOMA disqualified Windsor from the federal estate-tax exemption for surviving spouses. Windsor paid over 360,000 dollars in estate tax and then sued the Internal Revenue Service in federal court for denying her request for a refund. She claimed that DOMA violated the guarantee of equal treatment under the law that the Fifth Amendment's Due Process Clause enforced against the federal government. The District Court agreed, and ordered the IRS to pay Windsor with interest. The case eventually arrived at the Supreme Court through a peculiar process that presented a "procedural dilemma" calling into question the Court's power to hear and decide it.[6]

While Windsor's suit was pending in the District Court, the attorney general of the United States submitted a letter to the speaker of the House of Representatives under section 530D of Title 28 of the U.S. Code.[7] It notified the speaker that the executive would no longer defend the constitutionality of section 3 of DOMA. Such notices from the Department of Justice were not uncommon. But they usually came *after* a federal court's judgment adverse to the executive's defending the constitutionality of a law it was obligated to enforce. This letter came *before* any such decision.[8] And it meant that no party in Windsor's ongoing case was opposing her argument that DOMA was unconstitutional.

The letter said the president had determined "that heightened equal-protection scrutiny should apply to laws that classify on the basis of sexual orientation[,]"[9] implying that DOMA could not withstand such scrutiny. But the letter said also that while the executive would not defend the law, it would continue to enforce it. The United States "had an interest in providing Congress a full and fair opportunity to participate in the litigation[.]" At the same time, the president "recogniz[ed] the judiciary as the final arbiter of the constitutional claims raised."[10] Here was a stand-off between the executive and the legislature, with the president implicitly inviting the judiciary to declare the winner.[11]

Upon receiving the letter, the Bipartisan Legal Advisory Group ("BLAG") of the House of Representatives moved the District Court to allow it to intervene in Windsor's case and defend sections 3's constitutionality.[12] The District Court denied intervention as of right because the Department of Justice already represented the United States. But it allowed BLAG to intervene as an interested party. After the District Court ruled in Windsor's favor, both parties filed notices of appeal in the Second Circuit. While the appeal was pending before the Second Circuit, the solicitor general of the United States filed a petition for writ of certiorari at the Supreme Court. The Second Circuit then affirmed the District Court's decision. Its holding echoed the president's letter—section 3 of DOMA did not withstand the heightened judicial scrutiny courts must bring to laws classifying on the basis of sexual orientation.[13]

The United States' position posed a problem. It was the party nominally opposing Windsor, but it joined her in asking the high court to affirm the lower courts' decisions. It invoked the appellate jurisdiction of the Supreme Court, asking it to review the Second Circuit's decision, but it considered the decision correct. It was not asking the Court to change anything. Despite the fact that both parties asked the Court to hear the case, its peculiar posture raised the question of whether the federal judicial power could operate here at all, and the Court appointed an *amicus* to argue the contrary position that it was without jurisdiction.[14] The government's "agreeing with Windsor's legal contention but refusing to give it effect" had not divested the District Court of jurisdiction to resolve the controversy, because at that time Windsor's injury "was concrete, persisting, and unredressed."[15] But, the *amicus* argued, "Once the President agreed with Windsor's legal position *and* the District Court issued its judgment, the parties were no longer adverse."[16] They had no standing to appear in any further proceedings.[17] The Court should not rule on the merits of the case, because the United States sought "no redress from the judgment entered against it" below.[18] The judicial power could not operate here because there was no justiciable controversy.

***

The day before oral arguments in *Windsor*, the Court heard *Hollingsworth v. Perry*,[19] another same-sex-marriage case presenting a similar threshold issue. The case was about a California ballot initiative that amended the State's Constitution.[20] The amendment, "Proposition 8," had overruled a holding of the California Supreme Court that denying same-sex couples the right to marry violated the California Constitution's guarantee of equal protection. Proposition 8 limited the institution of marriage within the State to opposite-sex couples. It withstood a procedural challenge its opponents pushed all the way to the California Supreme Court, which held it was properly enacted.[21] Through their initiative process, the people of California had overruled the State's highest court on the issue of same-sex marriage.

Two same-sex couples—who were married in California *after* the California Supreme Court's ruling, but *before* the initiative that undid it—brought suit in federal District Court, naming as defendants the governor and attorney general of California and several executive officers of the State responsible for enforcing its marriage laws. The couples challenged the State's authority to rescind their marital status. Having granted this right, they claimed, the State could not take it away without violating the federal equal-protection guarantee of the Fourteenth Amendment.[22] The litigants in *Hollingsworth* and in *Windsor* invoked the same principle.

Like the federal Executive in *Windsor*, the State executive officials in *Hollingsworth* refused to defend the law in court, even as they continued to enforce it.[23] And as in *Windsor*, the state executives' refusing to defend the law prompted an intervention. The District Court allowed the "official proponents of the initiative"—as California law defined them—into the federal action to defend Proposition 8's constitutionality. After a bench trial on the merits, the court ruled that the law was unconstitutional and permanently enjoined the defendants, and anyone under their supervision, from enforcing it. No longer interested in defending the law, the State did not appeal the court's order to the Ninth Circuit.[24]

But the law's official proponents did.[25] "[T]he Ninth Circuit asked them[,]" for the same reason the Supreme Court appointed the *amicus* in *Windsor*, "to address why th[e] appeal should not be dismissed for lack of Article III standing[,]"[26] uncertain about whether they could invoke the federal judicial power. The Ninth Circuit "certified a question to the California Supreme Court: whether under . . . California law . . . the official proponents . . . possess[ed] either a particularized interest in the initiative's validity *or* the authority to assert the State's interest in [it.]"[27] The California Supreme Court answered the second half of the question. California law allowed them to assert the State's interest and defend the law—they could "defend [its] constitutionality . . . when the public officials charged with that duty refused[.]"[28]

The Ninth Circuit then ruled that "[a]ll a federal court need determine is that the state has suffered a harm sufficient to confer standing and that the party seeking to invoke the jurisdiction of the court is authorized by the state to represent its interest in remedying that harm."[29] It proceeded to the merits and affirmed the District Court. It held that Proposition 8 was unconstitutional "under the rationale of . . . *Romer*," according to which "the Equal Protection Clause require[d] the state to have a legitimate reason for withdrawing a right or benefit *from one group but not others*, whether or not it was required to confer that right or benefit in the first place."[30] Proposition 8, the court concluded, furthered no legitimate state interest.[31] Its *only* purpose was "to impose on gays and lesbians, through the public law, a majority's private disapproval of them and their relationships."[32]

When the official proponents of Proposition 8 petitioned the Supreme Court to review the Ninth Circuit's decision, the standing issue was again briefed and argued.[33] The same day the Court decided *Windsor*, it held in *Hollingsworth* that the Ninth Circuit had no authority to hear the case.[34] "Article III of the Constitution confine[d] the judicial power of federal courts to deciding actual 'Cases' or 'Controversies'."[35] An "essential aspect of this requirement [was] that any person invoking the power of a federal court must demonstrate standing to do so."[36] This in turn required "the litigant to prove that he suffered a concrete and particularized injury . . . fairly traceable . . . to the challenged conduct . . . likely to be redressed by a favorable judicial decision."[37] The Ninth Circuit had erred, because under this standard the intervenors had no standing at the Circuit Court.[38]

Federal law required a litigant to demonstrate a redressable injury, and "the District Court had not ordered the intervenors to do or refrain from doing anything."[39] They were no better positioned to meet the requirement of standing in federal court than any member of "the public at large" with an interest in "vindicat[ing] the constitutional validity of a generally applicable California law."[40] They sought no specific relief from the Circuit Court's judgment and thus "had no direct stake in the outcome of their appeal."[41] The U.S. Supreme Court had never before recognized the standing of such litigants, who "rais[ed] only a generally available grievance about government—claiming only harm to [their] and every citizen's interest in proper application of the Constitution and laws[.]" And it would not do so here.[42]

The Court vacated the judgment of the Ninth Circuit and remanded the case "with instructions to dismiss the appeal for lack of jurisdiction."[43] The final ruling was thus the federal District Court's. The same-sex couples won. The State could not rescind their marital status. Proposition 8 was unconstitutional. The State of California had not appealed the ruling, and the official proponents had no standing to challenge it. The justiciable controversy had resolved in the District Court.

Justice Kennedy dissented. He conceded that whether the official proponents had standing was a question of federal law.[44] But answering it required "a threshold determination of state law."[45] What mattered was "how California define[d] and elaborate[d] the status and authority of an initiative's proponents who [sought] to intervene in court to defend the initiative after its adoption by the electorate."[46] The State had undeniably "sustained a concrete injury, sufficient to satisfy the requirements of Article III, when a United States District Court nullified a portion of its State Constitution."[47] And "under California law, a proponent had the authority to appear in court and assert the State's interest in defending an enacted initiative when the public officials charged with that duty refuse[d] to do so."[48] The Court must, Kennedy insisted, recognize this State-conferred authority as sufficient to confer standing in federal court. This was "essential to the integrity of [the State's] initiative process."[49] Refusing to recognize the official proponents as the State's representatives, Kennedy said, "disrespect[ed] and disparag[ed]" California's own determination about who could appear and assert its interest in the validity of Proposition 8.[50]

The Court should be more deferential to California and to "the 26 other States that permit initiatives and popular referendums, . . . exercis[ing] their own inherent sovereign right to govern themselves."[51] Kennedy observed the "irony in the Court's approach to justiciability in this case. A prime purpose of justiciability [was] to ensure vigorous advocacy, yet the Court insist[ed] upon litigation conducted by state officials whose preference [was] to lose the case."[52] Any irony Justice Kennedy saw here would pale in comparison to his observation of it, in light of the justiciability analysis he would deploy in *Windsor.*

"[J]usticiability exists[,]" he claimed, "to allow disputes of public policy to be resolved by the political process rather than the courts[.]"[53] "The essence of democracy is that the right to make law rests in the people and flows to the government, not the other way around."[54] But "here," he complained, "the Court refuses to allow a State's authorized representatives to defend the outcome of a democratic election."[55]

> Of course, the Court must be cautious before entering a realm of controversy where the legal community and society at large are still formulating ideas and approaches to a most difficult subject. But it is shortsighted to misconstrue principles of justiciability to avoid that subject.[56]

As Kennedy would demonstrate in *Windsor*, it would not be so shortsighted to misconstrue them to *reach* it.

***

Writing for the Court in *Windsor*, Kennedy characterized the *amicus*' argument as "elid[ing] the distinction between . . . the jurisdictional requirements of Article III and the prudential limits on its exercise."[57] There was an important difference, he said, between "Article III standing, which enforces the Constitution's case-or-controversy requirement, . . . and prudential standing[.]"[58] The former required a specific injury, but the latter, Kennedy said, comprised "more flexible rules of federal appellate practice[.]"[59] A common-law judge would have here voiced skepticism. A judge would no doubt be hard-pressed to find a redressable injury where no party asked an appellate court to change a lower court's decision. And the tradition most certainly demanded an integrated and principled account of any judicial power exercised through such a thing as the "flexible rules of . . . practice" that Kennedy invoked here.[60] The Court would not offer one.

So eager was one faction of the Court to reach the merits of this case, the common law resorted to channeling its counseling restraint through Justice Scalia. In his dissent he agreed with the *amicus*. The Court "ha[d] no power to decide this case."[61] Article III of the Constitution, he said, gave to judges only the "judicial Power"—"a power to decide not abstract questions but real, concrete 'Cases' and 'Controversies'."[62] Windsor won in the District Court, and the United States did not contest the Circuit Court's decision. Now it asked the Supreme Court to affirm it. The Court should not be so tempted "to say what the law is[,]" Scalia warned, and ignore this most basic limitation on the exercise of judicial power.[63] "Only when a particular case is before us," he said, "a controversy that it is our business to resolve under Article III—do we have the province and duty to pronounce the law."[64]

But Justice Kennedy said the requirement of Article III standing was met here. There *was* an injury. The United States was not like the petitioners in *Hollingsworth*, because here in *Windsor* it "retain[ed] a stake . . . on appeal and in proceedings before" the Court.[65] "The judgment in question," he explained, "order[ed] the United States to *pay* Windsor,"[66] but it had not yet complied with the District Court's order.[67] The United States conceded that it *should* comply with the lower court's orders but wanted this Court to say that it *must*. "That the Executive may welcome this order to pay the refund," he said, "if it is accompanied by the constitutional ruling it wants does not eliminate the injury to the national Treasury if payment is made, or to the taxpayer if it is not."[68] "It would be a different case[,]" Kennedy said, "if the Executive had taken the further step of paying Windsor the refund to which she was entitled under the District Court's ruling."[69] Unlike *Hollingsworth*, one party to the action still at least faced the prospect of a "particularized injury."

This thin justification for exercising the judicial power, Scalia observed, belied the Court's hunger to "tell everyone its view of the legal question at the heart of this case."[70] Citing the same page of precedent that Kennedy and *Hollingsworth* did to identify the requirements of standing, Scalia wrote, "Our authority begins and ends with the need to adjudge the rights of an injured party who stands before us seeking redress."[71] Like *Hollingsworth*, no party to this case sought redress from the appellate court's judgment.[72] "When a private party has a judicial decree safely in hand to prevent his injury," Scalia argued, "additional judicial action requires that a party injured by the decree seek to undo it."[73] "Article III require[d] not just a plaintiff (or appellant) who has standing to complain but an *opposing party* who denies the validity of the complaint."[74] The proper question, Scalia posed, was "whether there is any *controversy* . . . between the United States and Ms. Windsor."[75] And he observed that "[t]here [wa]s not."[76]

Kennedy concluded the "case present[ed] a justiciable controversy under Article III[.]"[77] He conceded there were "prudential problems inherent in the Executive's agreement with Windsor's legal argument[.]"[78] It "raise[d] the risk that instead of" a real controversy, the Court faced a "friendly, non-adversary, proceeding . . . [in which] a party beaten in the legislature [seeks to] transfer to the courts an inquiry as to the constitutionality of the legislative act."[79] But "unlike Article III requirements[,]" he explained, "the relevant prudential factors that counsel against hearing this case are subject to countervailing considerations [that] may outweigh the concerns underlying the usual reluctance to exert judicial power."[80] These factors were "matters of judicial self-governance . . . designed to protect the courts from deciding abstract questions of wide public significance . . . [when] other governmental institutions may be more competent to address the questions and even though judicial intervention may be unnecessary to protect individual rights."[81]

Here was the same irony Kennedy saw in *Hollingsworth*'s analysis. "Judicial intervention" was obviously "unnecessary to protect" the "individual rights" of any party to this action. Windsor's rights were vindicated in the District Court and no party asked any other court to change the decision. The United States already had what it asked the Court to give it—an order to pay a tax refund. The Circuit Court should have dismissed the appeal for lack of jurisdiction.[82] Like *Hollingsworth* this case should have gone no further than the District Court. The Court could reverse the mistake here and recognize that where the controversy had resolved the judicial power had ended. Just like the same-sex couples' victory in *Hollingsworth*, Windsor's at the District Court would be final.

But the litigants faded from view as they had in *Lawrence*, when Justice Kennedy's attention turned to the "hundreds of thousands of people registered in the 2000 census who have formed gay families, gay partnerships, many of them raising children[.]"[83] "Were this Court to hold that prudential rules require it to dismiss the case," Kennedy warned,

> rights and privileges of hundreds of thousands of persons would be adversely affected, pending a case in which all prudential concerns about justiciability are absent. . . . True, the very extent of DOMA's mandate means that at some point a case likely would arise without the prudential concerns raised here; but the costs, uncertainties, and alleged harm and injuries likely would continue for a time measured in years before the issue is resolved.[84]

"In these unusual and urgent circumstances," he said, "the very term 'prudential' counsels that it is a proper exercise of the Court's responsibility to *take* jurisdiction."[85]

How unmoored was the twenty-first-century Court from the constraints on judicial discretion inherent to the common-law tradition. The *sine qua non* of an Article III controversy was a party's injury that a court's ruling would redress. The common-law judge would have here invoked Cardozo, Harlan, and Souter to show *why* this was so. The parties' contending claims were the point of entry into the ordered-liberty analysis.[86] A judge needed them to juxtapose the competing interests and hone their levels of generality in light of the evidence developed in the record below. And the relief an aggrieved party sought exposed the *justiciable* controversy. Souter had shown in *Glucksberg* that the common-law analysis illuminated only the narrowest of issues on which a court was required to rule in determining which interest must give way to the other.[87] The tradition *limited* the judicial power to nullifying only an unreasonable legislative balance between clashing principles, already struck and *as applied* to someone whose resulting injury a court order could cure. The judicial power extended to "Cases" and "Controversies"—to *lawsuits.*[88] The tradition allowed its judges to say which party won, and obligated them to explain why.

There was no justiciable controversy at the Supreme Court.

> We have never before agreed . . . to say what the law is . . . where there is no controversy before us. In the more than two centuries that this Court has existed as an institution, we have never suggested that we have the power to decide a question when every party agrees with both its nominal opponent *and the court below* on that question's answer.[89]

> The further proceedings have been a contrivance, having no object in mind except to elevate a District Court judgment that has no precedential effect in other courts, to one that has precedential effect throughout the Second Circuit, and then (in this Court) precedential effect throughout the United States.[90]

There was a danger here that required "wise appreciation of the great role[] that . . . Separation of Powers ha[d] played in establishing and preserving American freedoms."[91] The case-or-controversy requirement limited the "judicial Power,"[92] and foolish discretion here might inappropriately extend it into the domain of national social policy.

The Court's decision to proceed to the merits, Kennedy said, did not mean this should be "a common practice in ordinary cases."[93] But "if the Executive's agreement with a plaintiff that a law is unconstitutional is enough to preclude judicial review, then the Supreme Court's primary role in determining the constitutionality of a law . . . would become only secondary to the President's."[94] But the executive's agreement with Windsor had obviously *not* precluded judicial review. Two federal courts had issued a judgment in her favor. Just not the *highest* one.

Kennedy was concerned about protecting Congress, too. "[I]t poses grave challenges to the separation of powers for the Executive at a particular moment to be able to nullify Congress' enactment solely on its own initiative and without any determination from the Court."[95] There had, of course, been a determination from *a* court. Just not one poised to decide so much more than the rights of the parties to a discrete controversy before it. Passing up this opportunity, Kennedy said, would "undermine[] the clear dictate of the separation-of-powers principle that when an Act of Congress is alleged to conflict with the Constitution, [i]t is emphatically the province and duty of the judicial department to say what the law is."[96]

Kennedy's "prudential jurisdiction" spotlighted the Supreme Court's "primary role in determining the constitutionality" of the Nation's laws,[97] not the common-law prerogative of the *judicial department* to say what the law is *only* when integral to adjudicating a discrete case or controversy.[98] Kennedy seemed to "have in mind one of the foreign constitutions that pronounce[d] such primacy for its" highest court and allowed it to exercise its power outside the bounds of a lawsuit.[99] But the judicial power of this Court was born of the Anglo-American common law—"the power to adjudicate, with conclusive effect, disputed . . . claims."[100] Scalia reminded the Court,

> [D]eclaring the compatibility of state or federal laws with the Constitution is not a separate, free standing role *at all*. We perform that role incidentally . . . when that is necessary to resolve the dispute before us. Then, and only then, does it become the province and duty of the judicial department to say what the law is.[101]

"The integrity of the political process would be at risk," Kennedy admitted, "if difficult constitutional issues were simply referred to the Court as a routine exercise."[102]

> But this case is not routine. And the capable defense of the law by BLAG ensures that these prudential issues do not cloud the merits question, which is one of immediate importance to the Federal Government and to hundreds of thousands of persons. These circumstances support the Court's decision to proceed to the merits.[103]

The Court had a duty, Justice Kennedy cautioned, to "insist upon that concrete adverseness that sharpens the presentation of issues [on] which [it] . . . depends for illumination of difficult constitutional questions."[104] But the intervenor's defending the law, the relative infrequency of this opportunity, and the urgent expectations of so many people not parties to the litigation, mitigated any concerns about abusing the judicial power. So in a prudential exercise of it the Court took jurisdiction and decided whether DOMA violated the due-process guarantee.

***

Windsor arrived at the Court as the States' democracies were changing. For some citizens, the possibility was unthinkable that "two persons of the same sex might aspire to occupy the same status and dignity as that of a man and a woman in lawful marriage."[105] But for others "came the beginnings of a new perspective, a new insight."[106] As of the date of the *Windsor* decision, eleven other states and the District of Columbia had "decided that same-sex couples should have the right to marry[.]" In those jurisdictions they could now "live with pride in themselves and their union . . . in a status of equality with all other married persons."[107]

Kennedy explained that when Windsor and Spyer "at first longed to marry," no State in the Union allowed it.[108] But their State had moved toward it, recognizing same-sex marriages sanctioned in other jurisdictions.[109] Along with some other States, New York eventually gave marriage to "same-sex couples who wish[ed] to define themselves by their commitment to each other."[110] The people of Windsor's home state and their elected representatives had come to see an injustice in denying marital status to same-sex couples—one they had not earlier perceived.[111]

Casey had suggested that a new understanding of what salient facts meant might require a "new choice of constitutional principle[.]"[112] A common-law judge would use this detail to consider whether the democratic decision in New York to recognize Windsor as a spouse represented a break from the traditions of the past, opening the door to claims resonant with already cognizable ones.[113] But Kennedy would instead follow the examples of *Michael H., Glucksberg*, and *Lawrence*. In *Windsor*, democracy in some of the States provided the "background" against which the constitutionality of "the design, purpose, and effect of DOMA should be considered[.]"[114]

The "definition and regulation of marriage," Kennedy said, "ha[d] been treated . . . by history and tradition . . . as being within the authority . . . of the separate States."[115] But it was not an exclusive one, and State and federal laws regulating marriage interacted. "Congress, in enacting discrete statutes, [could] make determinations that bear on marital rights and privileges."[116] Examples included federal laws designating beneficiaries of federal life insurance policies, what counted as a valid marriage to determine immigration status, and who qualified as the spouse of a Social Security beneficiary.[117]

These examples, Kennedy said, "established the constitutionality of limited federal laws that regulate the meaning of marriage in order to further federal policy."[118] DOMA was different; it had "a far greater reach[.]"[119] It "enact[ed] a directive applicable to over 1,000 federal statutes."[120] And it intervened not only into "the whole realm of federal regulations[,]" but also into the democratically enacted "laws of New York, and of 11 other States[,]" affecting "a class of persons" those laws "sought to protect."[121] "[A]ssess[ing] the validity of [this] intervention," Kennedy said, required a closer look at "the extent of the state power and authority over marriage as a matter of history and tradition."[122]

The States had to respect "the constitutional rights of persons," but within this limitation the "regulation of domestic relations . . . ha[d] long been regarded as a virtually exclusive province of the States."[123] The regulation of marriage was "central to state domestic relations law."[124] Controlling its definition was "the foundation of the States' broader authority to regulate the subject of domestic relations" generally.[125] When the Constitution was adopted, it "delegated no authority to the Government of the United States on the subject of" domestic relations,[126] and "the common understanding was that [these] were matters reserved to the States."[127]

As a consequence of this "allocation of authority," throughout the Nation's history the "Federal Government . . . ha[d] deferred to state-law policy decisions with respect to domestic relations."[128] Because there was "no federal law of domestic relations," when the operation of federal laws depended on the marital status of individuals, they often referred "to the law of the State which created those legal relationships[.]"[129] This federal deference to the States meant that while domestic-relations laws, including those controlling marital status, might differ from State to State, they were uniform within each. DOMA dismissed this "long-established precept that the incidents, benefits, and obligations of marriage [were] uniform for all married couples within each State[.]"[130] It thus "depart[ed] from [the] history and tradition of reliance on state law to define marriage."[131]

Although poised to consider whether DOMA offended the separation-of-powers principle, Justice Kennedy said it was "unnecessary to decide whether this federal intrusion on state power [was] a violation of the Constitution because it disrupt[ed] the federal balance."[132] Nor would his opinion address the lower courts' decisions, which like the courts in *Hollingsworth* had decided the issue under the equal-protection guarantee. Instead, *Windsor* would hone the doctrine that *Lawrence* had introduced. It would focus on the effect that DOMA had on the autonomy and dignity of a class of persons, and enforce against this government action the categorical prohibition of liberty's transcendent dimension.

The State's "historic and essential authority to define the marital relation" was still "of central relevance in this case[,]" even "apart from principles of federalism."[133] Because when it recognized and then allowed same-sex marriages, "New York was responding to the initiative of those who [sought] a voice in shaping the destiny of their own times."[134] And the State's "decision to give this class of persons the right to marry conferred on them a status and dignity of immense import."[135] DOMA used the State's classification for a "purpose" exactly "opposite," and took this state-conferred benefit away.[136] Precisely where the State sought to protect, DOMA "impos[ed] restrictions and disabilities."[137]

Kennedy said this "result require[d] th[e] Court to . . . address whether the resulting injury and indignity [was] an essential part of the liberty" that the

Fifth Amendment protected.[138] This strange description of the Court's obligation to review the statute begged the question before it and at the same time contained its answer. The law's negative impact required the Court to scrutinize it. At the same time, however, and consistent with *Lawrence*, *Windsor* would conclude that this same "resulting injury and indignity" to same-sex couples meant that DOMA was unconstitutional. The *Windsor* opinion thus completed the Court's post-*Griswold* conflating of the common-law's threshold question in due-process review with the dispositive one. DOMA's effect obligated the Court to scrutinize it *and* compelled the conclusion that DOMA violated the due-process guarantee. The Court must decide *whether* DOMA was unconstitutional because it *was*.

Like Justice Powell had done in *Moore* with regard to family, Kennedy emphasized the elevated social status of the marital institution. The State's interest in "defining and regulating" it, said Kennedy, "stem[med] from the understanding that marriage is more than a routine classification for purposes of certain statutory benefits."[139] *Lawrence* had recognized, after all, that the State could not punish "[p]rivate, consensual sexual intimacy between" same-sex couples, because this intimacy "form[ed] but one element in a personal bond that is more enduring."[140] And when New York recognized same-sex marriages performed in other jurisdictions as valid within its own, it "sought to give further protection and dignity to that bond."[141] The State gave "lawful status" to same-sex couples' post-*Lawrence* "lawful conduct."[142] This status was a "far reaching legal acknowledgment of the intimate relationship between two people, a relationship deemed by the State worthy of dignity in the community equal with all other marriages."[143] DOMA's "unusual deviation from the usual tradition of recognizing and accepting state definitions of marriage here," Kennedy said, "operates to deprive same-sex couples of" this status.[144] The State's decision to grant it "reflect[ed] both the community's considered perspective on the historical roots of the institution of marriage and its evolving understanding of the meaning of equality."[145]

Here was Kennedy's new doctrine at work—the history-and-tradition aspect of the personal-liberty inquiry coupled with an equal-protection component assimilating evolving social values. This was not a due-process analysis where the reasons for the law's impact were strictly scrutinized for fitness with how they had been applied. Like the *Lawrence* opinion and Scalia's dissent from it, *Windsor* would not consider any relation of means to ends. Nor was this an equal-protection analysis in which homosexual persons were members of a suspect class, subjecting legislation disparately impacting them to strict scrutiny. Certain government actions—those that stigmatized or demeaned persons (as members of a class), branding them as less equal than others—were categorically prohibited deprivations of liberty.

Like the Texas statute in *Lawrence*, the effect of DOMA was dispositive. Working backward from the law's consequences for same-sex couples, Kennedy found "strong evidence" of its unconstitutional purpose.[146] "DOMA seeks to injure," Kennedy said, "the very class New York seeks to protect."[147] The "avowed purpose and practical effect of the law here in question[,]" he wrote, "are to impose a disadvantage, a separate status, and so a stigma upon all who enter into same-sex marriages made lawful by the unquestioned authority of the States."[148]

Kennedy found support for this finding in DOMA's "own text" and in selections from the report of the House of Representatives where it originated.[149] The House Report on "the Defense of Marriage Act" indicated that Congress thought it "appropriate and necessary . . . to defend the institution of traditional heterosexual marriage."[150] The law's "purpose[,]" therefore, "[was] to discourage the enactment of same-sex marriage laws and to restrict the freedom and choice of couples married under those laws if they [were] enacted."[151] "The Act's demonstrated purpose [was] to ensure that if any State decide[d] to recognize same-sex marriages, those unions will be treated as second-class marriages for purposes of federal law."[152] Its "interference with the equal dignity of same-sex marriages, . . . conferred by the States in the exercise of their sovereign power," he explained, "was its essence."[153] "DOMA's operation in practice[,]" he observed, "confirms this purpose."[154]

Devoid of any scrutiny of means and ends, in this analysis the law's effect defined its purpose. Kennedy wrote, "DOMA's principal effect is to identify a subset of state-sanctioned marriages and make them unequal. The principal purpose is to impose inequality[.]"[155] The unequal purpose and effect of the law were pervasive, for it wrote "inequality into the *entire* United States code."[156] It "place[d] same-sex couples in . . . a second-tier marriage."[157] It "demean[ed]" them, even after *Lawrence* had affirmed that the Constitution protected their "moral and sexual choices[.]"[158] It "humiliate[d] tens of thousands of children . . . being raised by same-sex couples[,] mak[ing] it even more difficult for the children to understand the integrity and closeness of their own family[.]"[159] It "touche[d] many aspects of married and family life, from the mundane to the profound," including health care and insurance, status in bankruptcy proceedings and tax filing, veterans and social security benefits, the application of certain criminal laws, and federal financial aid.[160] All of this established, Kennedy concluded, "that the principal purpose and the necessary effect of this law are to demean those persons who are in a lawful same-sex marriage."[161]

"This requires the Court to hold," he wrote, "as it now does, that DOMA is unconstitutional as a deprivation of the liberty of the person protected by the Fifth Amendment of the Constitution."[162] Concluding his opinion, Kennedy presented a cryptic summary of how the equal-protection component of

Romer and *Lawrence* fit into this new personal-liberty doctrine: "While the Fifth Amendment itself withdraws from Government the power to degrade or demean in the way this law does, the equal protection guarantee of the Fourteenth Amendment makes that Fifth Amendment right all the more specific and all the better understood and preserved."[163]

> The federal statute is invalid, for no legitimate purpose overcomes the purpose and effect to disparage and to injure those whom the State, by its marriage laws, sought to protect in personhood and dignity. By seeking to displace this protection and treating those persons as living in marriages less respected than others, the federal statute is in violation of the Fifth Amendment.[164]

Perhaps this resurrected the Ninth Circuit's holding in *Hollingsworth*, which the Court had eviscerated on the standing issue. Regardless of whether the Constitution guaranteed marital status to same-sex couples, once a government granted it, a legitimate interest must justify withdrawing it, and mere disapproval of the relevant class did not qualify. But this was not the principle at work here in *Windsor*. In *Hollingsworth*, the Ninth Circuit had applied it following *Romer*; here, Kennedy used the personal-liberty doctrine that *Lawrence* introduced. It required no evaluation of any purpose proffered for the law, nor of any motive behind it. The problem with DOMA was its *consequences* to same-sex couples. It demeaned this class of persons, interfering with the autonomy of those who belonged to it and subjecting them to indignity. Like *Lawrence*, the government's means and objectives were irrelevant to the analysis. This case was about the undignified status the law imposed on a class of persons, and this determined its unconstitutionality.

Windsor clarified that due-process review under the Fifth Amendment included the same class-based analysis of *Lawrence*, finding in the Fifth Amendment's due-process guarantee the protection against stigmatizing legislation that *Lawrence* had found in the Fourteenth through *Romer*. The Constitution's promise of liberty prohibited laws controlling the destinies of individuals or demeaning them as members of a class of persons defining their own existence. But while these cases were clearly devoted to the "right to liberty" of one particular class—persons in same-sex intimate relationships—they did not explain why they qualified as a class for purposes of applying the doctrine, or who else might in other cases.

Like *Lawrence*, "history and tradition" played a central role in *Windsor*. And the history-and-tradition inquiry again focused on government action—both Congress's passing DOMA and the States' regulating marriage—rather than on an asserted liberty interest as in pre-*Lawrence* fundamental-rights cases. But unlike *Lawrence*, history and tradition did not reveal here any emerging awareness of what laws liberty prohibited. Here, it validated eleven

States' decisions to recognize same-sex marriages entered into in foreign jurisdictions—those that section 3 of DOMA defined out of existence for purposes of federal law. History affirmed the States' traditional authority to democratically confer the dignity attendant to marital status. In *Windsor* thus recurred the aspect of *Moore* from which Scalia, in *Michael H.* and relying on *Bowers*, had conjured the modern-conservative method. History and tradition in the American States revealed constitutional protection for a revered social institution.

Windsor did not turn on whether the federal congress invaded the province of a State's government without constitutional authority. The State of New York had exercised its traditional and historically sanctioned power to recognize Windsor and Spyer's Canadian marriage as valid within its jurisdiction. In doing so, it conferred on them a special status—the dignity that comes with marriage. Because they were a same-sex couple, DOMA took this away, demeaning them as members of a class of persons. This consequence violated the federal constitution's promise of liberty in its more transcendent dimension. This was not a federalism analysis—there was no "wise appreciation of the great roles that federalism and separation of powers ha[d] played in establishing and preserving American freedoms."[165]

In *Windsor*, just like *Lawrence*, there was no weighing of the liberty interest against the background of precedent. There was no countervailing interest against which to juxtapose it, to hone its breadth and isolate the discrete interest at stake. And there was no consideration of whether the government could defend its pursuit of its objective and proffer a rational connection to the means it chose to accomplish it. This law demeaned a class of persons, and, therefore, presumptively had no other purpose. "No legitimate purpose," Kennedy declared, "overcomes the purpose and effect to disparage and to injure those whom the State, by its marriage laws, sought to protect in personhood and dignity."[166] This was not an affirmation on appeal of a lower court's determination in this particular case. It was a categorical legal conclusion.

There was, therefore, no particularly careful scrutiny of any need asserted to justify the abridgment of a liberty interest basic to a free society. Although *Windsor* recognized BLAG's standing to offer arguments for the constitutionality of section 3, there was no need to address them. The opinion was rife with statements about the law's "purpose," but only mentioned one of the government's proffered objectives. And this was a quick offhanded dismissal of the argument that DOMA's definitional section provided uniformity to the U.S. Code for efficiency's sake. "DOMA's principal effect[,]" wrote Kennedy, "is to identify a subset of state-sanctioned marriages and make them unequal. The principal purpose is to impose inequality, not for other reasons like governmental efficiency."[167] *Windsor* presumed that DOMA's objective—its purpose—was to accomplish the prohibited effect. *Lawrence* had introduced this feature of Kennedy's new doctrine when it cited *Romer*, implying what the Ninth Circuit said later in *Hollingsworth*—the only possible motive behind a law with such a stigmatizing effect was a bare desire to harm.[168] And *Windsor* now found in the Fifth Amendment both this presumption and *Lawrence*'s categorical prohibition of such legislation.

This reversed the presumption-of-constitutionality principle the Court had recognized in repudiating the *Lochner* Era.[169] As Justice Souter had explained, "the enforceable concept of liberty would bar statutory impositions even at relatively trivial levels when governmental restraints are undeniably irrational as unsupported by any imaginable rationale."[170] But "[s]uch instances were suitably rare."[171] Hence the presumption of a rational connection between means and ends, and a corresponding burden on the party challenging democratic action to demonstrate the absence of one.[172] But *if* the party demonstrated that its "claim[] of arbitrariness . . . rested on . . . [an] interest[] requir[ing] particularly careful scrutiny of the state needs asserted to justify [its] abridgment[,]"[173] the burden shifted to the party defending the as-applied legislative resolution of order and liberty. "A State may not rest," at this point, "on threshold rationality or a presumption of constitutionality[.]"[174] This obligated a judge to strictly scrutinize the justification that a political majority proffered for the means it chose to pursue its objective. The common-law tradition presumed that democracy would *not* produce unconstitutional results unless its careful analysis revealed otherwise.

Windsor seemed to erase this presumption from personal-liberty doctrine. Both *Lawrence* and *Windsor* demonstrated that if a law had the prohibited effect, an apparently irrebuttable presumption of *un*constitutionality arose. Throughout Kennedy's opinion in *Windsor*, he explicitly equated the "purpose" and "effect" of DOMA, just as he had done implicitly with the Texas statute in *Lawrence*.[175] And the analysis in each case proceeded from the law's injurious effect and to its presumptively unconstitutional purpose. *Windsor* made this especially obvious, as DOMA's injurious effect obligated the Court to "scrutinize" it, and at the same time meant that "no legitimate purpose" could overcome its "purpose and effect"—its negative impact on the dignity of a class of persons.

In his dissent, Justice Scalia reminded the Court that the *amici* offered several plausible non-demeaning purposes for the law.[176] And he chastised Kennedy for addressing none of them. He observed that the Court's opinion "affirmatively conceal[ed] from the reader the arguments that exist in justification" for the law.[177] Scalia chose "just one of [the] defenders' arguments," and explained "the difficult choice-of-law issues" that DOMA ostensibly addressed.[178] Kennedy was obviously unconcerned with whether there was merit to this or any other justification proffered for the law. Scalia suggested the Court's not "even troubl[ing] to paraphrase or describe" the arguments presented for upholding DOMA made it easier to "maintain the illusion of the Act's supporters as . . . enemies of the human race,"[179] with no possible motivation for their position other than their "hateful hearts."[180]

Not surprisingly, Scalia cited *Glucksberg*. The Court's "opinion [did] not argue that same-sex marriage is 'deeply rooted in this Nation's history and tradition', . . . a claim," he said, "that would of course be quite absurd."[181] And, citing *Palko*, he suggested that it would be equally absurd to suggest "that a world in which DOMA exist[ed]" would be "one bereft of ordered liberty."[182] The "real rationale" of Kennedy's opinion, said Scalia, regardless of which "disappearing trail of its legalistic argle-bargle one cho[se] to follow, . . . [was] that DOMA [was] motivated by bare desire to harm couples in same sex marriages."[183] And he warned of the obvious ease with which the Court could—and inevitably would—reach the conclusion that all state laws denying marital status to same-sex couples had the same presumptively prohibited purpose and effect.[184] "It is[,]" he predicted, "just a matter of listening and waiting for the other shoe."[185]

Consistent with post-*Griswold* personal-liberty cases through *Lawrence, Windsor* unabashedly addressed far more than Edith Windsor's claim to her tax refund. And the throwaway limitation on the Court's holding—that it was "confined to those lawful marriages" that some States recognized as valid[186]—was all the more disingenuous in light of the extent of Justice Kennedy's next personal-liberty opinion. For the Court would finally meet the obligation that he had announced in *Lawrence*, and define the transcendent dimension of liberty for all within its reach.

NOTES

1. 133 S.Ct 2675 (2013).
2. *Id.* at 2682–2683.
3. *Id.* at 2683; *see also* 1 U.S.C. § 7.
4. 133 S.Ct. at 2683.
5. *Id.*
6. *Id.*
7. *Id.*
8. *Id.* at 2683–2684.
9. *Id.*
10. *Id* at 2684.
11. *Id.* at 2683. ("The letter . . . reflected the Executive's own conclusion, relying on a definition still being debated and considered in the courts[.]").
12. *Id.* at 2684.
13. *Id.*
14. *Id.*

15. *Id.* at 2685.
16. *Id.*
17. *Id.*
18. *Id.*
19. 133 S.Ct. 2652 (2013).
20. *Id.* at 2659.
21. *Id.*
22. *Id.* at 2660.
23. *Id.*
24. *Id.*
25. *Id.*
26. *Id.* (citing *Perry v. Schwarzenegger*, Civ. No. 10-16696 (C.A.9, Aug. 16, 2010)) (internal quotation marks omitted).
27. *Id.* (emphasis added).
28. *Id.* (quoting *Perry v. Schwarzenegger*, 628 F.3d 1191, 1193) (internal quotation marks omitted).
29. *Id.* (quoting *Perry v. Brown*, 671 F.3d 1052, 1072 (9th Cir. 2012)).
30. *Id.* (quoting *Perry*, 671 F.3d at 1083–1084) (emphasis in original).
31. *Id.* (citing *Perry*, 671 F.3d at 1095).
32. *Id.* (quoting *Perry*, 671 F.3d at 1095).
33. *Id.*
34. *Id.* at 2659, 2668.
35. *Id.* at 2661 (quoting U.S. Const. art. III sec. 2).
36. *Id.*
37. *Id.* (citing *Lujan v. Defenders of Wildlife*, 504 U.S. 555, 560–561 (1992)).
38. *Id.* at 2659, 2668.
39. *Id.* at 2662.
40. *Id.*
41. *Id.* (internal quotation marks omitted).
42. *Id.* at 2668.
43. *Id.*
44. 133 S.Ct. at 2668 (Kennedy, J., dissenting).
45. *Id.*
46. *Id.*
47. *Id.*
48. *Id.*
49. *Id.*
50. *Id.* at 2674
51. *Id.* at 2668.
52. *Id.* at 2674.
53. *Id.*
54. *Id.*
55. *Id.*
56. *Id.*
57. 133 S.Ct at 2685.

58. *Id.*

59. *Id.* at 2685–2686 (quoting *Deposit Guaranty Nat. Bank v. Roper*, 445 U.S. 326, 333 (1980)) (internal quotation marks and brackets omitted).

60. *Id.* at 2686.

61. 133 S.Ct. at 2697 (Scalia, J., dissenting).

62. *Id.* at 2698 (quoting U.S. Const. art. III sec. 2).

63. *Id.*

64. *Id.* at 2703.

65. 133 S.Ct. at 2686.

66. *Id.* (emphasis added).

67. *Id.*

68. *Id.*

69. *Id.*

70. 133 S.Ct. at 2698 (Scalia, J., dissenting).

71. *Id.* at 2699 (citing *Lujan*, 504 U.S. at 560 (1992)).

72. *Id.*

73. *Id.* at 2701.

74. *Id.* (emphasis in original).

75. *Id.* (emphasis added).

76. *Id.*

77. 133 S.Ct. at 2687.

78. *Id.*

79. *Id.* (quoting *Ashvander v. TVA*, 297 U.S. 288, 346 (1936) (Brandeis, J., concurring)) (internal quotation marks omitted).

80. *Id.*

81. *Id.* (quoting *Warth v. Seldin*, 422 U.S. 490, 498, 500 (1975)) (internal quotation marks omitted).

82. 133 S.Ct. at 2700 (Scalia, J., dissenting).

83. *Lawrence v. Texas*, No. 02-102, Tr. at 23:10–18; *see* discussion of *Lawrence v. Texas*, chapter 13, *supra*.

84. 133 S.Ct. at 2688.

85. *Id.* (emphasis added).

86. *See* discussion of *Palko v. Connecticut*, chapter 3, *supra*; discussion of *Poe v. Ullman,* chapter 4, *supra*.

87. *See* discussion of *Washington v. Glucksberg*, chapter 12, *supra*.

88. U.S. Const. art. III sec. 2.

89. 133 S.Ct. at 2700 (Scalia, J., dissenting).

90. *Id.*

91. *Griswold*, 381 U.S. at 501 (Harlan, J., concurring).

92. U.S. Const. art. III sec. 2.

93. 133 S.Ct. at 2688.

94. *Id.*

95. *Id.*

96. *Id.* (quoting *Zivotofsky v. Clinton*, 132 S.Ct. 1421, 1427–1428 (2012) (quoting *Marbury v. Madison*, 1 Cranch 137, 177 (1803))).

97. *Id.*
98. 133 S.Ct. at 2699 (Scalia, J., dissenting).
99. *Id.* at 2698–2699.
100. *Id.* at 2699.
101. *Id.*
102. 133 S.Ct. at 2689.
103. *Id.*
104. *Id.* at 2687 (quoting *Baker v. Carr*, 369 U.S. 186, 204 (1962)) (internal quotations omitted).
105. *Id.* at 2689.
106. *Id.*
107. *Id.*
108. *Id.*
109. *Id.*
110. *Id.*
111. *Id.*
112. *Casey*, 505 U.S. at 862.
113. *See Glucksberg*, 521 U.S. at 773–774, 777 (Souter, J., concurring).
114. 133 S.Ct. at 2689.
115. *Id.* at 2689–2690.
116. *Id.* at 2690.
117. *Id.*
118. *Id.*
119. *Id.*
120. *Id.*
121. *Id*
122. *Id.* at 2691.
123. *Id.* (citing *Loving v. Virginia*, 388 U.S. 1 (1967); quoting *Sosna v. Iowa*, 419 U.S. 393, 404 (1975)) (internal quotation marks omitted).
124. *Id.* (citing *Williams v. North Carolina*, 317 U.S. 287, 298 (1942)).
125. *Id.*
126. *Id.* (quoting *Haddock v. Haddock*, 201 U.S. 562, 575 (1906)) (internal quotation marks omitted).
127. *Id.* (quoting *Ohio ex rel. Popovici v. Agler*, 280 U.S. 379, 383–384 (1930)) (internal quotation marks omitted).
128. *Id.*
129. *Id.* (quoting *De Sylva v. Ballentine*, 351 U.S. 570, 580 (1956)) (internal quotation marks omitted).
130. *Id.* at 2692.
131. *Id.*
132. *Id.*
133. *Id.*
134. *Id.* (quoting *Bond v. United States*, 564 U.S. ____, ____ (2011) (slip op. at 9)) (internal quotation marks omitted; brackets in original); *see Bond*, 131 S.Ct. 2355, 2358–2359 (2011).

135. *Id.*
136. *Id.*
137. *Id.*
138. *Id.*
139. *Id.*
140. *Id.*
141. *Id.*
142. *Id.*
143. *Id.*
144. *Id.* at 2693.
145. *Id.* at 2693–2694.
146. *Id.* at 2693.
147. *Id.*
148. *Id.*
149. *Id.*
150. *Id.*
151. *Id.*
152. *Id.* 2693–2694.
153. *Id.* at 2693.
154. *Id.* at 2694.
155. *Id.*
156. *Id.* (emphasis added).
157. *Id.*
158. *Id.* (citing *Lawrence*, 539 U.S. at 558).
159. *Id.*
160. *Id.*
161. *Id.* at 2695.
162. *Id.*
163. *Id.*
164. *Id.* at 2696.
165. *Griswold*, 381 U.S. at 501 (Harlan, J., concurring).
166. 133 S.Ct. at 2696.
167. *Id.* at 2694.
168. *Lawrence*, 539 U.S. at 574 (quoting *Romer*, 517 U.S. at 634).
169. *See* discussion of *United States v. Carolene Products*, chapter 2, *supra.*
170. *Glucksberg*, 521 U.S. at 766 (Souter, J., concurring).
171. *Id.*
172. *See Carolene Products*, 304 U.S. at 152; *see also Lochner*, 198 U.S. at 68 (Harlan, J., dissenting) ("[W]hen the validity of a statute is questioned, the burden of proof, so to speak, is upon those who assert it to be unconstitutional.").
173. *Glucksberg*, 521 U.S. at 766 (Souter, J., concurring) (quoting *Poe*, 367 U.S. at 543 (Harlan, J., dissenting)) (internal quotation marks omitted).
174. *Id.*
175. *See* discussion of *Lawrence v. Texas*, chapter 13, *supra.*
176. 133 S.Ct. at 2707 (Scalia, J., dissenting).

177. *Id.*
178. *Id.* at 2708.
179. *Id.* at 2707–2708.
180. *Id.* at 2707.
181. *Id.* at 2706–2707.
182. *Id.* at 2707 (internal quotation marks omitted).
183. *Id.* at 2709 (internal quotation marks omitted).
184. *Id.* at 2710.
185. *Id.*
186. 133 S.Ct. at 2696.

Chapter 15

What Freedom Must Become

Justice Scalia did not have long to wait for the other shoe. It dropped two years later, when the Court decided *Obergefell v. Hodges*,[1] a set of consolidated cases from four States. Fourteen same-sex couples and two men whose same-sex partners were deceased challenged laws of their States that allowed only opposite-sex couples to marry.[2] Each State defined marriage like DOMA did, as a union between one man and one woman. The petitioners claimed that their States' denying them marital status "violate[d] the Fourteenth Amendment."[3] Post-*Windsor*, the due-process and equal-protection analyses were no longer distinguishable. Unlike *Lawrence* and *Windsor*, the Court in *Obergefell* need not specify in which clause the petitioners' claims sounded. It would decide these cases using "[t]he synergy between the two protections[.]"[4] The "interrelation of the two principles," the Court said, "furthers our understanding of what freedom is and must become."[5]

***

During oral argument, Justice Samuel Alito reacted incredulously to the petitioners' suggestion that the only possible purpose of excluding same-sex couples from the institution of marriage was to demean them. "You argue in your . . . brief," he said to counsel, "that the primary *purpose* of the Michigan law limiting marriage to a man and a woman was to demean gay people[.]" He asked, "Is that correct?"[6]

"The Michigan . . . statute and amendment," she answered, "certainly went out of their way to say that gay people were in some sense antithetical to the good of society."[7]

"[D]id . . . you say in your brief that the primary *purpose* of that was to demean gay people?"[8]

Although she responded to Justice Alito, she aimed her answer at another. "I think it has that *effect*, Your Honor."[9]

The United States appeared as *amicus* on behalf of the petitioners. The first words that the solicitor general spoke during his allotted time presumed that any scrutiny of the States' justifications was unnecessary.

"The opportunity to marry," he said, "is integral to human dignity. Excluding gay and lesbian couples from marriage demeans the dignity of these couples."[10]

And counsel for the respondents, during his argument, made a direct appeal to one justice in particular. "Justice Kennedy," he said, "to be perfectly clear, the State of Michigan values the dignity and worth of every human being, no matter their orientation or how they choose to live their life."[11]

***

Writing for the majority, Justice Kennedy presented a brief recapitulation of the Court's personal-liberty decisions—an even more truncated version than he had in *Lawrence.* Summarizing the merger of the incorporation and fundamental-rights doctrines, he first cited *Duncan*, noting that "[t]he fundamental liberties protected by [the Due Process] Clause include most of the rights enumerated in the Bill of Rights."[12] Then, citing *Eisenstadt* and *Griswold*, he explained that "these liberties extend[ed] to certain personal choices central to individual dignity and autonomy, including intimate choices that define personal identity and beliefs."[13]

As the post-*Griswold* fundamental-rights cases taught, the more broadly one described a liberty interest, the more likely it was to be found within the realm of personal liberty which the government may not enter. According to Kennedy, identifying rights within the realm was "guided by many of the same considerations relevant to analysis of other constitutional provisions that set forth broad principles rather than specific requirements."[14] The right to marry should be considered, therefore, as in the Court's prior cases—"in its comprehensive sense[.]"[15]

Citing Justice Souter's *Glucksberg* concurrence as an example, Kennedy explained that the proper inquiry in the Court's prior cases was whether "there was a sufficient justification for excluding the relevant class from the right."[16] Even leaving aside this misunderstanding of Souter's concurrence, counsel for the respondents had spent considerable time during oral arguments struggling to present a justification for limiting marriage to opposite-sex couples. But the *Obergefell* opinion would not evaluate it. Just like *Lawrence* and *Windsor*, what mattered here was the effect of the States' excluding members of "the relevant class[.]" This time, however, the Court's holding would do far more than categorically prohibit a particular government action.

***

Justice Breyer challenged counsel for the State of Michigan to provide a justification for excluding same-sex couples from "participat[ing] in [the] fundamental liberty" to marry. He said, "[W]e ask, why? And the answer we get is, well, people have always done it . . . . [o]r . . . because certain religious groups . . . think it's a sin[.] . . . And then when I look for reasons three, four and five, I don't find them. What are they?"[17]

"[T]he marriage institution," counsel responded, "developed to serve purposes that, by their nature, arise from biology." The purpose of marriage, he argued, and the State's interest in maintaining its "traditional definition," was to bind men and women who procreate to their biological children.[18] "[T]here's harm," he said, "if you change the definition because, in people's minds, if marriage and creating children don't have anything to do with each other, then . . . [y]ou expect more children outside of marriage."[19]

Justice Breyer asked, "[W]hat evidence is there of that?"[20]

As he had done in *Lawrence*, Justice Scalia tried to help. He suggested that the respondents need not point to any evidence. They had no "burden to show that it . . . will harm marriage between a man and a woman if . . . you allow two men or two women to marry[.]" The respondents' burden, Scalia said, was "simply to show that . . . the State's reason for [its policy] . . . has nothing to do with same-sex couples."[21]

Counsel agreed. Formulated under the *Glucksberg* method, the social practice of "same-sex couples marrying" was not a fundamental right. The presumption of constitutionality should, therefore, vindicate any plausible rationale connecting the legislative choice to the State's policy objective. "It's reasonable to believe," counsel insisted, that changing the definition of marriage "could have different results."[22] "Our point is that when you change something as fundamental as the marriage definition, . . . those changes matter."[23]

Justice Sonia Sotomayor wondered if this argument, even accepted on its own terms, could justify the States' policies. Was this mere suggestion—that some people might feel differently about the connection between marriage and procreation—a *plausible* rationale for the laws challenged here? She seemed to invoke Justice Souter's teaching that "the enforceable concept of liberty would bar statutory impositions . . . when governmental restraints are undeniably irrational as unsupported by *any* imaginable rationale."[24]

"Do we accept a *feeling*?" she asked. "[W]hy would that feeling, which doesn't make any logical sense, control our decision making?"[25]

***

Even while citing Souter's *Glucksberg* concurrence, Kennedy ignored its unambiguous refusal to identify unenumerated rights, whether described at the most specific level or in their comprehensive sense. The precision that reasoned judgment demanded, Souter had shown, counseled against calling any individual's interest a "right" unless the common-law method's careful scrutiny revealed that the State's interference with it, in the particular controversy before the Court, was unreasonable.[26] Only then did "the individual have anything legally enforceable as against the state's attempt at regulation."[27] This co-option of Souter's opinion seemed an insult to the memory of Justice Harlan, whose *Poe* opinion Kennedy cited to support the proposition that "the judicial duty to interpret the Constitution . . . . require[d] courts to exercise reasoned judgment in identifying interests of the person so fundamental that the State must accord them its respect."[28] Kennedy declared that "an enduring part of this judicial duty" was to "identif[y] . . . fundamental rights[.]"[29]

He acknowledged the respondents' argument that the Court should construe narrowly the right the petitioners claimed, using the modern-conservative method as applied in *Glucksberg*. The respondents "call[ed] for a 'careful description' of fundamental rights[,]" arguing that "the petitioners [did] not seek to exercise the right to marry but rather a new and nonexistent 'right to same-sex marriage'."[30] But *Glucksberg*, Kennedy explained, was an exception to the proper analysis.

> *Glucksberg* did insist that liberty under the Due Process Clause must be defined in a most circumscribed manner, with central reference to specific historical practices. Yet while that approach may have been appropriate for the asserted right there involved (physician-assisted suicide), it is inconsistent with the approach this Court has used in discussing other fundamental rights, including marriage and intimacy.[31]

Under the latter approach, the Court formulated fundamental rights more broadly. Consistent with modern liberalism's post-*Griswold* approach, Kennedy spurned the modern-conservative method's specificity without explaining why his broader alternative was better. But this version of the method's history-and-tradition inquiry, that he had suggested in *Lewis*, introduced in *Lawrence*, and developed in *Windsor*, would drive the analysis in *Obergefell*. And although this inquiry framed its object at a greater level of generality than the modern-conservative method, *Obergefell* would teach the same lesson as *Michael H.*, *Glucksberg*, *Lawrence*, and *Windsor*—properly identifying a fundamental right required surveying its history and tradition.

***

"From their beginning to their most recent page," Kennedy wrote, "the annals of human history reveal the transcendent importance of marriage."[32] Although the "ancient origins of marriage confirm[ed] its centrality," it had not "stood in isolation from developments in law and society."[33] Marriage had "evolved over time[,]" from a parentally arranged political, religious, and economic alliance, to a contract between a man and a woman.[34] And "[a] s women gained legal, political, and property rights," marriage changed from an institution that the law of coverture governed to one in which "women have their own equal dignity[.]"[35] "These . . . were not," Kennedy said, "mere superficial changes."[36] Marriage was not a static concept—it had undergone "deep transformations in its structure [that] affect[ed] aspects of [it] long viewed by many as essential."[37]

Throughout its history so far, marriage was admittedly always defined as "a union between two persons of the opposite sex."[38] But while "[h]istory and tradition [were] the starting point," they were "not in all cases the ending point" of the personal-liberty inquiry.[39] The history of marriage was only "the beginning of these cases."[40] "History and tradition guide and discipline this inquiry[,]" Kennedy said, "but do not set its outer boundaries. Th[is] method respects our history and learns from it without allowing the past alone to rule the present."[41] Although Kennedy's history-and-tradition inquiry had originated in the modern-conservative method, unlike it, his would not confine the protections of the Fourteenth Amendment to "rules fixed in the past[.]"[42]

"[T]he Court ha[d] long held [that] the right to marry [was] protected by the Constitution."[43] And as with other unenumerated substantive rights, "[c] hanged understandings of marriage" were "characteristic of a Nation where new dimensions of freedom bec[a]me apparent to new generations, often through perspectives that beg[a]n in pleas or protests and then [were] considered in the political sphere and the judicial process."[44] So the Court had "invalidated bans on interracial unions" in *Loving v. Virginia*, laws "prohibiting fathers who were behind on child support from marrying" in *Zablocki v. Redhail*, and "regulations limiting the privilege of prison inmates to marry" in *Turner v. Safley*.[45] New insights into the transcendent importance of marriage had illuminated for the Court the constitutional requirement to incrementally extend this fundamental right.

Kennedy saw a parallel "dynamic . . . in the Nation's experiences with the rights of gays and lesbians."[46] Up until the mid-twentieth century, same-sex intimacy was considered a crime "in most Western nations."[47] And "[f] or much of the 20th century . . . homosexuality was treated as an illness."[48] "In the late twentieth century," however, "following substantial cultural and political developments, same-sex couples began to lead more open and public lives and to establish families."[49] As "public attitudes" about homosexuality "shifted . . . toward greater tolerance . . . questions about the rights of gays and lesbians soon reached the courts, where the issue could be discussed in the formal discourse of the law."[50] The Court had initially upheld the criminalization of certain sexual acts in *Bowers*. But a mere "[t]en years later, in *Romer v. Evans* . . . the Court invalidated . . . Colorado's" attempt "to foreclose any branch or political subdivision of the State from protecting persons against discrimination based on sexual orientation."[51] And in *Lawrence*, "the Court overruled *Bowers*, holding that laws making same-sex intimacy a crime demean[ed] the lives of homosexual persons."[52]

Like *Michael H.* and *Glucksberg*, both *Lawrence* and *Windsor* taught that the history-and-tradition inquiry looked to developments in the States' laws for relevant background against which to assess the validity of a fundamental-right claim.[53] Kennedy observed that as these "new dimensions of freedom"—to marry and of same-sex intimacy—"had become apparent to new generations[,]" they had become apparent in the laws of some of the States. In 1993, the Hawaiian Supreme Court had held that Hawaii's law restricting marriage to opposite-sex couples was a sex-based classification subject to strict scrutiny under the Hawaiian Constitution.[54] "[T]his decision did not mandate that same-sex marriage be allowed, [but] some States[,] concerned by its implications[,] . . . reaffirmed in their laws that marriage [was] defined as a union between opposite-sex partners."[55] Other States came to "a different conclusion."[56] In 2003, Massachusetts became the first State to recognize the right to marry for same-sex couples as a state-constitutional guarantee.[57] Following this development, "some additional States granted marriage rights to same-sex couples, either through judicial or legislative process."[58]

The Court's precedents showed these new dimensions of freedom. Although "th[e] Court's cases describing the right to marry presumed a relationship involving opposite-sex partners,"[59] another line of "more instructive precedents . . . express[ed] constitutional principles of broader reach."[60] These principles, evident in cases like *Griswold* and *Lawrence*, "identified essential attributes of th[e] right [to marry] based in history, tradition, and other constitutional liberties inherent in this intimate bond."[61] Kennedy cited Harlan's *Poe* example again, this time for the proposition that "in assessing whether the force and rationale of its cases apply to same-sex couples, the Court must respect the basic reasons why the right to marry has been long protected."[62] Four broad principles that explained why marriage was a fundamental right also "compel[led] the conclusion that same-sex couples may exercise [it]."[63]

***

First, Kennedy explained, "the right to personal choice regarding marriage is inherent in the concept of individual autonomy."[64] *Loving* had recognized "[t]his abiding connection between marriage and liberty[.]"[65] Kennedy cited

Lawrence for the proposition that "choices concerning contraception, family relationships, procreation, and childrearing" were constitutionally protected because, like "decisions concerning marriage[,]" these were "among the most intimate that an individual [could] make."[66] "Through [the] enduring bond" of marriage, "two persons together c[ould] find other freedoms, such as expression, intimacy, and spirituality."[67] "[T]he decision whether and whom to marry [was] among life's momentous acts of self-definition."[68] "Choices about marriage[,]" Kennedy said, "shape an individual's destiny."[69]

The second relevant "principle in [the] Court's jurisprudence[,]" he continued, was the dignity-conferring power of marriage.[70] It "promised nobility and dignity to all persons, without regard to their station in life."[71] Kennedy explained that marriage "support[ed] a two-person union unlike any other in its importance to the committed individuals. This point," he said, "was central to *Griswold*['s]" holding that "the Constitution protects the right of married couples to use contraception."[72] *Lawrence* had similarly "confirmed a dimension of freedom that allows individuals to engage in intimate association without criminal liability[.]"[73] Like *Griswold*'s rejecting government action affronting the dignity of married couples, *Lawrence* had rejected government action affronting the dignity of same-sex couples whose "intimate conduct . . . [could] be but one element in a personal bond that is more enduring."[74] In this sense *Lawrence* stopped short of the constitutional promise that *Griswold* represented, merely freeing same-sex couples from their status as outlaws.[75] This was "a step forward, but it [did] not achieve the full promise of liberty."[76] And so *Windsor* taught that "[t]he right to marry . . . dignifie[d] couples"—whether same or opposite-sex—"who wish[ed] to define themselves by their commitment to each other."[77]

Citing *Meyer* and *Pierce*, Kennedy identified the "third basis for protecting the right to marry." He said, "[I]t safeguards children and families."[78] Justice Douglas had used *Meyer* and *Pierce* as support for incorporating unenumerated substantive rights.[79] Kennedy had used them much the same in *Lawrence*, as evidence of the "broad statements of the substantive reach of liberty" in the Court's precedent.[80] Now he used them more narrowly. The right to marry, he explained, "draws meaning from related rights of childrearing, procreation, and education."[81] "The Court ha[d] recognized these connections by describing the varied rights as a unified whole[ ]"[82] When the Court in *Zablocki* held, for example, that "prohibiting fathers who were behind on child-support from marrying"[83] violated due process, it referred to *Meyer*'s "right to marry, establish a home and bring up children" as a "central part of the liberty" that the Constitution protected.[84]

The laws in some of the States bolstered the relevance of this third principle. "Most States . . . allowed gays and lesbians to adopt, either as individuals or as couples, and many foster and adopted children [had] same-sex parents."[85] Kennedy emphasized that no parties to these cases disputed that "many same-sex couples provide[d] loving and nurturing homes to their children[.]"[86] And "hundreds of thousands of children . . . [were] being raised by such couples."[87] He concluded, "This provides powerful confirmation from the law itself that gays and lesbians can create loving, supportive families."[88] Kennedy seemed to suggest that to maintain as a unified whole the constellation of rights for which *Meyer* and *Pierce* stood—to marry, establish a home and raise children—same-sex couples, having been granted some of them in most States, must be permitted to exercise all of them.

But this was not the reason this third "principle and tradition" counseled against "excluding same-sex couples from marriage[.]"[89] Rather, the dignity the Constitution guaranteed to same-sex couples extended to their children. The existence of loving and supportive families comprising same-sex partners and their children showed that excluding these couples from marriage "conflicts with a central premise of the right to marry."[90] "Without the recognition, stability, and predictability marriage offers," Kennedy explained, these "children suffer the stigma of knowing [that] their families are somehow lesser."[91] The laws the petitioners challenged here, he said, "harm and humiliate the children of same-sex couples."[92]

Concern for these children was, of course, only one aspect of "the constitutional marriage right."[93] For no State had made "an ability, desire, or promise to procreate" a "prerequisite for a valid marriage."[94] And "[i]n light of" the "more instructive precedents" in which Kennedy had found "principles of broader reach"[95]—"precedent[s] protecting the right of a married couple *not* to procreate"—no one could say that "the Court or the States [had] conditioned the right to marry on the capacity or commitment to" have children.[96] Significantly, the *Obergefell* opinion did not connect this point to any consideration of the respondents' proffered justification for their laws, despite its begging for this very retort.

The "Court's cases and the Nation's traditions . . . ma[de] clear" the fourth and final principle compelling the conclusion that the Constitution guaranteed to same-sex couples the right to marry.[97] Kennedy explained, "[M]arriage is a keystone of our social order."[98] The Court had recognized this as long ago as 1888, when in *Maynard v. Hill*[99] it "explain[ed] that marriage is the foundation of the family and of society, without which there would be neither civilization nor progress."[100] "Marriage remains[,]" Kennedy said, "a building block of our national community."[101] "For this reason," he explained, "society pledged to support" married couples, "offering symbolic recognition and material benefits to protect and nourish th[eir] unions."[102] And while the States were free to vary the benefits they conferred on married couples, "throughout . . . history [they] made marriage the basis for an expanding list of governmental rights, benefits and responsibilities."[103] Entry into the institution of marriage was an aspect of full participation in the political community, and "the States . . . contributed to the fundamental character of the marriage right by placing [i]t at the center of so many facets of the legal and social order."[104]

The origin of Kennedy's history-and-tradition inquiry showed here again. The modern-conservative method had equated the fundamental status of unenumerated rights with the States' already recognizing them, attempting to eliminate federal constitutional protection for them against the States' legislative policies. Kennedy's method similarly related social order in the States to constitutional liberty—the States "contributed to . . . the marriage right['s] . . . fundamental character"[105]—although decidedly not to implement a majoritarian-positivist political ideology. Harlan had foreseen the danger of abandoning the precision, cautious moderation, and careful scrutiny of the common-law due-process tradition.[106] He had prophesied that *Griswold*'s quasi-incorporation would be used to restrict liberty as well as protect it.[107] Scalia fulfilled the prophesy, picking and choosing from among various nonconstitutional-law sources to reach foregone conclusions.[108] And Scalia's method in turn inspired Kennedy's, which now found results at the opposite end of the ideological spectrum.

With respect to the fourth principle, Kennedy concluded, "There is no difference between same- and opposite-sex couples[.]"[109] Because they were excluded from the institution of marriage, "same-sex couples [were] denied the constellation of benefits that the States ha[d] linked to marriage."[110] But the effect of this harm was not merely its "material burdens[.]"[111]

> As the State itself makes marriage all the more precious by the significance it attaches to it, exclusion from that status has the effect of teaching that gays and lesbians are unequal in important respects. It demeans gays and lesbians for the State to lock them out of a central institution of the Nation's society.[112]

> [L]aws excluding same-sex couples from the marriage right impose stigma and injury of the kind prohibited by our basic charter.[113]

Consistent with *Lawrence* and *Windsor*, the equal protection aspect of due process would further compel the States to permit same-sex couples to marry. Interpreting this principle, "the Court [had] recognized that new insights and societal understandings [could] reveal unjustified inequality within . . . most fundamental institutions that once passed unnoticed and unchallenged."[114] This had "occurred with respect to marriage" during the second half of the twentieth century, as the Court discovered "classifications denying the equal dignity of men and women" and "invalidated laws imposing sex-based inequality on marriage."[115] And "[i]n *Lawrence* the Court acknowledged the interlocking nature of [the] constitutional safeguards" of "liberty and equality[,]" and "drew upon [them] to define and protect the rights of gays and lesbians, holding that the State cannot demean their existence or control their destiny[.]"[116] "This dynamic," Kennedy said, "also applies to same-sex marriage."[117] "Under the Constitution," he concluded, "same-sex couples seek in marriage the same legal treatment as opposite-sex couples, and it would disparage their choices and diminish their personhood to deny them this right."[118]

***

Justice Kennedy mused aloud during oral arguments: "[T]he word that keeps coming back to me in this case is 'millennia'. I don't even know how to count the decimals when we talk about millennia. This definition [of marriage] has been with us for millennia. And it's very difficult for the Court to say, oh, well, . . . we know better."[119]

***

"There may be an initial inclination in these cases[,]" Justice Kennedy wrote, "to proceed with caution[.]"[120] But the Nation had waited long enough.

> When new insight reveals discord between the Constitution's central protections and a received legal stricture, a claim to liberty must be addressed.[121]
>
> The limitation of marriage to opposite sex couples may long have seemed natural and just, but its inconsistency with the central meaning of the fundamental right to marry is now manifest.[122]
>
> The right to marry is fundamental as a matter of history and tradition, but rights come not from ancient sources alone. They rise, too, from a better informed understanding of how constitutional imperatives define a liberty that remains urgent in our own era.[123]

Windsor had connected *Lawrence*'s constitutionally protected intimate bond for same-sex couples—their full right to sexual intimacy[124]—to the institution of marriage. And it had shown just how urgent was the liberty of same-sex couples to find this intimacy within it—so urgent that the Court *took* jurisdiction to declare DOMA unconstitutional.[125] And now, the coterminous evolutions of society's views toward marriage and same-sex intimacy, evident in some of the States' laws and the Court's precedents, converged here in *Obergefell*. A new right would rise from the Court's better informed understanding of these evolving liberties, and of how the constitutional imperatives of autonomy and dignity, derived from the due-process and equal-protection aspects of the Fourteenth Amendment defined them in the twenty-first century. A more transcendent liberty would now work a deep transformation in the structure of marriage, affecting another aspect of it long viewed by many as essential.[126]

The petitioners "ask[ed] for equal dignity in the eyes of the law."[127] And the judicial power would grant them this right. But it would not simply announce, as in *Lawrence*, that constitutional liberty categorically prohibited yet another state policy. Here, it would pronounce what the promise of its transcendent dimension required. And not just of the losing litigants. Nor for only the petitioners in these cases. In *Lawrence* and *Windsor*, the Court had shrugged off such limitations, vindicating the interests of hundreds of thousands of persons and tens of thousands of children. But *this* decision would touch over 300 million persons. This one was expressly for *every* State, all at once, throughout the Union.

> The Court, in this decision, holds same-sex couples may exercise the fundamental right to marry in all States. It follows that the Court also must hold—and it now does hold—that there is no lawful basis for a State to refuse to recognize a lawful same-sex marriage performed in another State on the ground of its same-sex character.[128]

The hollow holding of *Slaughterhouse* had undeniably resounded in Justice Scalia's *Michael H.* opinion. And now, as the Court resolved the civil-rights issue of the new century, the faint strains of a mid-nineteenth-century argument—one the *Slaughterhouse* majority had rejected—traversed the turns of two centuries to reverberate here.

> The tie between the United States and every citizen in every part of its own jurisdiction has been made intimate and familiar. To the same extent the confederate features of the government have been obliterated. . . . The purpose is manifest, to establish through the whole jurisdiction of the United States one people, and that every member of the empire shall understand and appreciate the fact that his [liberty] cannot be abridged by State authority[.][129]

Justice Kennedy had put the States, "in their closest connection with their members[,]" where they finally belonged—"under the oversight and restraining and enforcing hand of" a closely divided U.S. Supreme Court.[130]

***

Half a century ago, Justice Douglas had discovered a zone of privacy comprising penumbras emanating from some Bill of Rights provisions. During the thirty years after *Griswold*, the zone became a category of fundamental rights worthy of special protection. In the twenty-first century, *Griswold*'s mischievous spirit had found a willing host in Justice Kennedy, who discovered, emanating from some of these special rights, a transcendent dimension of liberty. According to this doctrine, like the modern-conservative method, democracy in some of the States helped illuminate what democratic actions this dimension of freedom prohibited. Democracy in the States might also help illuminate, sometimes, whether a right was fundamental and protected from state action. And here in *Obergefell*, democracy in the States helped illuminate not only what the States may *not* do, but also what the Court should decide they must.

As in *Lawrence* and *Windsor*, government actions that impacted the destiny of individuals or demeaned classes of persons were prohibited, regardless of their objectives or of the means employed to pursue them. This liberty promised individuals—at least as members of a relevant class—the freedom to define themselves and construct their own identities with dignity. These were surely unobjectionable precepts, resonant with basic values underlying American society. But they were presented here, again, as axioms with no principled account of their judicial application. This was simply a mixture of Kennedy's own opinions and various nonconstitutional-law sources—trends in legal scholarship, the laws of foreign nations and the American States, and society's views—yielding a twenty-first-century *metaphysic* of liberty.

The modern conservatives had ultimately failed to forge an "established method of substantive due-process analysis"[131] out of *Bowers*, *Moore*, *Michael H.*, and *Glucksberg*. Their attempt had spanned eleven years. But Justice Kennedy managed to establish, in about the same amount of time, a new doctrine of substantive liberty using *Lawrence*, *Windsor*, and *Obergefell*, drawing on his own contributions in *Romer* and *Casey*. And Justice Scalia's now-quarter-century-old attempt to skew personal-liberty jurisprudence toward conservative results provided the patina of analytic legitimacy covering Kennedy's new jurisprudence. History and tradition only furthered modern-conservative ends if one obeyed the stricture of "carefully describing" asserted liberty interests at "the most specific level."[132] But Kennedy had hedged against this constraint just two years after arriving at the Court, when he joined Justice O'Connor's *Michael H.* concurrence,[133] and then in *Lewis* presented a different view of history and tradition.[134] *Lawrence*, *Windsor*, and *Obergefell* showed just how differently it could be used in each case.

In *Lawrence*, recent history revealed an emerging awareness within the legal tradition that the basic human rights of autonomy and dignity invalidated laws like Texas's anti-sodomy statute. In *Windsor*, the power to confer the constitutional dignity of marital status belonged, as a matter of history and tradition, to the States, and DOMA's taking it away demeaned same-sex married couples in violation of the constitution's promise of liberty. And in *Obergefell*, the history of the marital tradition, and a corresponding history of society's views of gays and lesbians, revealed that withholding marriage's "transcendent importance" from same-sex couples had the same effect, and, therefore, the same unconstitutional purpose. History and tradition had been co-opted into the service of one ideology, and then co-opted into the service of another. Scalia had prepared the ground for Kennedy, who now sowed the seeds of opportunity for the next aspiring ideologue.

The problem that arose with *Griswold* persisted in *Obergefell*—outcome-dispositive tailoring of the levels of generality at which competing interests were stated. Justice Souter had shown that to solve it, common-law arbitrariness review juxtaposed the parties' claims with reference to the concept of ordered liberty, paying especially close attention to their details evident in the factual record of the case. But the Court had ignored this lesson. And, like the modern-conservative method, Kennedy's exploited the problem. He found in *Meyer*, for example, "broad statements of the substantive reach of liberty"[135] to describe its transcendent dimension, and the more narrow "rights of childrearing, procreation, and education"[136] to connect same-sex couples' enjoyment of these extant rights to the "constitutional marriage right"[137] understood "in its comprehensive sense[.]"[138] Like the Court's fundamental-rights cases, and *Lawrence* and *Windsor*, *Obergefell* relied on a special dimension of constitutional liberty and "rights"—some broad, some narrow—found within its realm. Illustrating the extent to which this problem had so completely captivated the Court, Chief Justice John Roberts, dissenting in *Obergefell*, insisted that "[t]he fundamental right to marry does not include a right to make a State change its definition of marriage."[139]

Obergefell displayed just how confused the Court's fundamental-rights jurisprudence had become. The respondents tried to use, for example, Justice Kennedy's consequentialism to support their own cause. They argued that "it would demean a timeless institution if the concept and lawful status of marriage were extended to two persons of the same sex."[140] The problem was not, Kennedy explained, any threat to the dignity of the marital institution that the petitioners' claims posed. The petitioners' "intent" was not "to demean the revered idea and reality of marriage."[141] "Their plea[,]" he explained, "is that they do respect it, respect it so deeply that they seek to find its fulfillment for themselves."[142] There *was* a purpose to demean here, but it was not the petitioners', and the effect of excluding them from the institution of marriage proved it.

The respondents took to its logical conclusion *Michael H.*'s and *Glucksberg*'s equating constitutionally protected liberties with democratically preapproved social practices. They claimed that the liberty interest at stake was theirs, not the petitioners'. Much like a renowned icon of modern conservatism had complained that "the courts . . . [were] depriving" the people of their "most precious freedom . . . to govern [them]selves democratically unless the

Constitution actually says otherwise[,]"[143] counsel argued, "[W]e're asking you to affirm every individual's fundamental liberty interest in deciding the meaning of marriage."[144] They were not interested, of course, in the Court's affirming *every* individual's liberty to decide the meaning of marriage—just enough of those who agreed with them to make a majority. Counsel insisted, "We're talking about the fundamental liberty interest in deciding the question of what marriage means."[145] The Court should not infringe upon the liberty of conservative majorities in the States.

This appealed to the majoritarian positivism with which Justice Scalia had infused the jurisprudence. Counsel for the respondents even denied, early in his oral argument, that the definition of marriage mattered at all. What mattered was protecting democracy in the States. "This case isn't about how to define marriage[,]" he said. "It's about who gets to decide that question. Is it the people acting through the democratic process, or is it the Federal courts?"[146] This argument easily persuaded Scalia, who lamented, as he had in *Lawrence*, the havoc upon American democracy that the Court's decision would wreak. Writing separately in dissent "to call attention to th[e] Court's threat to American democracy[,]"[147] Scalia, too, parroted Judge Bork:

> This practice of constitutional revision by an unelected committee of nine, always accompanied (as it is today) by extravagant praise of liberty, robs the People of the most important liberty they asserted in the Declaration of Independence and won in the Revolution of 1776: the freedom to govern themselves.[148]

The opening sentence of *Obergefell* summarized Kennedy's new doctrine of constitutional liberty: "The Constitution promises liberty to all within its reach, a liberty that includes certain specific rights that allow persons, within a lawful realm, to define and express their identity."[149] Like the *Lawrence* and *Windsor* opinions, this cryptic formulation begged the question. The opinion gave no account of any countervailing interest against which to juxtapose this new liberty's breadth. Nor any explanation of how to know which "specific rights" were "included" in its transcendent dimension, or of how to find the boundaries of the "lawful realm" within which it protected "persons" (plural) as they defined and expressed a collective "identity" (singular). These mysterious statements would undoubtedly produce unintended consequences, much like *Griswold* had a half century ago.

But *Obergefell* nevertheless clarified the analysis that *Lawrence* introduced and *Windsor* developed. It applied a doctrine of transcendent fundamental rights based on a presumption of unconstitutionality for laws with particular consequences. Marriage was a fundamental right, to be considered in its comprehensive sense. Laws excluding same-sex couples from marriage demeaned the relevant class of persons, affronted their dignity, and interfered with their right to define their own existences and control their own destinies. And no legitimate purpose could overcome this effect, because it was irrebuttably the unconstitutional purpose of the laws the petitioners challenged. The analysis only perfunctorily asked whether there was a sufficient justification for excluding the "relevant class"—here, same-sex couples—from exercising the fundamental right. This clearly was not a due-process analysis that scrutinized with particular care this exclusion for fitness with its "own ostensible justification."[150]

Nor could it be understood as an equal-protection analysis, strictly scrutinizing the States' denying a government-conferred benefit based on a suspect classification.[151] Nevertheless, while surveying the history of "the Nation's experiences with the rights of gays and lesbians[,]" Kennedy noted that in the mid-twentieth century homosexuality was classified as a mental disorder,[152] but in "more recent years . . . psychiatrists and others recognized that sexual orientation [was] both a normal expression of human sexuality and immutable."[153] He made another passing reference to immutability after insisting that the petitioners sought marriage for themselves "because of their respect—and need—for its privileges and responsibilities."[154] He wrote, "And their immutable nature dictates that same-sex marriage is their only real path to this profound commitment."[155] But these mentions of homosexuality as an immutable characteristic were not connected to the holding of the case, to any analysis of whether or why gays and lesbians or same-sex couples were a suspect class, or to any other explanation of how immutability influenced the analysis.

As it had in *Lawrence*, the harm principle briefly appeared in Kennedy's opinion. But it, too, remained unconnected to the holding, appearing well after it in dicta toward the end of the opinion. Finally acknowledging the argument that "allowing same-sex couples to wed will harm marriage as an institution by leading to fewer opposite-sex marriages[,]"[156] Kennedy wrote, "with respect to this asserted basis for excluding same-sex couples from the right to marry, it is appropriate to observe these cases involve only the rights of two consenting adults whose marriages would pose no risk of harm to themselves or third parties."[157] Like the mention of immutability, this cursory acknowledgment of the respondents' justification was no part of any analysis. Nor did it account for the breadth of the Court's holding, which expressly applied far beyond "these cases."

In his dissent, Chief Justice Roberts noticed this conclusory dismissal of the respondents' argument "near the end of [the majority's] opinion."[158] And he aptly compared it to an infamous period in the Court's troubled history of applying the due-process guarantee.

> This argument . . . echoes *Lochner*, which relied on its assessment that "we think that a law like the one before us involves neither the safety, the morals nor the

welfare of the public, and that the interest of the public is not in the slightest degree affected by such an act."[159]

But Justice Kennedy's jurisprudence was a *Lochner*-Era redux in a far more significant respect than his conclusory fact-finding about the alleged dangers of same-sex marriage. *Lawrence*, *Windsor*, and *Obergefell* now stood for a categorical constitutional prohibition of state policies that the Court determined affronted the fundamental rights to autonomy and dignity. The *Lochner*-Era cases had stood for a categorical constitutional prohibition of state policies the Court determined affronted the liberty to contract. Like the *Lochner*-Era cases Justice Souter had described, Kennedy's doctrine "harbored the spirit of *Dred Scott* in [its] absolutist implementation of the standard [it] espoused."[160] But unlike the *Lochner*-Era opinions, Kennedy's in *Obergefell* did not even "invoke[] a correct standard of constitutional arbitrariness review[.]"[161] There was no trace of the concept of ordered liberty and the traditional common-law analysis that implemented it. *Obergefell's* ontological account of the marriage right—"the right to marry is a fundamental right inherent in the liberty of the person"—and its absolutist application of it—"under the Due Process and Equal Protection Clauses of the Fourteenth Amendment, couples of the same sex may not be deprived of that right and that liberty"—made this clear.[162]

"Rejecting *Lochner*," Chief Justice Roberts said, "does not require disavowing the doctrine of implied fundamental rights. . . . But to avoid repeating *Lochner*'s error . . . our modern substantive due process cases have stressed the need for judicial self-restraint."[163] And like so many before him, Roberts quoted Harlan's *Griswold* concurrence to describe the "only way to ensure restraint in th[e] delicate enterprise" of due-process review.[164] But his dissent gave no indication that he understood the *Poe* example. To the contrary, he repeated Scalia's misquotation of Cardozo. The "theory" of substantive due process, he said, "is that some liberties are so rooted in the traditions and conscience of our people as to be ranked as fundamental[.]"[165] And like the modern conservatives, Roberts saw the Court's "precedents . . . requir[ing] that implied fundamental rights be objectively, deeply rooted in this Nation's history and tradition[.]"[166]

Roberts broke ranks with the modern conservatives in one significant respect. "The Court [was] right[,]" he said, that "[p]roper reliance on history and tradition . . . require[d] looking beyond the individual law being challenged."[167] He disagreed with Scalia's absurdly contradictory requirement that a constitutional liberty interest must be a social practice that the States had at least not outlawed if it were to trump a State's outlawing it. But he nevertheless insisted, quoting Justice Powell in *Moore*, that "an approach grounded in history imposes limits on the judiciary that are more meaningful than any based on an abstract formula" like Kennedy's.[168] Kennedy's professed "discipline in identifying fundamental rights," Roberts said, "does not provide a meaningful constraint on a judge[.]"[169] *Obergefell* exemplified the danger. "Expanding a right suddenly and dramatically [was] likely to require tearing it up from its roots."[170] The "aggressive application of substantive due process" here, Roberts concluded, "breaks sharply with decades of precedent and returns the Court to the unprincipled approach of *Lochner*."[171]

***

There were plenty of opinions dissenting from Kennedy's constitutional revolution.[172] But there were no concurring opinions offering any less radical alternative. In *Lawrence*, Justice O'Connor had offered an equal-protection analysis,[173] and only Justice Scalia made the fundamental-rights argument in his dissent—against recognizing the interest as worthy of heightened protection.[174] No one proposed an analysis from the common-law tradition. And there were no concurring opinions at all in *Windsor* and *Obergefell*. So broken from the tradition, the Court could see at this fateful moment in its history only two options. It could wield the judicial power to make liberal social policy, or defer to conservative majorities in the States.

***

If not for their bitterness, Justice Scalia's dissents might have held some sway. But even if one could ignore their vitriol, they exhibited the same hyper-defense of democratic process as the sole determinant of a law's legitimacy that he had adopted twenty-five years earlier. In them he sometimes aptly criticized Kennedy's incoherent justifications for discovering the "components of liberty in its manifold possibilities[.]"[175] But he resorted to what came across as angry ridicule, even insult. Disgusted with his colleagues in *Obergefell*, he called the Court's opinion "judicial Putsch" filled with "the mystical aphorisms of the fortune cookie."[176] If ever he joined such a disastrous opinion, Scalia said, "I would hide my head in a bag."[177] Sadly oblivious to his complicity in the very corruption of which he accused the Court, this caricature of a disgruntled conservative curmudgeon that Justice Scalia had become eclipsed whatever insights he offered.

***

As counsel for the petitioners in *Obergefell* finished her first argument before the Court, a protestor who had infiltrated the courtroom began screaming.[178]

"*If you support gay marriage*," he shrieked, "*then you will burn in hell for eternity!*"[179]

Order was quickly restored.

As the room fell silent, Justice Scalia quipped, "It's rather refreshing, actually."[180]

What happened to the dignity of which this institution had once been worthy? Near final was its capitulation to the lure of the limelight. To the temptation to speak from on high and say what the law is. To take center stage in the political life of the Nation. Having cast off the self-discipline the tradition demanded of its judges, and the humility the people had the right to expect of their highest court, it shone now as a technicolor specter of its former self. Defining the liberty of all here in the new millennium, it drew its own part in a twenty-first century political cartoon. Perhaps the time had indeed come, as it seems to for all things distinctly American, to put it on television.

NOTES

1. 135 S.Ct. 2584 (2015).
2. *Id.*
3. *Id.*
4. *Id.* at 2603.
5. *Id.*
6. *Obergefell v. Hodges*, No. 14-556, Tr. at 8:4–7.
7. Tr. at 8:8–11.
8. Tr. at 8:12–14.
9. Tr. at 8:15–16 (emphasis added).
10. Tr. at 28:13–15.
11. Tr. 49:18–50:2.
12. 135 S.Ct. at 2597 (citing *Duncan*, 391 U.S. 147–149).
13. *Id.* at 2597–2598.
14. *Id.* at 2598.
15. *Id.* at 2602.
16. *Id.* (citing *Glucksberg*, 521 U.S. at 752–773 (Souter, J., concurring); *id.* at 789–792 (Breyer, J., concurring)).
17. *Obergefell v. Hodges*, No. 14-556, Tr. at 42:19–43:4.
18. Tr. at 43:8–19.
19. Tr. 47:19–22.
20. Tr. 51:3–6.
21. Tr. 46:14–20.
22. Tr. 51:7–12.
23. Tr. 49:23–50:2.
24. *Glucksberg*, 521 U.S. at 766 (Souter, J., concurring) (emphasis added).
25. *Obergefell v. Hodges*, No. 14-556, Tr. at 42:19–43:4.

26. *Glucksberg*, 521 U.S. at 768 footnote 10 (Souter, J., concurring).
27. *Id.*
28. 135 S.Ct. at 2598 (citing *Poe*, 367 U.S. at 542).
29. *Id.*
30. *Id.* at 2602.
31. *Id.*
32. *Id.* at 2593–2594.
33. *Id.* at 2595.
34. *Id.*
35. *Id.*
36. *Id.*
37. *Id.* at 2595–2596.
38. *Id.* at 2594.
39. *Lewis*, 523 U.S. at 857 (Kennedy, J. concurring).
40. 135 S.Ct. at 2594.
41. *Id.* at 2598.
42. *See Duncan*, 391 U.S. at 176–177 (Harlan, J., dissenting) (citing *Hurtado*, 110 U.S. at 529).
43. 135 S.Ct. at 2598.
44. *Id.* at 2596.
45. *Id.* at 2598 (citing *Loving v. Virginia*, 388 U. S. 1 (1967); *Zablocki v. Redhail*, 434 U.S. 374 (1978); *Turner v. Safley*, 482 U. S. 78 (1987)).
46. *Id.* at 2596.
47. *Id.*
48. *Id.*
49. *Id.*
50. *Id.*
51. *Id.*
52. *Id.* (internal quotation marks omitted).
53. *See* discussion of *Lawrence v. Texas*, chapter 13, *supra*; *see* discussion of *United States v. Windsor*, chapter 14, *supra*.
54. 135 S.Ct. at 2596–2597.
55. *Id.* at 2597.
56. *Id.*
57. *Id.* (*citing Goodridge v. Department of Public Health*, 440 Mass. 309, 798 N.E. 2d 941 (2003)).
58. *Id.*
59. *Id.* at 2598.
60. *Id.*
61. *Id.* at 2598–2599.
62. *Id.* at 2599 (citing *Poe*, 367 U.S. at 542–553 (Harlan, J., dissenting)).
63. *Id.*
64. *Id.*
65. *Id.*
66. *Id.*

67. *Id.*
68. *Id.* (*quoting Goodridge v. Department of Public Health*, 440 Mass. 309, 322 (2003)) (internal quotation marks omitted).
69. *Id.*
70. *Id.*
71. *Id.*
72. *Id.* (citing *Griswold*, 381 U.S. at 485).
73. *Id.* at 2600.
74. *Id.* (citing Lawrence, 539 U.S. at 567).
75. *Id.*
76. *Id.*
77. *Id.* (quoting *Windsor*, 133 S.Ct. at 2689).
78. *Id.*
79. *See* discussion of *Griswold v. Connecticut*, chapter 5, *supra.*
80. *See* discussion of *Lawrence v. Texas*, chapter 13, *supra.*
81. 135 S.Ct. at 2600.
82. *Id.*
83. *Id.* at 2603.
84. *Id.* at 2600 (citing *Zablocki*, 434 U.S. at 384).
85. *Id.*
86. *Id.*
87. *Id.*
88. *Id.*
89. *Id.*
90. *Id.*
91. *Id.*
92. *Id.* at 2600–2601.
93. *Id.* at 2601.
94. *Id.*
95. *Id.* at 2598.
96. *Id.* at 2601 (emphasis added).
97. *Id.*
98. *Id.*
99. 125 U.S. 190 (1888).
100. 135 S.Ct. at 2601 (quoting *Maynard*, 125 U.S. at 211) (internal quotation marks omitted).
101. *Id.*
102. *Id.*
103. *Id.*
104. *Id.*
105. *Id.*
106. *See* discussion of *Griswold v. Connecticut*, chapter 5, *supra.*
107. *Id.*
108. *See* discussion of *Michael H. v. Gerald D.*, chapter 9, *supra.*
109. 135 S.Ct. at 2601.

110. *Id.*
111. *Id.*
112. *Id.* at 2601–2602.
113. *Id.* at 2602.
114. *Id.* at 2603.
115. *Id.* at 2590.
116. *Id.* (internal quotation marks omitted).
117. *Id.* at 2604.
118. *Id.* 2602.
119. *Obergefell v. Hodges*, No. 14-556, Tr. at 6:20–7:9.
120. *Id.* at 2605.
121. *Id.* at 2589.
122. *Id.* at 2590.
123. *Id.* at 2602.
124. *Lawrence*, 539 U.S. at 572.
125. *See* discussion of *United States v. Windsor*, chapter 14, *supra.*
126. *See* 135 S.Ct. at 2595.
127. 135 S.Ct. at 2608.
128. *Id.* at 2607–2608.
129. *Slaughterhouse Cases*, 83 U.S. at 53.
130. *Id.*
131. *Glucksberg*, 521 U.S. at 720.
132. *Michael H.*, 491 U.S. at 127 footnote 6.
133. 491 U.S. at 132 (O'Connor, J., concurring).
134. *Lewis*, 523 U.S. at 857 (Kennedy, J., concurring).
135. *Lawrence*, 539 U.S. at 564; *see* discussion of *Lawrence v. Texas*, chapter 13, *supra.*
136. 135 S.Ct. at 2590 (citing *Pierce*, 268 U.S. 510).
137. *Id.* at 2601.
138. *Id.* at 2602.
139. 135 S.Ct. at 2611(Roberts, J., dissenting).
140. 135 S.Ct. at 2594.
141. *Id.*
142. *Id.*
143. Robert H. Bork, *Slouching Towards Gomorrah* (New York: Harper Collins, 1996), 117.
144. *Obergefell v. Hodges*, No. 14-556, Tr. at 41:15–17.
145. Tr. at 42:3–5.
146. Tr. 41:12–15.
147. 135 S.Ct. at 2626 (Scalia, J., dissenting).
148. *Id.* at 2627.
149. 135 S.Ct. at 2593.
150. *Glucksberg*, 521 U.S. at 772–773 (Souter, J., concurring).
151. *See*, *e.g.*, *Perry v Schwarzenegger*, 704 F.Supp.2d 921, 997 (N.D.Cal. 2010) ("All classifications based on sexual orientation appear suspect, as the evidence

shows that California would rarely, if ever, have a reason to categorize individuals based on their sexual orientation. Here, however, strict scrutiny is unnecessary. Proposition 8 fails to survive even rational basis review."); *see also Korematsu v. United States*, 323 U.S. 214, 216 (1944) ("It should be noted, to begin with, that all legal restrictions which curtail the civil rights of a single racial group are immediately suspect. That is not to say that all such restrictions are unconstitutional. It is to say that courts must subject them to the most rigid scrutiny.").

152. 135 S.Ct. at 2596.
153. *Id.*
154. *Id.* at 2594.
155. *Id.*
156. *Id.* at 2606–2607.
157. *Id.* at 2607.
158. 135 S.Ct. at 2622 (Roberts, J., dissenting).
159. *Id.* (quoting *Lochner*, 198 U.S. at 57).
160. *Glucksberg*, 521 U.S. at 760–761 (Souter, J., concurring).
161. *Id.* at 761.
162. 135 S.Ct. at 2604.
163. 135 S.Ct. at 2618 (Roberts, C.J., dissenting).
164. *Id.*
165. *Id.*
166. *Id.*
167. *Id.*
168. *Id.* (quoting *Moore*, 431 U.S. at 504 footnote 12).
169. *Id.*
170. *Id.*
171. *Id.* at 2618–2619.
172. In *Casey*, Justice Stevens filed an opinion concurring in part and dissenting in part; Justice Blackmun filed an opinion concurring in part, concurring in the judgment in part, and dissenting in part; Chief Justice Rehnquist filed an opinion concurring in the judgment in part and dissenting in part, that Justices Scalia and Clarence Thomas joined; Justice Scalia filed an opinion concurring in the judgment in part and dissenting in part, that Chief Justice Rehnquist, and Justices White and Thomas, joined. In *Lawrence*, Scalia filed a dissenting opinion that Chief Justice Rehnquist and Justice Thomas joined; Justice Thomas filed a dissenting opinion of his own. In *Windsor*, Chief Justice Roberts filed a dissenting opinion; Justice Scalia filed a dissenting opinion that Justice Thomas joined and Chief Justice Roberts partially joined; Justice Alito filed a dissenting opinion that Justice Thomas partially joined. In *Obergefell*, Chief Justice Roberts filed a dissenting opinion that Justices Scalia and Thomas joined; Justice Scalia filed a dissenting opinion that Justice Thomas joined; Justice Thomas filed a dissenting opinion that Justice Scalia joined; Justice Alito filed a dissenting opinion that Justices Scalia and Thomas joined.
173. *Lawrence*, 539 U.S. at 579 (O'Connor, J., concurring).
174. *Id.* at 586 (Scalia, J. dissenting).
175. *Lawrence*, 539 U.S. at 578.

176. 135 S.Ct. at 2630 footnote 22 (Scalia, J., dissenting).

177. *Id.*

178. *Obergefell v. Hodges*, No. 14-556, Tr. at 27:21 (transcribed as "(interruption)").

179. "*Obergefell v. Hodges* Docket Number: 14-556-Question-1," Supreme Court of the United States, 27:09–27:30, https://www.supremecourt.gov/oral_arguments/audio/2014/14-556-q1.

180. *Obergefell v. Hodges*, No. 14-556, Tr. at 28:5–6.

Epilogue

Deeply rooted in our nation's history and tradition is the insight that our democracy is a liberal one, in which the people rule themselves so that each person will be free. Our ancestors aimed collective political action at an individualistic goal, and enshrined the complementary values of democracy and liberty in their Declaration of Independence. After positing the self-evident truths of equality and the "rights to life, liberty, and the pursuit of happiness,"[1] they described the purpose of government as "secur[ing] these rights[,]" and found its authority in the democratic consent of the governed.[2]

When our forbears chose democracy as the antidote to unjust monarchy, they did not merely trade one tyrant for another. They knew that democracy was no panacea for injustice—it has its own shortcoming. A majority might run roughshod over a minority. This concern is as old as the American political experiment. Arguing in favor of ratifying the Constitution, James Madison wrote,

> Complaints are everywhere heard from our most considerate and virtuous citizens, equally the friends of public and private faith, and of public and personal liberty, that our governments are too unstable, that the public good is disregarded in the conflicts of rival parties, and that measures are too often decided, not according to the *rules of justice* and the rights of the minor party, but by the superior force of an interested and overbearing majority.[3]

Our tradition aspired to eradicate tyranny altogether with a non-positivist rule of law, the people's original consent to which trumps any temporal democratic majority that violates it. Our tradition plainly teaches that governments derive their *just* powers from the governed's consent,[4] so the law cannot be merely what the sovereign says it is.[5] Neither a personal monarch nor an impersonal majority may "authorize manifest injustice by positive law."[6] We cherish democracy, but it is not worth sacrificing the individualized pursuit of happiness. And we accept a democratically legislated social order *because* within it we find protection for our liberties. Some legislative acts are *ultra vires*—those that unjustly impinge on our basic freedoms, regardless of the democratic authority that otherwise sanctions them. And a special rule of justice—one born of the law that "iss[ues] from the life of the people"—prohibits the tyranny of any majority attempting to govern beyond the scope of our consent.[7]

When order and liberty clash in a discrete controversy, our tradition obligates our judges to evaluate the balance our democracy has struck (even unconsciously) between them.[8] A judge must determine whether one legislative resolution of these contenders, as applied to the supplicant before the court, was fair, evaluated against a basic value underlying the society in which the controversy happened: in *this* polity, individual freedom is *why* the people govern themselves. This demands a precise balance of order and liberty. And in American constitutions, we find the textual distillation of the common-law guarantee for testing it—*no majority may deprive any person of liberty without due process of law*.[9]

Our most basic liberties—"the purposes (of securing) which [we] enter into society"[10]—are not absolutes. But when in their pursuit of social order political majorities interfere with them, they must have reasons of overriding importance. A majority cannot claim, "We are the government," to justify imposing on a liberty the government exists to protect. A government made to protect liberty cannot justly be used to destroy it. Mere majoritarian imprimatur is a woefully insufficient justification for such a substantial imposition. Such an abuse of power is so repugnant to our tradition that it justifies altering or abolishing government.[11] Each person has agreed with every other that a majority may prescribe reasonable restraints on even fundamental liberties. But no one has consented to a majority utterly subverting them.[12] The people reserved to *themselves* the power over their basic liberties. It does not belong to any legislature. It resides, finally, not with the States, but with *the people*.[13]

Over a quarter-century ago, modern conservatism rejected our tradition, insisting that law is the positive sanction of a majority. For a social practice to be a fundamental right, majorities in the States must have thought it so for a long time. At the very least, a liberty's proponent must show that there is *not* a long list of very old laws in the States denying it protection. And every claim to liberty fails when described at the most specific level at which we might find in the Nation's history a relevant tradition already protecting it. An individual's presence in federal court is the first indication that she should seek to vindicate her interest back in the State that she accuses of violating it.[14]

The choice that modern conservatism gave us—either limit unenumerated rights to those the States already protect, or, anything goes—was a distraction from what really happens in these controversies. Individuals seek refuge in the federal constitution from onerous laws their own States' legislators passed. They invoke a fundamental principle of justice assimilated over centuries into the Anglo-American common law. Like every other person in this nation, these litigants never consented to any government arbitrarily infringing their basic liberties. And the Fourteenth Amendment's due-process guarantee is the cause of action for asking a federal court to enforce this principle against a State.

Majorities in the American States express moral values through their laws. The health and safety, general welfare, and moral integrity of society in the States are *their* concerns. The people of them are entitled to further their vision of how to accomplish these objectives through legislative policy. But if in pursuit of their ends they employ means that interfere with a fellow citizen's basic liberty, they must have an overriding interest in social order to justify it—one "sufficiently compelling to place within the realm of the reasonable [their] refusal to recognize the individual right asserted[.]"[15] Otherwise they pretend to exercise a power they never had. Such a legislative act is arbitrary—impossible to justify in terms of how we are ordered. *All* members of the political community grant to the legislature its power, and it is not a power to impose on their basic liberties arbitrarily.[16] The people cannot capitulate to purposeless restraints, because they consent to *this* democracy to *prevent* them.[17]

No one has consented to any majority treading on basic freedoms without an overwhelming justification that appeals to liberty's complement: a democratic social order established *to protect it*. The legislative process that is due—literally, *owed as a moral obligation to*[18]—those who consent to this democratic republic demands nothing less. As applied in a particular controversy, the means chosen to order society are "not immune to distinctions turning on" their "collateral consequences" in pursuit of their precise ends.[19] Where they impact a basic liberty, the means must fit reasonably with the pursuit of a legitimate democratic objective.[20] Without such a justification, the majority's pursuing its objective—even one constitutionally reserved to the State—cannot withstand the strict scrutiny of the common-law judge.

The due-process guarantee actualizes a "vital principle[] inherent to our free governments,"[21] and stands as a bulwark against attempts—whether born of malice, ignorance, mistake, or some other human frailty—to exercise the legislative power beyond the limits that its "nature and ends" will tolerate.[22] It obligates a judge to *determine* "an obnoxious and flagrant abuse of legislative power."[23] And it authorizes *overruling* it.[24] But this is a correction carefully made—one "deeply rooted in reason and in the compelling traditions of the legal profession."[25] This practice is "fused in the whole nature of our judicial process."[26] It is the practice of reasoned judgment.[27]

"[L]ike any . . . judgment dependent on common-law method," its persuasive force accords with "the usual canons of critical discourse."[28] The common-law judge feels the gravity of the tradition's accumulated decisions weighing on the principles to which the clashing interests before him appeal, whose relative dignities he must evaluate in this new example.[29] He brings "close criticism . . . to the details"—in the record of *this* case—"of the opposing interests" the parties present.[30] He looks simultaneously to prior cases for analogues of the "relationships" between these interests and "the historically recognized principles" that give them their weight.[31] Thus juxtaposed at the nexus of fact and law, the parties' claims—the breadth of each honing the other—together point to the discrete controversy the Constitution authorizes our judge to resolve.[32] And he induces from his forbears' examples *how* to apply the principle that must live in *this* one—a principle ever-capable of broader application than the specific mischief that calls it forth each time.[33]

The common-law judge seeks a fresh understanding of the relationship between order and liberty at this evolving boundary between the domains of these venerable principles.[34] Each proper demonstration of the due-process inquiry reveals a unique controversy in our nation's history where a judge determined whether these paradoxically situated fundamental values either sat finally in the equipoise of reasonableness, or, the specific application of their democratic resolution necessarily gave way to the bulwark against arbitrary legislation that is the due-process guarantee.[35] This is what the judge decides. *Judicial discretion* limits the judicial power. Our tradition demands this of our judges, and the people "ha[ve] the right to expect [it] from those" to whom they have "entrusted [the] ultimate judicial power."[36]

We lost this practice in the twentieth century. The formulaic convenience of the incorporation doctrine lured the Court away from the tradition of reasoned judgment. Ignoring Article III's grant of the judicial power to decide discrete cases and controversies,[37] it legislated criminal procedures for all the States in the Union. A nation committed to civil rights and equal treatment under the law brought itself closer to realizing these values. But the consequences were grave for federal jurisprudence and for the Court as an institution. A novel doctrine revealed a general interest in privacy rooted in the Bill of Rights.[38] It did not take long for this "right" to bloom into a conceptually spatial, capacious repository for unenumerated rights worthy of special protection. An elegant tradition of reasoning was reduced to a crude inquisition—whether an asserted right belonged in this new and special category. While its conservative counterpart defiled "history and tradition" to steadfastly answer "no" every time, modern liberalism chanted mantras of "history and tradition," "autonomy and dignity," and "purpose and effect," until the "more transcendent dimension" of "a realm of personal liberty" appeared—one the government is forbidden to enter under any circumstances.[39]

The great common-law giant is now the stuff of legend. The sage—rest his soul—is dead. The quiet hero has vanished. And the concept of ordered liberty is forgotten. None of our justices seem to hear the words our last common-law judge gave us. There they sit, staring up at an edifice of fundamental rights, struggling to evaluate another claim that yet another jagged piece is missing. Wondering whether the right to do *this* should be "extended" to include the right to do *that*. Peering into the realm of personal liberty, soothsaying its more transcendent dimension, announcing categorical constraints on democratic action and what social policies throughout the Nation the Constitution's promise of liberty requires. Or, refusing to engage in this overreach—or to fulfill their responsibility—and embracing the only alternative apparent to them, deferring to conservative democratic majorities in the States as the touchstone of federal constitutional protections.

***

The hero of this story slung a stone of powerful insight at a behemoth of misapprehension born of opposed political ideologies. Each exploited the concept of ordered liberty. Both corrupted our jurisprudence as our justices betrayed the tradition to which their fidelity rightfully belonged. A compelling institution once presumed to safeguard the integrity of its reasoning is now taken for granted as a social-policy arbitrator—one tainted with legal-celebrity ego and salted with partisan schtick. We should ask ourselves at what cost—to the integrity of the judiciary, to the legitimacy of its highest court, and to the rule of law in America—we have purchased the vindication of such important liberties.

We stand at the edge of an abyss the divide leaves us, staring wistfully into the gloom. We long for something. Although the dust of forgetting covers it, and the cobwebs of neglect occlude our view, we fix our gaze upon the stone. Perhaps it is because we have looked so intently that we can begin to make out an inscription it bears. We come closer together, blow away the dust, and read it. It says:

The Tradition is a Living Thing

We hope this is a tribute inscribed on a monument to the wisdom of the common law, reminding us to heed it. But we have reason to fear these words are an epitaph etched into a memorial. We might stand before a tombstone above where reasoned judgment is laid to rest, interred in a ground that our nation, obsessed with partisan political identity, has forgotten. And so we wonder, at its end, whether the tale now told has been a eulogy, leaving us to pay our respects with eyes downcast in mourning. Or, if it fades into a glimmer of hope, coaxing us to lift our heads to the horizon and watch for the next incarnation.

NOTES

1. *Declaration of Independence* (US 1776).
2. *Id.*
3. James Madison, "The Same Subject Continued: The Union as a Safeguard against Domestic Faction and Insurrection," *New York Daily Advertiser*, November 22, 1787 (emphasis added).
4. *Declaration of Independence* (US 1776) ("That to secure these rights, Governments are instituted among Men, deriving their just powers from the consent of the governed[.]").
5. *Hurtado v. California*, 110 U.S. 516, 536 (1884).
6. *Calder v. Bull*, 3 U.S. 386, 388 (1798) (Chase, J., concurring).
7. "The common law is the will of mankind, issuing from the life of the people." Hartley Burr Alexander, 1873–1939.
8. *See Glucksberg*, 521 U.S. at 764 (Souter, J., concurring).
9. *See* U.S. Const. amend. V; U.S. Const. amend. XIV § 1.
10. *Poe*, 367 U.S. at 541 (Harlan, J. dissenting) (quoting *Calder v. Bull*, 3 U.S. 386, 388 (1798) (Chase, J., concurring) (parenthetical is Harlan's)).
11. *See Declaration of Independence* (US 1776) ("That whenever any Form of Government becomes destructive of these ends, it is the right of the People to alter or to abolish it[.]").
12. *Slaughterhouse Cases*, 83 U.S. at 111, 114 (Bradley, J., dissenting).
13. U.S. Const. amend. X.
14. *See* discussion of *Michael H. v. Gerald D.*, chapter 9, *supra.*
15. *Glucksberg*, 521 U.S. at 766 (Souter, J., concurring).
16. *See* John Locke, "Of the Extent of the Legislative Power," in *Second Treatise of Government, Chapter XI, § 135*, ed. C.B. MacPherson (Indianapolis and Cambridge: Hackett Publishing Company, Inc., 1980), 70–71.; *see also Poe v. Ullman*, 367 U.S. 497, 543 (1961) (Harlan, J., dissenting).
17. *See Declaration of Independence* (US 1776) ("That to secure these rights, governments are instituted among men . . .").
18. *Oxford Dictionary of English* (2nd ed. revised 2009).
19. *Glucksberg*, 521 U.S. at 772 (Souter, J., concurring).
20. *See Meyer v. Nebraska*, 262 U.S. 390, 399–400 (1923).
21. *Calder*, 3 U.S. at 388 (Chase, J., concurring).
22. *Id.*
23. *Id.*
24. *See id.*
25. *Poe*, 367 U.S. at 544–545 (Harlan, J., dissenting).

26. *Id.*
27. *See Casey*, 505 U.S. at 849.
28. *Glucksberg*, 521 U.S. at 769 (Souter, J., concurring).
29. *See id.*
30. *Glucksberg*, 521 U.S. at 769 (Souter, J., concurring).
31. *Id.*
32. *See* U.S. Const. art. III, sec. 2.
33. *See Weems v. United States*, 217 U.S. 349, 373 (1910).
34. *See Glucksberg*, 521 U.S. at 770 (Souter, J., concurring).
35. *See Hurtado v. California*, 110 U.S. 516, 532 (1884).
36. *Rochin v. California*, 342 U.S. 165, 171–172 (1952).
37. U.S. Const. art. III, sec. 2, cl. 1.
38. *See Griswold v. Connecticut*, 381 U.S. 479 (1965).
39. *See Moore*, 431 U.S. at 499; *Casey*, 505 U.S. at 847; *Lawrence*, 539 U.S. at 572.

Bibliography

Balkin, Jack. *Living Originalism*. Cambridge: Belknap Press of Harvard University Press, 2011.

Barnett, Randy E. "Who's Afraid of Unenumerated Rights?" *University of Pennsylvania Journal of Constitutional Law*, no. 9 (October 2006): 1–22.

Bork, Robert H. *Slouching Towards Gomorrah*. New York: HarperCollins, 1996.

Carpenter, Dale. *Flagrant Conduct*. New York: W.W. Norton & Company, 2012.

Cooley, Thomas M. *The General Principles of Constitutional Law in the United States*, edited by Andrew C. McLaughlin. Boston: Little, Brown, and Company, 1898.

Corwin, Edward S. *Liberty Against Government: The Rise, Flowering, and Decline of a Famous Judicial Concept*. Baton Rouge: Louisiana State University Press, 1948.

Cover, Robert M. *Justice Accused: Antislavery and the Judicial Process*. New Haven and London: Yale University Press, 1975.

CSPAN.org. "Souter Confirmation Hearings." http://www.c-span.org/video/?13979-2/souter-confirmation-hearings.

Ledewitz, Bruce. "Justice Harlan's Law and Democracy." *Journal of Law & Politics*, no. 20 (Summer 2004): 373–461.

Locke, John. *Two Treatises on Civil Government*. Vol. 9. G. Routledge and Sons, Limited, 1887.

Locke, John. "Of the Extent of the Legislative Power." In *Second Treatise of Government, Chapter XI, § 135*, edited by C.B. MacPherson, 70–71. Indianapolis and Cambridge: Hackett Publishing Company, Inc., 1980. (*Second Treatise of Government* was originally published in 1690.)

Madison, James. "The Same Subject Continued: The Union as a Safeguard Against Domestic Faction and Insurrection." *New York Daily Advertiser*, November 22, 1787.

Maitland, F.W. *The Constitutional History of England*, edited by H.A.L. Fisher. Cambridge: University Press, 1908.

Oxford Dictionary of English. 2nd ed. revised, 2009.

Scalia, Antonin. "Originalism, The Lesser Evil." In *Judges on Judging*, edited by David M. O'Brien, 209–217. Thousand Oaks: CQ Press, 2004.

Senate.gov. "Hearings Before the Committee on the Judiciary, United States Senate, One Hundred First Congress, Second Session on the Nomination of David H. Souter to be Associate Justice of the Supreme Court of the United States." S.Hrg. 101-1263, Sep 13, 14, 17, 18, 19, 1990. https://www.govinfo.gov/content/pkg/GPO-CHRG-SOUTER/pdf/GPO-CHRG-SOUTER.pdf.

Senior, Jennifer. "In Conversation: Antonin Scalia." https://nymag.com/news/features/antonin-scalia-2013-10/.

Supreme Court of the United States. "Obergefell v. Hodges Docket Number: 14-556-Question-1." https://www.supremecourt.gov/oral_arguments/audio/2014/14-556-q1.

Toobin, Jeffrey. "Swing Shift: How Anthony Kennedy's Passion for Foreign Law Could Change the Supreme Court." https://www.newyorker.com/magazine/2005/09/12/swing-shift.

Toobin, Jeffrey. *The Nine*. New York: Knopf Doubleday Publishing Group, 2008.

Tribe, Lawrence H. *American Constitutional Law*, third edition. St. Paul: Foundation Press, 1988.

Whitehead, Alfred North. *Science and the Modern World*. New York: Free Press, 1925.

Yarbrough, Tinsley E. *John Marshall Harlan: Great Dissenter of the Warren Court*. New York: Oxford University Press, 1992.

List of Cases

Adamson v. California, 332 U.S. 46 (1947)
Akron v. Akron Center for Reproductive Health, Inc., 462 U.S. 416 (1983) (*Akron I*)
Alberts v. California, 354 U. S. 476 (1957)
Allgeyer v. Louisiana, 165 U.S. 578 (1897)
Anderson v. Celebrezze, 460 U.S. 780 (1983)
Aptheker v. Secretary of State, 378 U.S. 500 (1964)
Ashvander v. TVA, 297 U.S. 288 (1936)
Baggett v. Bullitt, 377 U.S. 360 (1964)
Baker v. Carr, 369 U.S. 186 (1962)
Bank of Columbia v. Okely, 17 U.S. 235 (1819)
Bank of the State v. Cooper, 10 Tenn. 599 (1831)
Barbier v. Connolly, 113 U.S. 27 (1884)
Barenblatt v. United States, 360 U.S. 109 (1959)
Bartels v. Iowa, 262 U.S. 404 (1923)
Bartemeyer v. Iowa, 18 Wall. 129 (1874)
Bearden v. Georgia, 461 U.S. 660 (1983)
Board of Education v. Barnette, 319 U.S. 624 (1943)
Bond v. United States, 131 S.Ct. 2355 (2011)
Bowers v. Hardwick, 478 U.S. 186 (1986)
Boyd v. United States, 116 U.S. 616 (1886)
Brown v. Levee Comrs., 50 Miss. 468 (1874)
Brown v. Mississippi, 297 U.S. 278 (1936)
Buchalter v. New York, 319 U.S. 427 (1943)
Bush v. Gore, 531 U.S. 98 (2000)
Butchers' Union Co. v. Crescent City Co., 111 U.S. 746 (1884)
Calder v. Bull, 3 U.S. 386 (1798)

Campbell v. Sundquist, 926 S.W.2d 250 (Tenn. App. 1996)
Cantwell v. Connecticut, 310 U.S. 296 (1940)
Carey v. Population Services International, 431 U.S. 678 (1977)
Chambers v. Florida, 309 U.S. 227 (1940)
City of Chicago v. Rumpff, 45 Illinois 90 (1867)
Cleveland Board of Education v. Lafleur, 414 U.S. 632 (1974)
Collins v. Harker Heights, 503 U.S. 115 (1992)
Commonwealth v. Wasson, 842 S.W.2d 487 (Ky. 1992)
Corfield v. Coryell, 6 F. Cas. 546 (1823)
County of Sacramento v. Lewis, 523 U.S. 833 (1998)
Cruzan v. Director, Missouri Dept. of Health, 497 U.S. 261 (1990)
Cummings v. State of Missouri, 4 Wall. 277 (1866)
De Jonge v. Oregon, 299 U.S. 353 (1937)
Dent v. State of West Virginia, 129 U.S. 114 (1889)
Deposit Guaranty Nat. Bank v. Roper, 445 U.S. 326 (1980)
De Sylva v. Ballentine, 351 U.S. 570 (1956)
Dred Scott v. Sanford, 19 How. 393 (1857)
Duncan v. Louisiana, 391 U.S. 145 (1968)
Eisenstadt v. Baird, 405 U.S. 438 (1972)
Ex Parte Garland, 4 Wall. 333 (1866)
Farrington v. Tokushige, 273 U.S. 284 (1927)
Fiske v. Kansas, 274 U.S. 380 (1927)
Fletcher v. Peck, 6 Cranch 87 (1810)
Frank v. Mangum, 237 U.S. 309 (1915)
Gideon v. Wainwright, 372 U.S. 335 (1963)
Gitlow v. New York, 268 U.S. 652 (1925)
Goodridge v. Department of Public Health, 440 Mass. 309, 798 N.E. 2d 941 (2003)
Goshen v. Stonington, 4 Conn. 209 (1822)
Griffin v. Illinois, 351 U.S. 12 (1956)
Griswold v. Connecticut, 381 U.S. 479 (1965)
Grosjean v. American Press Co., 297 U.S. 233 (1936)
Gundling v. Chicago, 177 U.S. 183 (1900)
Gryczan v. State, 283 Mont. 433, 942 P.2d 112 (1997)
Haddock v. Haddock, 201 U.S. 562 (1906)
Hagar v. Reclamation Dist., 111 U.S. 701 (1884)
Hamilton v. Regents, 293 U.S. 245 (1934)
Hebe Co. v. Shaw, 248 U.S. 303 (1919)
Herbert v. Louisiana, 272 U.S. 312 (1926)
Herndon v. Lowry, 301 U.S. 242 (1937)
Herring v. State, 119 Ga. 709 (1904)
Hooper v. California, 155 U.S. 648 (1895)

Hurtado v. California, 110 U.S. 516 (1884)
In re Kemmler, 136 U.S. 436 (1890)
In re Oliver, 333 U.S. 257 (1948)
Irvine v. California, 347 U.S. 128 (1954)
Jegley v. Picado, 349 Ark. 600, 80 S.W.3d 332 (2002)
Kahler v. Kansas, 140 S.Ct. 1021 (2019)
Kalloch v. Super. Ct., 56 Cal. 229 (1880)
Kepner v. United States, 195 U.S. 100 (1904)
Kidd v. Pearson, 128 U.S. 1 (1888)
Klopfer v. North Carolina, 386 U.S. 213 (1967)
Korematsu v. United States, 323 U.S. 214 (1944)
Kovacs v. Cooper, 336 U.S. 77 (1949)
Kramer v. Union Free School District, 395 U.S. 621 (1969)
Lawrence v. Texas, 539 U.S. 558 (2003)
Lawton v. Steele, 152 U.S. 133 (1894)
Lochner v. New York, 198 U.S. 45 (1905)
Lovell v. Griffin, 303 U.S. 444 (1938)
Loving v. Virginia, 388 U.S. 1 (1967)
Lujan v. Defenders of Wildlife, 504 U.S. 555 (1992)
Malloy v. Hogan, 378 U.S. 1 (1964)
Mapp v. Ohio, 367 U.S. 643 (1961)
Marbury v. Madison, 1 Cranch 177 (1803)
Martin v. Struthers, 319 U.S. 141 (1943)
Maynard v. Hill, 125 U.S. 190 (1888)
Mayor of the City of Hudson v. Thorne, 7 Paige 261 (1838)
Maxwell v. Dow, 176 U.S. 581 (1900)
McCulloch v. Maryland, 4 Wheat. 316 (1819)
Meyer v. Nebraska, 262 U.S. 390 (1923)
Michael H. v. Gerald D., 491 U.S. 110 (1989)
Missouri v. Lewis, 101 U.S. 22 (1879)
Montana v. Egelhoff, 518 U.S. 37 (1996)
Moore v. City of East Cleveland, 431 U.S. 494 (1977)
Moore v. Dempsey, 261 U.S. 86 (1923)
Mugler v. Kansas, 123 U.S. 623 (1887)
Munn v. Illinois, 94 U.S. 113 (1877)
Murray's Lesee v. Hoboken Land Co., 18 How. 272 (1855)
NAACP v. Alabama, 357 U.S. 449 (1958)
NAACP v. Button, 371 U.S. 415 (1963)
Near v. Minnesota ex rel. Olson, 283 U.S. 697 (1931)
New York Central R. Co. v. White, 243 U.S. 188 (1917)
Nixon v. Condon, 286 U.S. 73 (1932)
Nixon v. Herndon, 273 U.S. 536 (1927)

Norman v. Reed, 502 U.S. 279 (1992)
Norwich Gaslight Company v. The Norwich City Gas Company, 25 Connecticut 19 (1856)
Obergefell v. Hodges, 135 S.Ct. 2584 (2015)
Ohio ex rel. Popovici v. Agler, 280 U.S. 379 (1930)
Olmstead v. United States, 277 U.S. 438 (1928)
Palko v. Connecticut, 302 U.S. 319 (1937)
People v. Adamson, 27 Cal.2d 494 (1946)
Perry v. Brown, 671 F.3d 1052 (9th Cir. 2012)
Perry v. Schwarzenegger, Civ. No. 10-16696 (C.A.9, Aug. 16, 2010)
Perry v. Schwarzenegger, 628 F.3d 1191 (9th Cir. 2011)
Perry v Schwarzenegger, 704 F.Supp.2d 921 (N.D.Cal. 2010)
Pierce v. Carskadon, 16 Wall. 234 (1872)
Pierce v. Society of Sisters, 268 U.S. 510 (1925)
Planned Parenthood of Southeastern Pennsylvania v. Casey, 505 U.S. 833 (1992)
Poe v. Ullman, 367 U.S. 497 (1961)
Pointer v. Texas, 380 U.S. 400 (1965)
Powell v. Alabama, 287 U.S. 45 (1932)
Powell v. State, 270 Ga. 327, 510 S.E.2d 18 (1998)
Presser v. Illinois, 116 U.S. 252 (1886)
Price v. Illinois, 238 U.S. 446 (1915)
Prince v. Massachusetts, 321 U.S. 158 (1944)
Railroad Comm'n Cases, 116 U.S. 307 (1886)
Reno v. Flores, 507 U.S. 292 (1993)
Robinson v. California, 370 U.S. 660 (1962)
Rochin v. California, 342 U.S. 165 (1952)
Roe v. Wade, 410 U.S. 113 (1973)
Rogers v. Peck, 199 U.S. 425 (1905)
Rowan v. State, 30 Wis. 129 (1872)
Schloendorff v. Society of New York Hospital, 211 N.Y. 125 (1914)
Schware v. Board of Bar Examiners, 353 U.S. 232 (1957)
Shapiro v. Thompson, 394 U.S. 618 (1969)
Sherbert v. Verner, 374 U.S. 398 (1963)
Skinner v. Oklahoma, 316 U.S. 535 (1942)
Slaughterhouse Cases, 83 U.S. 36 (1872)
Snyder v. Massachusetts, 291 U.S. 97 (1934)
Sosna v. Iowa, 419 U.S. 393 (1975)
South Carolina v. Barnwell Bros., Inc., 303 U.S. 177 (1938)
Standard Oil Co. v. Marysville, 279 U.S. 582 (1929)
Stromberg v. California, 283 U.S. 369 (1931)
Sweezy v. New Hampshire, 354 U.S. 234 (1957)

Taylor v. Porter & Ford, 4 Hill (N.Y.) 140 (1843)
Thornburgh v. American College of Obstetricians and Gynecologists, 476 U.S. 747 (1986)
Turner v. Safley, 482 U.S. 78 (1987)
Twining v. New Jersey, 211 U.S. 78 (1908)
United States v. Carolene Products Co., 304 U.S. 144 (1938)
United States v. Windsor, 570 U.S. 744 (2013)
Village of Belle Terre v. Boraas, 416 U.S. 1 (1974)
Wagner Electric Mfg. Co. v. Lyndon, 262 U.S. 226 (1923)
Walker v. Sauvinet, 92 U.S. 90 (1875)
Warth v. Seldin, 422 U.S. 490 (1975)
Washington v. Glucksberg, 521 U.S. 702 (1997)
Washington v. Texas, 388 U.S. 14 (1967)
Weeks v. United States, 232 U.S. 383 (1913)
Weems v. United States, 217 U.S. 349 (1910)
Wiemann v. Updegraff, 344 U.S. 183 (1952)
West Coast Hotel Co. v. Parrish, 300 U.S. 379 (1937)
West v. Louisiana, 194 U.S. 258 (1904)
Westervelt v. Gregg, 12 N.Y. 202 (1854)
Whitney v. California, 274 U.S. 357 (1927)
Wilkinson v. Leland, 2 Pet. 627 (1829)
Williams v. Illinois, 399 U.S. 235 (1970)
Williams v. North Carolina, 317 U.S. 287 (1942)
Wolf v. Colorado, 338 U.S. 25 (1949)
Worcester County Trust Co. v. Riley, 302 U.S. 292 (1937)
Wynehamer v. People, 13 N.Y. 378 (1856)
Yick Wo v. Hopkins, 118 U.S. 356 (1886)
Zablocki v. Redhail, 434 U.S. 374 (1978)
Zivotofsky v. Clinton, 132 S.Ct. 1421 (2012)

Index

About the Author

Matthew W. Lunder is an attorney and writer whose deep interest in process philosophy and systems theory pervades his work. After graduating summa cum laude with a degree in political science from the University of California at Los Angeles, near his birthplace, he earned a juris doctor with honors from the University of Montana School of Law. The idea that became *The Concept of Ordered Liberty* originated in a philosophy of law course, and after graduating, Mr. Lunder was afforded the opportunity to teach and develop it while serving as a law clerk for the federal judiciary. He now lives in Baltimore, Maryland, and is a trial attorney at the U.S Department of Justice.

www.ingramcontent.com/pod-product-compliance
Ingram Content Group UK Ltd.
Pitfield, Milton Keynes, MK11 3LW, UK
UKHW041841031026
15587UKWH00002B/933

9 781793 626349